JILL MESSENGER:
OUT OF BODY

Volume I of a Trilogy

JILL MESSENGER:
OUT OF BODY

RUSS MASON

Two Moons Press

JILL MESSENGER: OUT OF BODY

© 2008 Russ Mason

Cover Illustration by Maria Whitehead

Cover and Interior Design by Ted Ruybal

PB ISBN 13: 978-0-9791263-5-5
LCCN 2008936525
First Edition
1 2 3 4 5 6 7 8 9 10

For information, please contact:
Wisdom House Books
15455 Dallas Parkway, Suite 600
Dallas, Texas 75001
Tel. 214-566-9590

www.wisdomhousebooks.com

Two Moons Press
A Division of Wisdom House Books

For Laurie

American Airlines Flight 182 flew over southern Ohio, destined for Columbus. It was a small commuter airplane with sixteen passengers aboard. The flight, which had originated in Richmond, was on schedule, and everything was as it should be. However, although the pilots and passengers were unable to see her, a woman in a nightgown was flying alongside them, a few feet from the airplane's starboard windows. The woman smiled at the people in the airplane, but they had no idea she was there. As the landing gear swung down, the woman gracefully turned and headed southeast, her nightgown trailing soundlessly behind her.

CHAPTER ONE

Marietta, Ohio – Saturday morning

The phone rang sharply, jarring Jill Messenger awake. She slowly opened her eyes and peered at the clock on the table beside her bed: 8:45 a.m. The phone rang again and as Jill reached for it, her hand knocked a glass off the table's edge and onto the floor. It landed with a thump but didn't break. Jill picked up the receiver and stretched the cord to where she lay.

"Hello," she sighed.

"Hey, Jill, it's going on nine. Are you coming?" It was Sara Hopkins, her friend who lived across the street.

"Oh Sara, I'm sorry," Jill replied, her speech slurred. "Give me ten minutes."

Sara picked up on Jill's speech and knew that she had spent another night with the bottle. *What a shame*, thought Sara. *Everything had been going so well . . . until the accident.*

Jill had not yet recovered; when her husband and young son had died while on a skiing trip in Colorado, she had really lost it, and Sara's efforts to help her went unheeded.

"Listen, no rush. There's hardly anybody here, so eat some breakfast. Come when you can."

"OK. *Sorry*, Sara. I'll be there soon."

Jill, a woman in her late forties, had an expressive face, large liquid blue eyes, light brown hair, and a dimple on her right cheek. She stood 5'5" and was once strikingly pretty. That is, when she was vibrant and healthy; now she was neither.

She clunked the receiver back on its cradle, lay back on the pillow, and rubbed her eyes. She felt terrible. It wasn't just the vodka; it was the certainty that her life was plummeting in a downward spiral, out of her control. She was powerless. It was only a matter of time before she joined her husband Dave and son Jamie in the vast blackness of death. She wondered what would become of Cathy, her daughter, a junior at the University of Virginia. Cathy would be the last survivor of this unfortunate family.

Cathy had been devastated when Jill called to tell her about the accident, but she handled it with quiet grace—maybe because she studied psychology, or maybe because she was just more resilient than Jill. Cathy had established a new life in Charlottesville; she had made friends at college and felt the promise of a bright future. But for Jill, the vodka helped. It made her numb, senseless, which is what she wanted most—not to *feel* anymore.

She was not looking forward to helping Sara with the garage sale. She felt rotten; her head throbbed, and she knew she

2

looked wretched. Her face was puffy, and her hair needed washing. She did not want to set foot outdoors, but she had promised her friend—perhaps her only friend—that she would help.

Sara had been divorced two years previously and did not enjoy the single life. The scarcity of eligible men in Marietta was frustrating and annoying. After the solemn funeral last January for Dave and Jamie, a closeness had grown between Jill and Sara. Jill had needed a shoulder to lean on, and Sara had been there for her. She made Jill casseroles and soup, helped with the housework, and provided fresh boxes of Puffs when Jill ran out. It was during this period that Jill began to drink, heavily and every day. At first she had been able to walk the short blocks to Weber's Market—the only liquor store in Marietta. But then, after a couple of weeks, she had pleaded with the owner to deliver a case of 110 vodka. The man had reluctantly agreed.

Sara had done her best to keep Jill positive and active, but it was a losing battle. Jill had retreated and sought refuge in her vodka. Nevertheless, Sara had continued to call with the latest gossip, and she had cheerfully tried to get Jill to go shopping with her. None of it had worked so far, except one thing: Jill's promise to help with Sara's garage sale. Jill had said she would help, and Sara had called several times to remind her. Jill knew she *had* to go, to actually set foot outdoors. And now that the day had arrived, it was terrifying.

Jill stepped over to her bedroom window and peered through the Venetian blinds. Sara was right: there were only a few people in her driveway and front yard, poking around the tables laden with stuff for sale.

Dear God, look at all the junk.

Citizens of Marietta had donated things to help Sara raise money for the Washington County Library Bookmobile. Jill suddenly thought of her own dwindling bank account. The $100,000 from her husband's life insurance had been eaten up by airfare and lodging for her and Cathy in Colorado—to claim the bodies—an expensive funeral, a catered wake, the minister's fee, cemetery arrangements, mortgage payments, and car insurance. Now Jill had less than $3,000 left. She didn't want to think about it. She didn't want to think about anything. She had to get ready to help Sara.

Her once lovely bedroom was now in filthy disarray. Clothes were flung carelessly on chairs; shoes, socks, and magazines were strewn about the floor. The rest of the house was just as bad. It was an airless, smelly, messy pit. Since the funeral, Jill had rarely done laundry, nor had she made the slightest attempt to keep order. Near the back door of the kitchen were overflowing garbage cans and a stack of empty Red Baron pizza boxes. There were bugs crawling on the kitchen floor.

The living room, once comfortable and inviting, was now a mess. The nautical teak coffee table, a wedding gift, was laden with several containers of half-eaten Chinese food, menus, an overflowing ashtray, a stack of unread magazines, and the smeared remote controls to the television and DVD player. The sofa had a tattered plaid blanket wadded into a ball at one end, and three beige corduroy toss pillows were scrunched up at the other. It was a place where Jill would drink, smoke, eat take-out food, watch TV, and eventually pass out. But on some nights, such as the previous one, she made it upstairs and into bed.

Twenty-five minutes later, Jill, wearing an old T-shirt, jeans, a nylon windbreaker, large sunglasses, and a Cleveland Indians cap pulled down low, moved out her front door onto the broad gray porch and breathed in the coolish June air. It felt pretty good.

Jill liked this section of Marietta; it was a real neighborhood. The two-story clapboard houses were solid and reassuring under the tall elms. At the lower end of Sixth Street was Marietta College, a venerable, smaller version of Harvard. Its red brick buildings with white trim were set among the trees in a tidy, picturesque campus. The people of Marietta were friendly without gushing or prying. There were good places to eat and shop, and there were plenty of things to do. Jill and her husband had visited all of these, back when he was around to enjoy them with her.

Jill and Dave also owned a boat, a 26-foot cabin cruiser, which they had docked in the Muskingum River. Marietta was at the confluence of the Muskingum and Ohio Rivers; the Muskingum was fairly small and murky, and it emptied into the broad Ohio. When the kids were young, they had taken day trips down the Ohio River. Those had been sun-filled, idyllic days, full of laughter. But now the *Keuka Maiden* sat in silent storage. One of the last things Dave had said to Jill was that he was looking forward to spring, and to putting the boat back in the water. Jill had been glad; she loved the boat and being on the water.

She reflected on how her life had been transformed in an instant—the moment Dave and Jamie's car slipped off the road in Colorado, snuffing out their beautiful lives. Her life also ended that day; now she was just marking time.

Jill shoved her fists into her jacket pockets and moved down the porch steps and across the smooth brick street toward Sara's driveway. As she approached Sara's house, Jill saw more than a dozen people moving quietly around the tables in the driveway and front lawn, looking at the assortment of collectables. On the tables were glassware, cups and saucers, a tray of utensils, old telephones wrapped with their cords, stadium cushions, portable radios with missing knobs, boxes of books, and a box of LP records. In the driveway were snow tires, old golf clubs on a tarnished cart, wooden baseball bats, folding lawn chairs, several sets of skis, a few assorted chairs of various sizes, and a large stereo system. There were two racks of clothing—mostly women's apparel—and a few men's jackets. There was nothing of great value, but that wasn't the point. People had donated things to help Sara's fundraising efforts.

Sara, standing behind a card table, saw Jill and waved, pointing to a lawn chair beside her. Jill nodded as she moved up the driveway toward Sara, a youthful fifty-five years old. Sara was 5'4" and had curly blond hair and a busty hourglass figure. Sara was a flirt, but she always stopped there. Many of the men in Marietta would have given anything to have a fling with Sara, but she was still "waiting for Mr. Right." One lousy failed marriage was enough. She didn't want another. And yet, 55 and living in Marietta, Sara had begun to secretly wonder, *Who am I going to have to settle for?* All that she saw available were balding guys with potbellies and bad teeth.

Sara lived in her parents' rambling house, directly across from Jill's, and she worked at the Washington County Library, a job that didn't pay well. As a result, Sara babysat, taught guitar and piano lessons, and did odd jobs to make ends meet. And yet, although she found money to be extremely tight in her home, she was generous enough to hope her yard sale would bring in a few hundred dollars to help keep the Bookmobile in service.

"Listen, why don't you sit here and take the money?" Sara asked. Then, leaning into Jill's ear, she whispered, "Are you OK?"

"I'll be fine. I *am* fine," said Jill.

"Did you get something to eat?"

"I had a protein shake," Jill lied.

Sara frowned. "You call that food? Somebody brought a box of Hostess Cupcakes. They're fantastic. Help me, for God's sake, before I eat 'em all."

Jill smiled faintly and sat down. She opened the box of cupcakes. Quite a few were left, but they did not look appealing. A wasp buzzed near Jill and she lurched back.

"Relax, honey," soothed Sara. "It won't sting you."

Jill pulled her cap down and reset her chair as the wasp flew away. She didn't like them one bit. Bees were OK, but not wasps.

Her spirits improved as the garage sale progressed. Breathing the fresh air and talking with some of the neighbors made her feel better. She took a cupcake from the box, removed the cellophane wrapper, and bit into it tentatively. It was sugary and filled with sweet, creamy goo. She shoved the rest into her mouth and licked her fingers. Sara watched and nodded approvingly.

As the day began to wane, Jill grew weary and anxious to leave. Sara sensed this, stepped over to her, and said, "Just a little while longer, honey. I'm makin' some good money today."

It crossed Sara's mind to ask Jill if she had anything to sell, but she suspected it would be more than Jill could bear. She thought of this because the golf clubs and cart had sold for $100, and Jill probably still had her husband's clubs, along with his kayak, ski equipment, and other sporting gear.

At 4:30, Jill said, "Sara, I'm tired. I have to go."

"I understand. I'm tired myself. Let me give you some money for your help."

"Oh no," Jill said, shaking her head. "I couldn't do that. Not after all you've done for me."

"Take a twenty. That'll get you a pizza or something," Sara said while thrusting a folded bill into Jill's pale hand. "It's the least I can do. Is there anything here you want?"

Jill scanned what was left on the tables. Nothing had especially appealed to her when she looked earlier, and now there wasn't much left.

"No, I don't think so. Thanks anyway."

Sara took a quick stroll around the tables. Her eyes fell on a shoebox that held some CDs, a CD player, and headphones. She picked it up and handed it to Jill. "Here, take this."

"What is it? CDs?"

"Yeah. And a player, too."

"Well, OK. Thanks." She put the box under her arm. "See you later." She gave a little wave as she headed across the street.

"Call if you need anything," Sara said, but Jill barely heard her. She was going home to drink and to forget.

By 10:00, Jill was curled up on the couch in the living room, watching a TV movie that starred Kiefer Sutherland. Even though his character was mean, she liked his face. An open pizza box sprawled on the coffee table; three slices were gone, and the crusts had been set back in the box. Bottles of vodka and tonic water sat on the table in front of her. She had started the evening with ice cubes in her glass, but now she was drinking the vodka straight with a trickle of tonic. Her eyelids grew heavy, and she could barely see the television; her head lolled to one side.

This was the feeling she loved.

This . . . is the way to go.

Jill was dimly aware that the TV movie had ended because a man was talking about the weather and pointing to a map of southeastern Ohio. Fighting off sleep, Jill couldn't decide whether to crash on the couch or go upstairs to bed. The bed was more sensible; she was never comfortable sleeping on the couch, especially in her clothes. She usually woke up with a cramp in her neck.

She reached for the remote, pushed a button, and the TV went black. The living room was now dark, illuminated only by the glow of the streetlights through the unwashed windows. The darkness didn't bother her; she had navigated her way upstairs in the dark before. Tonight would be no different.

She rose unsteadily to her feet, poured some vodka into the glass, and began to weave toward the staircase. When she reached the bottom of the stairs, she gripped the railing with her right hand, holding her drink in the left, and began a slow, unsteady climb. When she had nearly reached the top, her right foot missed, coming down hard on the step below. This knocked her off balance, and she tried to grab the banister. But it was too late—she toppled, sloppily tumbling backwards down the stairs, somersaulting until her head slammed into the hardwood floor.

Eleven hours later, Jill was awakened by the sound of steady electronic beeps. She opened her eyes slightly and looked around a semidark room, disoriented.

A hospital? What happened?

She tried to remember: had she been in an accident? Then she saw that she had an IV in her left wrist, and she sensed the unmistakable feeling of a catheter.

Oh great.

Then she dimly noticed someone sitting in a chair across the room. It was Sara.

"Sara?"

Sara had dozed off, and now she stirred, breathing in sharply.

"Oh. *Jill*," she said huskily, lifting herself slowly out of the chair and moving to the side of the bed. "Glad you woke up. I was a little concerned."

"What happened?"

"You don't remember?"

Jill shook her head, wincing at the pain this slight movement caused.

"Looks like you fell downstairs and smacked your head on the floor. It must have happened last night after the yard sale. I came by around eleven this morning, and when you didn't answer the door, I looked through the window and saw you. I called 911."

"Oh."

"I talked with the doctor. I think they're going to keep you here for a couple days," said Sara. "I also called Cathy. I didn't know how serious your injuries were. Or are."

"*Oh shit*," moaned Jill. "What did the doctor say?"

"You had a pretty bad concussion, and he ran some tests. He'll tell you. But at least you woke up."

Sara paused, not knowing what to say next. Then, tactfully, she said quietly, "It's none of my business, but you might want to take care of yourself a little better."

Jill nodded. She didn't want to take care of herself. And now Cathy was leaving school to visit her. Not good. As she was thinking this, Sara stuck her head out into the hall and called to Dr. Ryan, who was just across the hall.

Kevin Ryan, MD, entered a few moments later, switched on the overhead lights, and went over to Jill. He was a tall, beaming man in his mid-forties, with dark, close-cropped hair and a relaxed manner. He smiled at Jill and asked, "Jill Messenger. How are we doing this morning?"

"I have a headache," said Jill, looking into Dr. Ryan's bright blue eyes. "Other than that, I feel like crap."

Sara gave a little wave to Jill and pointed toward the hallway as she stepped out.

"I'm not surprised. You hit your head pretty hard. The CAT scan showed a subdural, so we're gonna have to keep an eye on you for a day or two."

"Is that what I have?" asked Jill.

"Well . . ." began Dr. Ryan, "you're not exactly in top

shape. The fall brought you in here, but we'll need to run some more tests."

"OK."

Dr. Ryan took out a penlight and shined it into Jill's eyes. "Look here, please," he said, and Jill looked at his finger. He shined the light into Jill's left ear, and then her right. Then he switched off the light and put it into his pocket.

Dr. Ryan pulled a chair up to the side of Jill's bed and looked earnestly at her face. She looked drained.

"You have some dehydration, some malnutrition. We did a blood workup, and you had almost no nutrients in your bloodstream, and that can be serious. Your heart was throwing PVCs, but we've got them under control now."

"What's that?" asked Jill.

"It's an arrhythmia," said Dr. Ryan. "Everybody has them from time to time, but I think yours were caused by a lack of magnesium. Have you been eating at all?"

"Cupcakes," Jill said warily, with a slight smile.

"I mean solid food," said Dr. Ryan. "When was your last good meal?"

"Does pizza count?"

"Seriously. Any idea?"

Jill shook her head.

"A couple of days ago?" asked Dr. Ryan.

"Maybe . . . January?" she said, looking away.

Dr. Ryan nodded sympathetically. "Well, your IV drip is bringing your vitamin and mineral levels back up. It's going to take a few days to get you back to normal. I've asked for a special diet for you, and I want you to eat everything. And I want you to drink a lot of water."

"OK."

"Are you listening to me?"

"You bet. Every word."

"A neurologist will be checking you. We need to figure out if the fall did any damage beyond the subdural."

"OK," Jill responded. "I just feel awfully tired."

"Sleep as much as you want. It's good for you."

Jill slept the rest of the day, dead to the world.

Monday

Jill's daughter Cathy was a mousy young woman of 21. She was 5′6″ and slender, wore horn-rimmed glasses, and had a large mop of light brown hair that hid much of her face. She was bright, perceptive, and quiet; she usually walked with her arms folded in front of her, her gaze downward. Cathy felt close to her mother, and she called every Sunday evening at 6:00. She knew that her mother stayed sober for these calls, usually. But she also knew that her mother had a problem with alcohol—a bad one—that had suddenly become full blown after the ski trip accident. Prior to that, Cathy had rarely seen her mother even finish a glass of wine at dinner. But now, as she and Sara began to clean the house on Sixth Street, a deep sadness befell each of them. Their dear witty friend had gone, and an alcoholic slob had taken her place.

"I drove all night, and when I went to see her this morning when I got here, I couldn't believe how much Mom had changed," said Cathy sadly. "She didn't even look like herself. It was so hard to be there with this . . . strange woman."

"But you're going back, right?" asked Sara as she picked up several old, sticky, Chinese food containers from the coffee table and dropped them into a black trash bag.

"Oh yeah, oh yeah. I have to," sighed Cathy. "She's my mom; she needs me. I should have been around more. I had no idea how bad . . ."

"Don't beat yourself up. Nobody knew."

"I guess."

"I think she'll be better now. Now that we know; now that the doctors know. We can keep an eye on her until she gets back on her feet."

"Yeah, but I'm down in Charlottesville," sighed Cathy.

"I'll keep you posted. Don't worry. We'll get through this and your mom will recover."

"Yeah. Well, let's hope."

"I'm gonna have to call for one of those dumpster things," sighed Sara as she dragged the black trash bag back toward the kitchen. "There's just too much stuff for the garbage cans, and we haven't even made a dent."

"It's awfully kind of you to do this for Mom," said Cathy.

"She's my friend. Besides, I owe her," said Sara. "Her and your father. This is the least I can do."

"Owe?"

Sara slumped into one of the kitchen chairs and wiped her forehead with her shirt. Then she cast a brief glance toward Cathy and began to speak in a weary voice.

"Well, I've been divorced for a couple of years now. You remember Bill? Everybody does."

"Well, sure. He gave me a Tinker Bell watch one Christmas," replied Cathy.

Sara smiled grimly. "That was more than he gave me. You know what I got? Promises. Just promises. Some men are good at that, honey, and that's all you get."

Cathy nodded.

"But your mom and dad stepped up when I was left high and dry. That jerk just walked out one Thanksgiving day to buy cupcakes and that was it. No goodbye, no see-ya-later—nothing."

"What did you do?"

"I went a little nuts that day," said Sara softly. "I was *pissed*. I threw the turkey and the mashed potatoes and the squash all over the kitchen. I smashed the nice table I had set. I screamed a lot. I picked up a knife, and if he had set foot in the door, I would have cut his goddamn heart out. That's when your mom and dad came. They heard me yelling from across the street, and they came and got me. I was hysterical. I loved that man with everything I had, and he just *left*?"

"I remember that day. You had dinner with us," said Cathy. "I think we ate the cranberry sauce you made."

Sara laughed and wiped away a tear.

"Yeah—the only thing I didn't throw."

"You came over for Christmas that year, too," remembered Cathy.

"Jill and Dave saved me. I learned what true friendship is: to be cared for without expectation. Your folks went above and beyond for me. So . . . that's why I'm helping your mom today."

"Thanks for telling me all that," Cathy said. "I didn't know."

Sara stood up and sniffed. "Now, my dear, we have to get this house in order."

"Maybe we could get a couple of people to help clean the house? Or help with the laundry?"

"Honestly, it might be easier to just toss everything and get her new clothes," said Sara.

"Oh no," replied Cathy. "Mom wouldn't like that. That would really embarrass her. She'll probably be mortified we're doing this much."

"I know a lady who'll help. And my neighbor Jack has a Shop-Vac we can use, I'm pretty sure."

Cathy nodded.

"And you know what else?" Sara said, wiping her brow with the back of her hand. "We should get your mom a new mattress."

"How much will it cost?" asked Cathy, quietly, as she rinsed her hands at the kitchen sink.

"I don't know," replied Sara. "Five hundred bucks? Most places deliver. I know a guy over the river who sells beds. We used to play guitars together. I think he'll help us out."

Cathy looked around, assessing what remained to be done. A lot, and she was clearly needed, but this kind of manual labor was not for her.

"It's almost time to go back and see Mom. I'm gonna change and go to the hospital. You want to come?"

Sara shook her head. "Not right now. There's just too much stuff to get out of here, and everything needs to get scrubbed."

"All right," Cathy replied as she headed for the stairway.

"Hey, why don't you take this box of CDs to her? I gave 'em to her for helping at the sale the other day. They might help pass the time."

"OK."

When Cathy entered her mother's room at Marietta Memorial Hospital, Jill was still dozing, her head turned toward the window.

"Hi, Mom," Cathy said, her voice just above a whisper, as she switched on the overhead florescents.

Jill took a deep breath and stirred awake.

"Hey, Pumpkin," Jill mumbled as she slowly turned to face Cathy. "Oh, please turn off the lights."

Cathy switched them off and said, "Mom, how are you feeling?" She set the shoebox of CDs on a chair and moved to another chair closer to the bed.

"I feel like I'm in a . . . time warp, Cathy. Everything is just endless. The *food* . . ."

"How's your head?" asked Cathy.

"It hurts. Not as bad as before, though. The neurologist said I had, ah, something. Not serious but they're keeping me here. How long are you going to stay?"

"I don't know. Summer session starts in a couple of weeks, and I am supposed to tutor some entering freshmen. Kids from Charlottesville," said Cathy.

"I hope they're paying you," said Jill.

"I get two credits for it, so I guess. It's only three hours a week. I want to find something else to do, though. I was thinking of interning at a TV station—there's a job in local news at the NBC affiliate."

"Intern—that means no pay, right?" asked Jill, wearily.

"Well, you get a stipend. I'm just thinking about it. I really don't want to waitress anymore."

"Don't blame you."

Jill sat up and rubbed her eyes. "What's that on the chair?"

"CDs. Sara wanted me to bring them to you. There's a little player here, too. If you want them."

"Oh, right," remembered Jill. "Yeah, she gave them to me. I don't know what they are."

"I'll see," said Cathy as she moved to the box and picked it up. Then she returned to her chair, set the box on her lap, and took out a CD.

"There's quite a few. They all look the same." She held the CD up to the light to read the cover. "'The Madison Institute. The Discovery Voyage, Disc One.' Hmm. Sounds like historical stuff."

"Too bad. I was hoping to cha-cha," Jill said, smirking.

Cathy looked at the other CDs.

"There's a whole set of these, whatever they are. I think there's, like, ten or so. They all say '*Voyage of Discovery*.' The CD player looks barely used. The headphones are really cool. Look, Mom."

Cathy held up a pair of black Sony headphones that had big, cushiony ear cups. Jill looked at them and blinked.

"These are, like, professional. I wouldn't mind having them."

"You want 'em, you take 'em," murmured Jill.

"I want to hear what's on this," Cathy said as she inserted disc one into the player and plugged in the headphones. She pushed the play button and waited expectantly as Jill looked on.

"I hear a babbling brook . . ."

"Perfect," Jill said.

"Oh wait!" exclaimed Cathy. "A man is talking. He says that I am going on a journey of discovery and . . . all I need to do is to listen . . . and to pay attention. If I fall asleep, it's OK . . ."

Cathy pressed the stop button and took off the headphones. "I don't know what this is, but it sounds pretty neat. You should try it."

"Maybe I will," said Jill. "Put it on the table, Cath. Would you mind getting me some ice?"

"Sure."

"It's down the hall in one of the . . ."

"I know where it is," Cathy replied as she stood up, set the player on the table, and left the room.

When Cathy returned, she was somber, almost on the verge of tears. Jill noticed immediately that something was wrong.

"What is it, Honey?"

"Mom," began Cathy as she sat in the chair across from the bed. She looked down, into the bucket of ice she held, and spoke in a quiet, emotion-filled voice. "I've already lost Jamie and Dad. I don't think I could take it if I lost you, too. I know it hurts. It hurts me too, but life has to go on for you and me. It has to. You could have killed yourself, falling downstairs because you were loaded. I can't handle this, Mom. You're all I've got. This is a lousy situation for you and me. You have to stop drinking. I don't know what's involved, but I will support you all the way. You're my mom and I love you. I don't want you to die."

Jill nodded, touched by Cathy's words.

"When Jamie and your father were killed, you were a great comfort to me; so were Sara and everybody else. But then you went back to college and everybody else left me . . ." Jill grabbed a tissue from a box beside the bed and blew her nose. "I was alone. Alone in the big house that had once been so full of fun and life and laughter. Now there was nothing. Nothing. Everybody was gone. It was like being in a tomb. My life had ended, too. And if I had found a gun, I would have used it."

"Oh, don't say that!" cried Cathy.

"That's how I felt. Empty. As though my guts had been taken out, and I was just this empty . . . thing. Not a person, not a woman, not a mother. Just a *thing*. I didn't know what to do."

Jill wiped her eyes and blew her nose again.

"Yeah. I know. Drinking is bad. It may kill me. But, if it's any consolation, these past couple of days have opened my eyes . . . a little. I realized this morning that this is the first day in a long time that I don't have a hangover. This is the first time I can actually *taste* the food. This is the first day in a long time that I can see things clearly and feel the love from you and Sara and the compassion from the people in the hospital. Because after the burial, on that frozen day last winter, I went numb. I was in shock. I don't know how I got through it. I was like a zombie. And then everybody just . . . left. And there I was, with Dave's clothes still hanging in the closet, and Jamie's bed still made, waiting for him to return. His baseball cards are still on top of his dresser. I can't bring myself to even touch them . . ."

She started to cry. Cathy got up and hugged her mother. They held each other for a long time, both crying.

"I don't want to lose you!" Cathy said shakily.

"I know. I don't want to lose you either. We will get through this. And I will do my best to stop . . . drinking."

"That's all I can ask," Cathy said, her voice thick. "You promise?"

"I promise, Pumpkin."

It was past midnight, and Jill was wide awake. She pressed a button for the nurse and then reached for the remote control that turned on the television. The TV flickered on. Not much of interest: talk shows, infomercials, and a movie on *Lifetime*, which she'd seen and hated. She finally settled on a program that showed rugged fishermen at sea, hauling in big steel mesh crates of king crab.

Inez, a young Latina nurse, popped her head around the corner. "Hey, Jill," she said. "What can I do for you?"

"I need something to put me out. I want to go to sleep."

"Didn't I bring you a sleeping pill at ten?"

"Yeah, but I don't think it worked. Maybe it was a really old pill," Jill said. "I'm wide awake."

"I can't give you another one until 2:00 a.m. Sorry. I'll check back then, and if you're still awake, then I'll give you one. How's that?" the nurse said, smiling.

"What can I say, Inez? You have the pills."

"You got that right," Inez chuckled. "I'll check back in a couple of hours." She gave Jill a little wave, turned, and left the room.

Jill turned her gaze back to the television. She realized that this was the first time in a long while that she was able to watch

TV clearly, without the buzz of vodka. She wasn't particularly fond of this new clarity; she had grown accustomed to the warm fuzzy dullness. But something had changed. Was it the fall? The attention she was receiving in the hospital? The nourishing food and vitamins she was getting? She felt better than she had in a long time: stronger, more resilient.

On TV, the ship was rocking, and the men clad in orange rain slickers were having a hard time keeping their balance and bringing the huge cage down the side of the boat and into the chute. But the cage soon locked into place and was secure. Then one of the men pulled a handle, and scores of king crab splattered onto a flat surface, their pink legs and claws twitching.

One of the fishermen smiled and gave a thumbs-up to the camera as the program faded to *The Discovery Channel* logo before going to commercial.

Discovery, remembered Jill.

She looked at the player and headphones on the table where Cathy had left them. She picked up the player and looked at it. Easy enough to use, she thought. Just one big play button and three other little buttons. She set it on her lap, grabbed the remote control for the TV, and switched it off. Then she put the headphones on, pressed the play button, and lay back on her pillow.

As she closed her eyes, Jill heard a babbling brook, as Cathy had said. It sounded wonderful—soothing and restful. She could fall asleep listening to this, no problem. Then Jill heard the voice of an older man, maybe a grandfather. It was a soothing voice, one she liked.

You are going on a voyage of discovery. All you need do is to listen . . . and to pay attention. If you fall asleep, that is perfectly all right. You won't miss a thing. As you listen to the soothing sounds of the stream, make yourself as comfortable as possible—on your back, on your side, or even sitting up—whatever is best for you . . ."

As the man continued to talk, another sound began to whoosh through both of Jill's ears, a series of low tones that seemed to swirl inside her head. The tones continued, and Jill was instructed to mentally picture a strong box with a heavy lid. Into this box she was to put any worries, cares, or concerns. These concerns, she was told, would only "get in the way." She was given a few moments to do this.

Amid the background of the babbling brook and the deep swirling tones, Jill imagined an old-fashioned wooden captain's chest made of dark oak with a curved top.

What would she put into it? She thought of a photograph of Dave, Jamie, Cathy, and herself, and she put that into the trunk. Then she thought of Sara and of others she knew in Marietta, and she put them in as well. Dr. Ryan, Nurse Inez, the others—all went into the trunk. Next, she imagined her wallet, with its dwindling supply of cash, and the man at the bank—they went into the trunk, too. Last, she pictured a bottle of vodka and dropped it in silently. Then she closed the heavy lid and latched it, using the two bulky clasps on the front. Then, as instructed, she mentally turned away from the trunk and waited for the next instruction. She lay in complete blackness, bathed in the sounds, for what seemed to be a long time. She grew sleepy and was beginning to nod off, but then something happened.

Her body grew rigid and began to vibrate. It wasn't unpleasant, but Jill couldn't fight it. Her body was buzzing as though she were lying on a vibrating bed. It seemed to last for several minutes, growing in intensity. Then it stopped abruptly.

Jill looked around, disoriented. She was no longer in her bed; she was somewhere else.

Where am I?

It was dark, and she peered around, trying to get her bearings. She felt like she were floating. Was she dreaming?

She looked down and saw a woman in a hospital bed, lying on her back, with headphones on her head, eyes closed.

Oh God, no . . . That's me.

Was she dying? Was she dead?

What is happening?

She waved her arms and flailed around, panic stricken, hovering just below the ceiling. She tried to call out, but her voice sounded distant and feeble. She felt cold terror, and there was no way out. She had died. Just when she was starting to feel good.

Suddenly back in her bed, Jill sat up, sweaty, disoriented, and deeply shaken. She reached for the white control that had the call buttons and pushed the nurse button repeatedly until Inez came running down the corridor and into Jill's room.

"What's the problem?" asked Inez.

"I think I just died," said Jill, trembling.

Inez rolled her eyes and moved to check Jill's pulse. "Now why would you say that?"

"I was up there—on the ceiling—and I couldn't get back. It was terrible. I wasn't in my body."

"You want me to call the doctor?"

"Didn't you hear me?" insisted Jill. "*I was out of my damn body, and I was floating on the ceiling! I was dead!"*

"I've heard about that," said Inez soothingly. "Sometimes that happens to people in surgery, while they're on the operating table. Oh boy. But it looks like you made it back OK."

"Yeah, for *now!*" cried Jill.

"I'll page the doctor on call," Inez said as she rushed out of the room and into the corridor.

The doctor on duty was Thomas Bellino, M.D., a young resident from Columbia Presbyterian Medical School. He was of Italian descent, with an olive complexion, dark curly hair, a narrow face, and a boyish grin.

"I'm going to give you a sedative so you can get some sleep," Dr. Bellino told Jill. "But first, I want you to tell me what happened."

Jill recounted the events, her voice trembling. She had been listening to a CD, some kind of guided meditation, when she went rigid, blacked out, and suddenly found herself floating near the ceiling of her room. She had no idea how long she was out, but she was petrified, especially after seeing her own body lying in the bed beneath her.

Dr. Bellino nodded sympathetically and then said, "I've heard about this. It happens sometimes in surgical situations. Accidents, too. Normally when patients are as upset as you are, I would call for a psych exam, but you're not the first person this has happened to. In fact, I knew of a case in which a woman was in a car accident and felt that she was out of her body from the time of the crash until she woke up in intensive care. She saw the whole thing."

"Did she die?" asked Jill.

"No," smiled Dr. Bellino. "If she'd died, I wouldn't have known about her experience."

"Well, *duh*," grimaced Jill.

"There's a doctor over at Selby General . . . I forget his name now, but he's from India, I think. He's board certified in holistic medicine, and he does Reiki, Healing Touch. Does outstanding orthopedic work, too. Interesting guy. I bet he could help you figure this out. The thing for you to do is not to worry about it. Get some sleep. I'll request a consult for you."

"Well, OK," Jill said. "Thank you. Very much. I just have this dread I won't wake up the next time."

"I am positive you'll be fine," Dr. Bellino soothed, and he patted Jill on the shoulder as he got up to leave.

"Hope so."

Tuesday

The next morning, a little after 9:30, Jampa Singh strode down the corridor of the hospital, headed for Jill Messenger's room. Dr. Singh was small, dapper, slightly pudgy around the midline, and he had a head of thick curly black hair and twinkly raccoon-like eyes. He wore black slacks, a light blue shirt, and, despite the heat of summer, a Harris tweed jacket.

As Dr. Singh entered Jill's room, Inez was just finishing drawing a tube of blood.

"Mrs. Messenger? Good morning! I am Jampa Singh, and I am on staff over at Selby General. Dr. Bellino paged me this morning and asked if I would see you. So, how are you doing?"

Jill smiled at Dr. Singh: such effervescence was rare and, today, welcome.

"*Well . . .*" began Jill.

"I hear you had a little adventure last night," exclaimed Dr. Singh as he pulled up a chair beside Jill. "Tell me about it."

As Inez departed, Jill explained what happened, and her fear of what it may mean or imply. When she had finished talking, Dr. Singh asked to see the CD she had been listening to. Jill pointed to the box, which was now on the chair at the foot of the bed. Dr. Singh picked it up, returned to his chair, and looked at the CDs with great interest. At last he spoke.

"Tell me," he began. "Do you think there is any connection between the CD you were listening to and your floating on the ceiling?"

"I hadn't thought about that," said Jill. "I was just listening to a man talking, and I started to fall asleep. That's when the vibrations started."

"I see," Dr. Singh said slowly. "OK. Let me ask you: are you familiar with The Madison Institute?"

"No," replied Jill. "Doesn't ring a bell."

"That's where your CDs came from," began Dr. Singh. He paused for a moment and then began to speak. "There was a man named Robert Madison, and he lived with his wife and kids in Connecticut. And, one night he had an out-of-body experience, just like the one you had . . ."

"I don't think . . ." began Jill, but Dr. Singh waved a hand to cut her off.

"I know about these things, so just listen, please. Mr. Madison went out of body, just like you. It was the *same* thing. He was on the ceiling, and he thought he was dead. He was *terrified*. He talked to doctors; they could tell him nothing. His OBEs, or out-of-body experiences, continued, and Mr. Madison came to realize that he would not be harmed. He was safe! And then he became excited at the possibilities; and he learned how to use his wonderful new ability. He went all kinds of places, made many important discoveries, and went on to write books and start a school. Believe it or not, out-of-body experiences are actually fairly common. They are just not talked about very much."

"I can't believe that," said Jill. "I felt like I was dying. Honest."

"So did Mr. Madison. So does everyone. It's called the threshold, and it is difficult to cross. But everybody goes out of body while they are dreaming. They just don't remember it."

"This is all . . . baffling. I never heard of this kind of thing before—*ever*. I don't know what to think. Whatever that was last night, it just . . . *changed* me. And now you're telling me it's harmless?"

"Yes. And I am also telling you that you have a valuable resource in this box. These CDs are used by many people to achieve an out-of-body state, though I think you may be the first person in Marietta to do it. You are certainly the first I'm aware of."

"Well," said Jill, "It's nice to be first at something. But it *scared* me. You must know that. I'm still scared."

"Everyone is. Think of being on a big roller coaster. The first ride is frightening beyond belief. But the next one isn't quite so bad. And by twenty or thirty times, you're used to it. It's nothing."

"*Hmm*," mused Jill as she looked at the box of CDs.

Dr. Singh smiled and said, "I know you're being discharged today. If you decide to use these CDs in the future—and I hope you will try—feel free to call me if you have any questions or problems. Here's my card. Good luck, Mrs. Messenger!"

He started for the door, but Jill spoke.

"Have you ever had these experiences yourself?" asked Jill, suddenly curious.

The doctor turned, leaned close to Jill, and spoke in a low voice.

"Yes. Long ago, when I was a boy. I used to go out all the time! I went everywhere—I flew over the treetops. I went into the past, into the future, everywhere!"

"*Really?*"

"Oh yes. Many times. But that was long ago," he said, smiling. "Believe me, it's just wonderful, and . . . I guess the main thing I am telling you is, don't worry. It won't hurt you, and it can lead to some great adventures."

Dr. Singh stood up, buttoned his jacket, and handed the box of CDs to Jill.

"May I ask you something?"

"Sure."

"Who have you told about your . . . experience?"

"I told the nurse, Dr. Bellino . . . that's it."

Dr. Singh nodded. "Well," he began, leaning in, "I wouldn't tell anyone else."

"Why not?" asked Jill.

"People are funny. I just wouldn't say anything."

"OK. Well, thanks a lot," replied Jill as Dr. Singh nodded, turned, and left the room.

Three hours later, Sara's red minivan rolled to a stop in front of Jill's house. Its doors opened, and Cathy, Sara, and Jill got out and stepped to the sidewalk. Jill was carrying her dark teal duffel.

"Cathy and I took the liberty of tidying up a bit," Sara said offhandedly as she climbed the steps to the front porch.

"Oh, I wish you hadn't," replied Jill.

Inwardly, she was pleased but mortified. She knew the state the house has been in, but at the time she didn't care. Now she did, and—thanks to Cathy and Sara—they were giving her a fresh start.

She thought briefly of Dr. Singh. She liked him. Whatever temptation she might have felt to tell Cathy and Sara about her brief experience on the ceiling of her room was replaced by the wisdom of Dr. Singh's admonition. She'd keep quiet. She hadn't decided whether to risk another out-of-body experience, but Dr. Singh had piqued her interest. For some reason, flying over treetops seemed appealing.

"Ta-da!" exclaimed Cathy as she opened the front door and motioned for Jill to enter.

"Hope you like it," laughed Sara. "We stopped short of repainting."

Everything gleamed—the floors, the furniture, the lamps. The house even smelled fresh and clean. Tears came to Jill's eyes. She turned and hugged Sara and then Cathy.

Later that evening, after Cathy left to drive back to school, Jill sat on her couch, smoking a cigarette. A bottle of vodka stood on the polished coffee table, and a glass of ice cubes sat beside it.

Feels good to be back.

She switched on the TV and poured vodka into the glass until it was half full. Then she took a sip. It made her shudder. She always shuddered at the first sip, as the alcohol made its presence known. She glanced at her watch: 11:08 p.m. Cathy would be almost back to Charlottesville by now. Jill loved her, but she was glad to be alone, in her house, drinking again. It was comfortably familiar, but she knew she'd have to be careful. No more hospital visits. The coroner, maybe, but not the hospital.

The TV news was on, and the top stories were about the upcoming Sternwheel Festival and the NASCAR races down in Athens, a few miles south of Marietta. After the lead stories, the news showed a local reporter standing in a field near the Muskingum River, talking about a Brownie troop: "One hundred local Brownies are going to have their summer jamboree right here, on the banks of the Muskingum River," said the woman. "Starting this Friday, the girls will sleep in tents, cook their own meals over campfires, and have a lot of fun."

Jill had a slight feeling, a premonition, about the girls, but then she dismissed the thought and took another sip of vodka. She shuddered again. This time she didn't like the feeling. It felt foreign, like an invading army that was out to get her.

She stood up, took the drink and the bottle, and walked back to the kitchen. She set the bottle on the counter and poured the vodka down the sink, then rinsed out the glass. She returned to the living room, picked up the remote control, and switched off the TV. Then she moved to the lamp on the table at the end of the couch and switched it off. Jill moved upstairs quickly.

She entered her bedroom, switched on the light, and saw her duffel bag at the end of the bed. She moved to the duffel bag, zipped it open, and took out a handful of clothes, some papers from the hospital, and the shoebox containing the CDs, player, and headphones. She gathered the clothes, moved to her closet, and opened the door. The wicker hamper was empty—quite a surprise! She dropped the laundry into the hamper and replaced the lid. Then she took the empty duffel bag and put it on the top shelf. She returned to her bed, picked up the CD player and headphones, set them beside her pillow, and switched on the light beside her bed. She noticed how clean everything was and she smiled. She was lucky to have such a good daughter and friend.

A few minutes later, Jill was in her nightgown, lying on her bed, wearing the headphones. She was nervous and excited. She thought about Dr. Singh. What if she went out of body and couldn't get back? He had said that lots of people do it and that she would be fine. *Well*, she thought, *there's only one way to find out.*

She lay back and pressed the play button. It made a little whirring sound, and then she heard the babbling brook. She liked this sound. She wondered if they made a CD of just the babbling brook; she would love that. Then she heard the grandfatherly voice of Robert Madison:

You are going on a voyage of discovery. All you need do . . . is to listen . . . and to pay attention. If you fall asleep, that is perfectly all right. You won't miss a thing. As you listen to the soothing sounds of the stream, make yourself as comfortable as possible—on your back, on your side, or even sitting up—whatever is best for you . . .

As before, low tones began to swirl through Jill's head as she was instructed to picture the strong box with a heavy lid. She began to relax as she pictured the large wooden trunk, the same as the one she had pictured two nights before. She opened the heavy top and was soon putting things into it: Dave, Jamie, Cathy, her wallet, her bottle of vodka, her checkbook. That was enough.

Jill mentally turned away from the trunk and waited for the next instruction as the sounds continued to play. She began to doze off, but then Robert Madison's voice soothingly reappeared. She was to breath in energy, with her eyes open, so that it filled her entire body. Then, eyes closed, she was to breathe out the old, stale, used-up energy. As she breathed out, she was to hum or make a tone. *Seems kind of odd*, thought Jill, *but what the heck?* As Jill began to inhale, mentally filling herself with energy, she heard voices on the CD humming one single note. It was low, and the voices sounded like monks. There were no words, just a low *Ahhhh*. Jill followed along, breathing in and saying *Ahhhh* as she exhaled. Her body began to tingle. She could feel it along her legs, her arms, and her fingertips. She was suddenly sleepy, as if each exhalation took something from her. Then the vibrations began, and . . .

She *let go*.

Now Jill was floating on the ceiling of her room. She looked down and saw herself lying peacefully on her bed with the big black headphones on her ears. She was a little anxious, but she wasn't afraid. She waved her arms and tried to move, but she seemed stuck near the ceiling. She reached up with her right hand to push herself off, but her hand went through the ceiling, as if it were only a shadow. Jill looked surprised and then withdrew her hand. She closed her eyes and concentrated. Now she was floating just above the floor at the foot of her bed, looking at herself.

This is very cool.

She turned and floated toward her bedroom door. When she arrived, she reached for the knob, but her hand couldn't grasp it.

How do I get out?

Then she put her hand through the door until her arm disappeared up to the elbow. She put her other hand through the door in a similar manner. When both arms were extended through her bedroom door, she closed her eyes, scrunched up her face, and moved effortlessly through it. Now she was hovering over the carpet outside her bedroom.

Is this really happening?

She turned, scrunched up her face again, and forcefully dove back through the bedroom door. However, because of the strength of her intention, she sailed right through the door, across her bedroom, and through the outside wall. She had a brief sensation of the wall and bricks as she passed through them. Now she was hovering twenty feet over Sixth Street and was suddenly concerned that someone would see her:

Hey, there's Jill Messenger in her nightgown!

What the hell is she doing up there?

She looked around at the peaceful street. Everything seemed to radiate with an inner glow: the trees, the houses, the moon and stars.

This is like a real, beautiful dream.

She thought briefly of Dave and Jamie, and—for a moment—Jill had a distinct vision of them standing together in a beautiful park, smiling at her.

"We're OK, Mom," said Jamie. "Don't worry!"

"Hi, Honey! *Love you!*" said Dave.

All of a sudden, Jill was in blackness, spinning down a tunnel. Then she felt the pressure of the pillow and the headphones. She was back. She sat up in bed, flung off the headphones, and began to sob.

They were OK.

Wednesday

The next morning, Jill sat at her kitchen table. Before her was her mug of coffee, her cordless phone, and Dr. Singh's business card. She dialed his number and waited through several rings. Then she heard the familiar, cheery voice: "Hello. You have reached the offices of Dr. Jampa Singh. Unfortunately, I am not available to take your call, but I would be pleased to call you back."

Jill left a brief message and hung up. She needed some answers. She also needed money. She decided to drive to town.

Jill had liked Marietta ever since she and Dave moved there from upstate New York several years before. It was a picturesque town located on the Ohio River across from West Virginia. The population of Marietta was 12,000, but Jill always felt like it was smaller. When she walked along the broad streets of downtown, there were only a few pedestrians and not much traffic. She liked that. She and Dave could walk into any restaurant and get a table right away. Well, not Tampico's Mexican restaurant on a Friday night, but usually at the other places. People were friendly and didn't snoop; that was another thing she liked. There was a mix of cultures, too: northeast sensibility, southern hospitality, and a kind of western twang to it all. Marietta, with its modest levees, was a popular stop for sternwheel riverboats, which added a touch of history. The summer before, she, Dave, Jamie, and Cathy attended the Sternwheel Festival. Her friend Sara had gotten a job near the waterfront in a little booth selling Belgian waffles. Jill, Dave, and the kids had eaten lunch that day at the River House, a historic building that faced the Ohio River. Those were pleasant memories.

But they were in the dim past as Jill drove down Third Street to see Robert Guerra at Frontier Bank. She needed a second mortgage—or some kind of financial assistance—to tide her over until a new source of income could be found. She thought about substitute teaching, but it was June, so there would be no work until the fall. And, even then, getting a permanent sub position wasn't assured. She could always temp or do secretarial work at Chevrol, the company for which Dave had worked. She knew many people at the company, and they had been kind to her when he died. Dave's retirement package amounted to $20,000, which was quickly swallowed up by Cathy's tuition at the University of Virginia.

Robert Guerra had only been in Marietta for a few years; prior to that, he had worked at another Frontier Bank elsewhere in Ohio. Not that it mattered. Jill and Dave liked him. He was pleasant to them, and he was sharp as a tack. When Dave had been working, making the monthly payment of $1,500 was manageable. But now . . . well, she would just have to see.

"Jill!" exclaimed Robert as she entered his office at the back of the bank. "How are you doing?" A striking man in his mid-fifties, Robert was Jill's contact at Frontier Bank. He had dark curly hair with streaks of grey and was immaculately dressed in a navy blue suit, pale blue shirt, and yellow tie. Even though he stood 5′6″, he seemed taller, more imposing.

"OK," replied Jill with a half smile.

They shook hands, and some of Robert's cologne remained with her. It smelled good.

"Here, sit down!" Robert told her as he motioned toward the chair in front of his desk. "Did I hear something about you being in the hospital? Is everything all right?"

"I'm fine. Just took a spill, that's all," said Jill, looking down.

"Oh, gee," nodded Robert. "Wouldn't want anything to happen to you!" There was a brief pause, and then he added, "So, what can I do ya for?"

Jill explained that she might need a second mortgage, or some kind of loan to see her through the summer, and that she was hoping to get some kind of employment—teaching, maybe—in the fall.

"Listen, Jill, listen. Don't worry. We'll take care of you. You and Dave were practically my first customers when I got here!"

"I guess that's right," said Jill.

For the next twenty minutes, they discussed various ways the bank might be able to help her over the short term, without going into a second mortgage. He was kind and pleasant, and he made her laugh with his cheerful good humor. It was the first time Jill had laughed in a long while.

Then Robert offered the advice that, once Jill was solvent again, she might think about getting a financial advisor, someone who would place her money in solid, high-yield accounts: stocks, bonds, T-bills. Jill didn't know about any of that, but said, "Well, maybe."

"My brother-in-law, Ernie. Guy's a whiz. I placed some money with him five years ago, and he's doubled it."

"Wow."

"So that's something to think about down the road," smiled Robert.

"I guess it is," said Jill, nodding.

The conversation hit a lull. Then Robert suddenly spoke, his eyebrows high, "Say, Jill. Do you like horse racing?"

"I guess," she replied. "Why?"

Robert smiled and leaned forward. "I'm planning to go to the races on Saturday. And, if you would like to have a day out, I would be honored. I don't like going alone all that much, even though I sometimes see a few friends out there."

"Well, maybe," said Jill.

Robert took one of his business cards from a little holder on the front of his desk, flipped it over, and wrote on the back of it. Then he handed it to Jill.

"Here's my card. I put my home phone on the back. You can call me any time." Robert smiled pleasantly at Jill. "No pressure. Just a fun day at the races. We can sit in the clubhouse—very nice, air-conditioned. They have nice lunches there, too. Very pleasant." Then he paused, unable to sense what Jill was thinking. "Of course it's fun down in the grandstand, too. You can walk out on the flat area and stand right by the rail at the finish line. Those horses sure make a racket."

"I don't know, Robert . . ."

"Call me Bob," Robert smiled.

"OK, Bob," smiled Jill. "It might be a little early for me to do something like that. On the other hand, it might be just what I need."

"Well, as I said, no pressure," smiled Robert. "I'm going to go anyway, so whatever you decide is OK by me."

"Thanks. I'll call you one way or the other."

Robert stood up and extended a hand to Jill. She shook it again, and then Robert walked her out of his office. When she reached the street, Jill sniffed her hand.

Bob sure wears nice cologne.

When Jill arrived home, she found a message on her answering machine. She pressed the button, and Dr. Singh's cheery voice filled the kitchen. "Hello, Mrs. Messenger. I was wondering about you! How are you doing? I'll be at Marietta College all day, so feel free to give me a call or even stop by; I have an office on the second floor of the Rickey Science Center, room 215. Thank you!" Because Marietta College was only a short distance away, not far from Jill's house, she decided to wander down and visit Dr. Singh.

The day had become warm and slightly humid, typical for this time of year. Jill walked down Sixth Street until she arrived at the entrance to Marietta College. She entered the pretty campus and found the Science Center on the right, down an outdoor stairway. Soon, she was in the brightly lit foyer, where she took the elevator to the second floor. In a few moments, Jill was tapping on the edge of a door frame. Dr. Singh sat up with a start.

"Ah, there you are! I just left you a message, and here you are. Come in!"

Jill smiled and said, "Yes, I got it. I decided to come see you. I hope you don't mind."

Dr. Singh quickly stood up, buttoned his jacket, and

grabbed a stack of papers and notebooks from his other chair. "Please. Have a seat."

Jill moved toward the chair, but Dr. Singh put the papers back and announced, "I have a better idea! Let's get some coffee and cake."

In a few minutes, Jill and Dr. Singh were walking across the campus of Marietta College toward Gilman Hall, which had a modern dining area on the ground floor.

As they walked toward the hall, Dr. Singh said, "Tell me. Have you had more experiences like the one the other night?"

"Yes, I have," began Jill. "Last night. You were right. It's very exciting, once I got past the idea that I wasn't in danger."

"Oh no. It's safe, so long as your physical body is not disturbed."

Jill nodded, "That's good."

"So you had no problem getting out and about?"

"Well," began Jill. "I am not doing it consciously. At least I don't think so, but I listened to the CD last night with the intention of . . ."

"That's the secret," interrupted Dr. Singh, smiling broadly. "Intention is everything. You hold the intention, but don't force it. Just hold it lightly. Ah, here we are, our campus refectory."

Jill and Dr. Singh entered Gilman Hall and turned right into the gleaming dining area. Soon they were settled at a table with cups of coffee and spicy carrot cake. Dr. Singh looked at Jill with his large, dark eyes and asked, "So! What happened? I am most curious about this." He was still jovial, but now his question seemed to have a deeper purpose.

Jill took a sip of coffee and glanced around to make sure

nobody else was within earshot. Then she leaned forward and said quietly, "Well. I was on the ceiling, just as I was in the hospital . . ."

"Yes?"

"But then I imagined myself standing at the foot of my bed, and, suddenly, there I was." Dr. Singh was about to speak, but Jill held up a finger. "Then I was able to, well, *float* . . . right through my bedroom door, like it was a shadow."

"Very good," nodded Dr. Singh.

"Then I kind of lost control because I wanted to just go back into my room, but I ended up out in the street. Well, over it. And that felt kind of weird, just hovering over the pavement like that."

"That kind of thing just takes a little practice," said Dr. Singh. "You said it before: *intention.* That is what counts." He was leaning in toward Jill, interested. "You know, you are the first person I have met in a long time who has taken to it. I thought you would have been put off by the experience in the hospital, but I can see you're a brave young woman."

"Well, I'm not that brave *or* young. But what I am is curious. If such a thing is possible, then why aren't more people doing it?"

Jill looked around again. The dining room was nearly empty, except for a table of matronly foodservice workers, absorbed in their conversations.

"You may not believe this, but everyone does it."

"No way."

"Absolutely," smiled Dr. Singh. "But they are asleep, and their astral travels happen while they are in a dream state. Oh, people leave their bodies and go lots of places. They see old friends, visit places they used to live, all sorts of things. But usually they do not remember these occurrences . . . unless they remember flying, even flying in a plane."

"I see," said Jill pensively. "I was just wondering if my . . . ability was somehow influenced by my head injury."

"Possibly," said Dr. Singh. "I didn't see your chart, so I don't know. I guess you had some kind of subdural trauma, but I can't say for sure whether that's what caused it. But, if I had to guess, Mrs. Messenger, you had these abilities long before you bumped your head. Everyone has similar abilities, but most don't know it. And those who do know aren't always that interested."

"Well," said Jill quietly. "When I was little, I used to see things . . . people, places. They were strange to me, and I thought I was making them up. When I got older, I didn't see them. That's another thing. Every once in a while, I kind of . . . well, know . . . if something is going to happen. I get a little mental . . . picture."

Dr. Singh nodded and smiled slightly.

"So," he began, "it seems you have some talent in the extrasensory."

"No, I wouldn't call it a talent. It's nothing I ever tried to do. It just happens. But something else happened last night," continued Jill. "I don't know if it was real or if I was imagining it. It happened just before I woke up."

"Tell me about it," replied Dr. Singh.

"I was thinking about Dave and Jamie, my husband and son. They were killed this past January in an accident. They were out skiing in Colorado over New Year's, and their car slid off the road and went down into a ravine. So it's been difficult, for many reasons.

Anyhow, I thought of them as I was hovering over the street . . . and then, suddenly, I think I saw them. I mean, I had a clear, distinct image of the two of them standing together. And then Jamie said that he and dad . . . were OK and that I shouldn't worry."

Dr. Singh nodded thoughtfully. Then he asked, "Did you see them in any particular surroundings? Were they in a setting that was familiar to you?"

Jill thought for a moment and said, "No. They looked like they were in some beautiful place outdoors. There were trees and a blue sky, and . . ."

"*Ahh*," nodded Dr. Singh. "Yes. I know, from experience, many people who pass over go to a place called the Garden. It's kind of a way station. It's a place people often go after they die. They meet their mothers, grandfathers, old friends, lots of people. Sometimes the new arrivals wait until they are joined by other friends or family members . . ."

"Are you serious?" asked Jill.

"Totally," nodded Dr. Singh.

"What about heaven and hell?" she whispered.

"Oh, there's no hell," smiled Dr. Singh. "At least not in the spirit world."

Then he paused for a moment before continuing.

"Well, I wasn't completely accurate. There is such a thing as hell, but it's on earth. People who live in horrible conditions, without hope. *That* is hell."

"But what about heaven?" she asked. "I had hoped that Dave and Jamie would be up there by now. Sounds kind of odd, I know, but that is what I hoped."

"Well," began Dr. Singh, "without going into too much controversy, I can pretty much assure you that we're all part of the oneness, creation, God, call it whatever you like. We have existed since creation, and our salvation, or *continuity* might be a better word, is a done deal."

Jill nodded. "I hope that's true."

"You have the ability to find out for yourself, you know," said Dr. Singh, quietly.

"How do I do that?"

"Just keep on doing what you're doing. You will learn a great deal."

Jill looked out the window for a moment and then she peered directly at Dr. Singh. "You told me the other day that it was possible to travel into the past, the future. Is that right?"

Dr. Singh smiled. "Certainly. Once you are free of physical matter, there is no time or space. You can go wherever you want."

"How do I do that?" asked Jill earnestly.

"Well, I can't exactly give you a map, but I can tell you that holding the intention will move you toward your goal. Let's say you wanted to see a famous historical figure like . . . George Washington. Once you are out of body, if you hold the intention of seeing him, you may be suddenly at his side."

"Wow," said Jill.

This is exciting.

"When you are ready, it might be good for you to visit your husband and son. It would give you some good insight into the nature of reality," said Dr. Singh.

"I thought about it," said Jill, quietly, "but I'm not quite sure if I'm ready for that yet."

"When the time is right, you will know. In the meantime, you have a wonderful opportunity to explore. I envy you. And I hope you will keep me apprised of your progress," smiled Dr. Singh.

"I will," Jill assured. "You're the only one I can talk to about this."

Dr. Singh glanced at his watch.

"Oh dear. I have a meeting in ten minutes. Sorry, but I just remembered, and Dr. McCaffrey is not a man one keeps waiting."

Jill smiled. "No, that's fine. I have things to do also. But I'll be in touch."

"I hope so, Jill Messenger," Dr. Singh said as he started to leave. Then he turned to her, put his hands together, bowed slightly, and said, "Namaste!"

Jill bowed back to Dr. Singh with a goofy smile.

Saturday

"Gee, I thought the track would be more crowded than this," Robert said with a quizzical smile.

"Well, there's the big NASCAR car race down in Athens," offered Jill. "That's on this weekend."

"Oh right," nodded Robert. "I forgot about that."

She looked down at her program for the day's race and wondered about the best way to use her new "information." The previous night she had gone *out* twice. The first time, she wanted to get used to flying around the neighborhood.

45

That was *quite* a kick.

She lifted out, flew through her bedroom wall, and sailed across the street, straight into Sara's house. She saw Sara, propped up in bed, watching TV and eating Pepperidge Farm Milanos. Then Jill moved out, up, and soared over the treetops. Everything looked so soft and sweet and twinkly from high up—the trees looked like broccoli.

Flying was better than she could possibly have imagined. It was like being in a dream, but she could see clearly and just go. It was sweet and beautiful.

Jill soared over the Lafayette Hotel toward the west side of Marietta, but she became disoriented once she passed the Becky Thatcher riverboat moored in the river. Nothing looked familiar. She wasn't particularly concerned because she remembered what Dr. Singh had told her; she would be OK no matter what. She closed her eyes and held the intention to return home.

She felt the pillow and knew that she'd made it back, safe and sound. She took a deep breath and smiled to herself. Then she got out of bed and padded downstairs to get *The Marietta Times* off the coffee table.

Earlier in the day, Jill had folded the paper to the racing page of the sports section and had looked at the list of entries for Saturday. She went back upstairs and put the newspaper at the foot of her bed. Then she climbed back to her pillow, lay down, and put on the headphones . . .

You are going on a voyage of discovery . . .

There was that nice, familiar voice and the tones.

She was soon out of her body, floating at the foot of her bed, the racing page before her. She couldn't pick it up, but she could see the date at the top of the page. She lightly held the intention of being at the races the next day, seeing the big scoreboard in the middle of the infield.

Suddenly, Jill was transported to the flat spectator area, directly across from where the winning horses' numbers were posted. She watched the board, trying to memorize the numbers as they flashed before her.

There are too many! I can't remember them all!

Holding her intention, Jill went back and saw the results of the first race. It was a trifecta, and she saw the numbers of the three winning horses as they flashed on the board: 5, 3, 9. She could remember them. She *would* remember them.

Jill was back on her bed now, very tired. She gently removed the headphones, set them on the table with the player, got under the covers, and immediately fell asleep.

"So, do you know anything about horse racing?" asked Robert, snapping Jill out of her reverie.

"Well, a little," smiled Jill. She looked at Robert. He was wearing that nice cologne again, and he was nattily attired in a tan Palm Beach suit and a light blue shirt, open at the neck.

"It's pretty easy, but there is a science to it," said Robert, matter-of-factly. "The program lists all the information: how old the horse is, the statistics for the jockey, how many races the horse has won, the track conditions . . . you read all this stuff, and then you watch the board to see what the odds are. The odds change, you know. You could bet a horse that is 9 to 1, but by post time, it's 4 to 1."

"Doesn't seem fair," said Jill. "If I place a bet at 9 to 1, and the horse wins, then that's what I should win, right?"

"In theory, yes," nodded Robert. "But this is called paramutual wagering, and that's why it changes. Still, you can probably do OK if you bet smart."

Nevertheless, she was nervous.

"So, *Bob*, were you going to give me twenty dollars to bet?" asked Jill, coyly.

"Oh right," said Robert. He took out his wallet and handed a twenty to Jill. "Don't bet it all on the first race. I would be happy to place a bet for you. That way you wouldn't have to go up to the windows and wait in line."

"What's a trifecta?" asked Jill as she looked at the program.

"It's a fancy word for throwing your money away," laughed Robert.

"No, I'm serious," Jill said. "What is it?"

"That is where you pick the first three horses in a given race. Not all races have trifecta wagering, but the first one does. But Jill, if you only get two of the three horses correct, you still lose your money. You have to get all three, in the order they cross the finish line. It's almost impossible. Even seasoned gamblers avoid it."

"I was just wondering," smiled Jill.

A few minutes later, Jill approached the betting window, placed the twenty dollar bill before the cashier, and said, "Trifecta, please. Five, three, nine."

The cashier swept the twenty under the gate and said,

"How much are you betting?"

"Twenty," said Jill, looking around.

The cashier punched some buttons on a machine, and a little pink ticket popped out. It read: *Mid-Ohio Racing—Race One—Trifecta—5-3-9—$20.00.*

"Thanks," said Jill, sweeping the ticket into her hand and moving back toward the clubhouse where Robert was waiting, sipping a vodka and tonic.

When she approached the table, he looked up, smiled, and said, "So, what horse did you bet on?"

"It's a secret," smiled Jill. "Don't want to jinx myself."

"Smart," nodded Robert approvingly. "Never tell anyone how you bet."

The first race was a one-mile race for two-year-olds. This meant the starting gate was directly in front of the grandstand. The gate, a long series of small cages, was moved into position by a boy driving a gray tractor with red fenders. The horses were behind it, down the track, each carrying a jockey wearing colorful silks. The number five horse, *Joss*, was a beautiful black thoroughbred with the jockey attired in green and white. Despite the beauty of the animal, the odds were long: 15:1. The number three horse, another long shot at 9:1, was a dapple gray horse named *T-For-Now*; its jockey wore bright red with baby blue. The number nine horse, a chestnut named *Dreamcatcher*, snorted and danced around on the dirt, shying at the gate. This horse was the place favorite at 3:1; the jockey wore black-and-white silks.

Jill peered through Robert's binoculars to see the horses, and she wondered if anybody else had made the same bet. And, for a brief moment, she wondered if she was a fool.

Soon the mounts were in the gate, and somewhere an electric bell rang. Jill clasped her hands together and squeezed. There was a momentary pause.

Then the gates slammed suddenly open, the announcer cried, "They're off!" and the horses shot out, jockeys leaning forward in an extended crouch. As the horses approached the first turn, there was a sea of horse rumps, all jostling for position.

They're so fast!

As she stood with Robert, watching the horses race down the back stretch and then around the clubhouse turn, Jill tingled with excitement and anticipation. It was hard to see who was in the lead, and the roar of the crowd made hearing the announcer difficult. Robert was watching intently through the binoculars, saying, *"Come on, come on . . ."*

When the horses streaked past the finish line, Jill could barely breathe. She had won. Five-three-nine was the correct order, just as she had seen.

I can do it!

"How'd you do?" asked Robert. But Jill just silently shook her head.

"Hey, what did you expect? Pick a winner the first race?"

Soon the sweaty horses and their jockeys ambled back toward the paddock, accompanied by stewards on sturdy mounts. The winning horse, the proud, gleaming black thoroughbred, moved delicately toward the winner's circle. There were smiles, flowers, and the flashes of cameras. It was a clean win: no bumps, protests, or photo finishes. The winners had crossed the line, just as Jill had foreseen. For the spectators, the biggest surprise was that *Joss* won and that *T-For-Now* placed. But sometimes there are big surprises at the track, which is why they found thoroughbred racing so exciting.

The tote board flashed the winning amounts and announcer that the race was "official." The trifecta paid $720 for a two-dollar win ticket. Jill wanted to leap up and scream *Holy crap!*—but she couldn't. She sat politely, barely able to control herself.

"I went bust," smiled Robert. "I had a show bet on *Night Train*, number seven. He was doing good for a while, but hey, that's the breaks. Two bucks down the drain. How'd you do?"

"Two bucks down the drain," replied Jill, her voice quivering.

Robert picked up on the tone of Jill's answer and said, "Oh, don't take it so hard. It's only two dollars."

"Right," Jill said.

She had never been so thrilled.

CHAPTER TWO

Las Vegas, Nevada

Patrick Waterhouse strode across the expansive lobby of the Starlight Resort and Casino, heading toward the registration desk. He was about sixty and was a 5'11", fit gentleman with close-cropped hair. Waterhouse was dressed in a navy blue Pierre Cardin blazer, tan slacks, and a white polo shirt open at the neck. In one hand, he carried a well-worn brown leather attaché case, and he rolled a Henk titanium suitcase with the other. At this time of the morning, 7:30, the lobby was nearly empty. Despite this, a short, stocky man carrying an umbrella and wearing a dark overcoat suddenly slammed into Waterhouse from the back, pitching him forward. The end of the umbrella jabbed into the back of Waterhouse's lower calf. By the time Waterhouse turned to see who it was, the man was careening down the lobby.

It was no accident.

Whoever the man was, he had been sent to deliver something. Waterhouse realized that no matter how carefully he planned, they could find him. As he straightened his jacket, Waterhouse wondered: was this a hit or just a drill? Either way, he didn't like it.

But it didn't surprise him either.

After registering at the Starlight desk, Waterhouse took the elevator up to the eighth floor. The elevator gleamed of polished walnut and gold and smelled of lemon. He felt his leg where he had been hit, but he was unable to ascertain whether any damage had been done.

When the elevator doors slid back, he stepped out and moved down the plush, deserted hallway. He arrived at room 812 and slid his card into the key slot. It clicked open and Waterhouse entered, tentatively. The room was clean and quiet. He moved inside, set the attaché case on the bed, opened it, and took out a small electronic scanner. He swept the room for bugs and cameras. It was clean. Next, he picked up the phone and punched three digits. A familiar voice answered immediately.

"Good morning," said the voice.

The voice was that of Herbert "Bud" Grant, a friend since Vietnam days. Grant was a good looking, slightly stocky man of fifty-eight. He stood 5'10", had short, dark hair, a round face, and a youthful bearing.

"Room 812," replied Waterhouse. "The door's ajar. Don't touch anything once you get here. Looking forward to seeing you, old friend."

"Same here, Captain. I'll be right there," said Grant.

Grant had arrived the night before and had blown $400 at the blackjack table. He had also gotten fairly drunk, but he was surprisingly sober this morning. He smelled adventure.

Waterhouse's door was open when Grant entered, calling, "Captain?"

"Hey, Bud. Over here," said Waterhouse. "Close the door."

Grant shouldered the door closed and moved into the room.

Waterhouse was standing by the window, his pant leg rolled up, revealing thick padding wrapped with an Ace bandage around his lower calf.

To Grant, Waterhouse had aged pretty well. He was still in good shape, but his hair had touches of gray. He looked tired.

"Been a while," said Grant.

"Too long, my friend," replied Waterhouse, smiling at Grant. "I hope we can see more of each other now that I am . . . well, maybe, unemployed."

"Really?" said Grant. "What's the story?"

"Can't say for sure. Let's just call it a hunch."

"OK," smiled Grant, shaking his head.

They smiled at each other.

"So what's with the padding?" asked Grant.

"I got jabbed with the end of an umbrella about 10 minutes ago. It might have been an accident, but I'm pretty sure I was targeted. Come here and take a look. See if there's a little dart or spot on the bandage."

"You always have the most delightful experiences," smiled Grant. "How did you know this was going to happen?"

Waterhouse raised a finger to his temple and pointed.

"Silly me," smiled Grant. "How else?"

"How else indeed."

"But if you're so psychic, why haven't you won the Lotto?" asked Grant as he knelt to look at Waterhouse's leg.

"What makes you think I haven't?" said Waterhouse.

"No shit?" exclaimed Grant.

"Haven't won millions, but never needed to. 'Stay under the radar,' that's my motto." He looked down at his leg. "See anything?"

"There's a little indentation here. What happened?"

"I was blindsided," said Waterhouse. "Guy bumps into me, almost a body-block, and jabs me with the umbrella."

"See his face?" asked Grant.

"No," replied Waterhouse. "I need you to unwrap the bandage for me . . . carefully."

"OK," said Grant.

"I can probably find him if I need to. I think he's just a flunkie," said Waterhouse. "Anyway, it makes things a whole lot easier for me."

"Makes what easier?" asked Grant.

"My disappearing," Waterhouse replied.

Grant unhooked the metal clasp that was holding the Ace bandage tight around Waterhouse's calf. As he unraveled it, the small spot became more evident, like a wet stain.

"Yeah, I think he got you with something," Grant said quietly.

"That was the idea."

Grant unwound the ace bandage and saw black fabric over some padding.

"What's this black stuff?" he asked.

"Kevlar 29. And underneath that is padding from an old Thinsulate vest. So they can *try*, but they are not gonna get me," smiled Waterhouse.

"You saw this beforehand?"

"Yep, pretty much," laughed Waterhouse. "Give me a minute to change, and we're out of here. I'll fill you in later."

"Did you see who it was?"

"No faces."

"Well, you're OK," Grant said. "Mind if I smoke?"

Waterhouse paused. Then he said, "I think that would be a fine idea."

"Huh?" replied Grant.

"Tell you later."

Waterhouse checked the blinds and then took off his clothes. He had wrapped his legs and arms with padding and Kevlar, and he wore a Kevlar vest under his polo shirt. Now he removed these layers and began to redress.

"Where are you parked? Down below?" asked Waterhouse, as he pulled up his pants.

"Yup," replied Grant.

"We'll take the stairs down and then walk into the garage down the ramp," Waterhouse said.

"OK."

Waterhouse lifted the Henk suitcase onto the bed, opened it, took out a large plastic shopping bag, and unfolded it. Then he picked up the vest, the Kevlar cloth, and the padding and placed it in the bag. He took out a fat fountain pen and moved into the bathroom. He knelt in front of the tub, unscrewed the top of the pen, and poured blood carefully around the drain.

Grant watched with interest.

"What is that?" asked Grant.

"My blood," replied Waterhouse.

He splattered the tub with more drops. Then he turned on the shower and quickly rinsed the blood from the tub and the drain.

"Why do that if you're only going to wash it away?" Grant asked.

"Oh there'll be traces. If they go to the trouble of finding them, then they'll think something *else* happened to me," replied Waterhouse as he stood up. He took a little piece of toilet paper from the roll, pressed it against the barrel of the pen, and gave the pen a hard shake. A little drop of blood spread into the tissue. He wadded it up and threw it into the toilet.

"There. A little appetizer."

Grant shook his head and smiled.

"You think of everything," he said approvingly.

"If I didn't . . . I would be no more." Then Waterhouse smiled, relieved, and asked, "You got us an airplane?"

"Absolutely. Sweet little Cessna 421 with a thousand mile range."

"How much?"

"A friend let me borrow it. I just need to return it with a full tank."

"Nice friend," said Waterhouse as he glanced around the room.

"So, who wants you out of the way?" asked Grant.

"I haven't done a full scan on that, but for now, let's just get out of here. Bring a blanket?"

"In the car."

"Good. You're good with details."

"Yeah, well, it's a horse blanket," quipped Grant.

Waterhouse smiled and shook his head.

A few minutes later, Grant eased the rented black Buick up from the underground parking garage and headed south. Waterhouse lay on the back floor, curled up under the blanket. When Grant had gone a few blocks, he pulled the car over. Waterhouse got out and switched into the passenger seat.

"Where we going?" asked Waterhouse.

"I am taking you to the Black Bear Diner," smiled Grant.

"You've been there before, I gather," smiled Waterhouse.

"A few times. It's OK," nodded Grant.

"You're the captain," nodded Waterhouse.

After a short pause, Grant asked, "Think anybody will be looking for you?"

"Oh yeah," said Waterhouse impassively. "Unless I am wrong, there will be people in the room within the hour."

"Think they'll find the blood?"

"I'd be disappointed if they didn't. Your cigarette smoke will definitely tell them someone else was in there. So that worked out well."

"See? Smoking has its benefits," smiled Grant as he eased the car onto West Tropicana.

"I like this car."

"Me too. Always liked Buicks," nodded Grant.

"Still play guitar?" Waterhouse asked.

"Oh yeah," smiled Grant. "Every day."

"You know, Bud. I don't have too many regrets, but I always wished I had taken up an instrument."

"I thought you played sax or clarinet or something."

"Yeah, but I never liked it though. I always saw myself as a piano player. But . . ."

"Here we are, Captain."

The Black Bear Diner was a modern, beige-front place set back from the road. As they entered, a pretty waitress with too much makeup smiled and said, "Good morning! Sit anywhere you like. I'll be right over."

"You know, they have these really fantastic keyboards now that can just teach you how to play," said Grant

"Really?"

"Yeah! I got one."

Waterhouse and Grant moved toward a back booth and slid into it as the waitress handed them menus.

"The breakfast specials are inside," she said. "I'll give you a couple of minutes. Coffee?"

"Please," Waterhouse said.

After the waitress departed, Waterhouse asked Grant, "So you're still with IBM, I gather?"

"Oh yeah," nodded Grant. "Good challenge, good money. Nice part of New York. I'm about thirty minutes from Roscoe, New York, which has the best trout fishing in the East."

"That a fact?" asked Waterhouse.

"Oh yeah. Fly fishermen come from all over the world; it's just great. And it's unspoiled."

"Do they fly in?"

"Not bad," smiled Grant.

"Do they get hooked?"

"You're a comedian now?"

"I don't know," smiled Waterhouse. "Just feeling a little punchy."

"Yeah," replied Grant.

The men sat quietly for a moment and looked at the menus.

"So tell me again what you do at IBM," said Waterhouse. "You told me once, but I forgot the details."

"Mostly, I try to get machines to think like people," said Grant, looking into his coffee. "It's called the AI group. Artificial Intelligence."

"And . . .?"

"Well, some of the stuff we do is classified, so I can't really . . . Besides, they're moving me to another division, and that one is *really* hush-hush."

"Say no more," smiled Waterhouse. "Well, whatever it is, I bet you're good at it."

"Wish I were better," smiled Grant. "So, what's the story? Are you out of commission now?"

Waterhouse nodded. "I think so. All I can tell you is that I saw some things I wasn't supposed to see. If there's a downside to psychic surveillance, it's that you don't know what you're gonna get. And I saw some things a little bit like the stuff you and I used to look at a few years ago. Anyhow, I'm pretty sure that's the reason."

"So, what's next?"

"I am going to disappear . . . for a while. That's why I need your help, to get out of here."

"Well, we're all set. You're gonna love this airplane," smiled Grant as he sipped his coffee.

Waterhouse looked up and scowled at the loud country music that was blaring from overhead speakers. He said to Grant, "Why do they always play such loud music?"

"Bothers you?" asked Grant.

"Yeah. I like it quiet," replied Waterhouse, looking around, feeling trapped. "I feel like I'm in a . . ."

"Be right back," said Grant.

He slid out of the booth and walked to the front door, then out to the car. He opened the trunk and took something out of a small carry-on bag. Then he closed the trunk and reentered the diner, concealing a small box in his hand.

Grant saw the waitress deliver two mugs of steaming black coffee to the table, and he waited for her to move away before returning to the booth. As he returned to his seat across from Waterhouse, Grant looked around carefully before setting the box on the table. It looked electronic, whatever it was; it contained a small antenna, a round meter, switches, buttons, and a couple of LEDs.

"Whatcha got?" asked Waterhouse, curious.

The overhead music twanged incessantly.

"A little something for these precious moments," smiled Grant, picking up the box.

He flipped the switch and the round meter became illuminated. Grant looked around to make sure the waitress was nowhere in sight. He adjusted a knob until the needle on the dial was pointing directly at 12:00.

Grant looked at Waterhouse, his eyes twinkling merrily. Then he whispered, "T-minus three . . . two . . ."

He pressed a button on the box, and the overhead music suddenly stopped. The Black Bear Diner became eerily quiet.

Waterhouse opened his eyes wide and cocked his head.

"You did that?" he whispered.

Grant raised his eyebrows and said, "*May-be.*"

Waterhouse broke into a grin.

"Where'd you get it?"

"Made it," said Grant, with schoolboy pride. He took a sip of his coffee.

"No shit," smiled Waterhouse approvingly. "How's it work?"

Grant looked around again and moved the box out of sight. Then he looked at Waterhouse.

"I just tune into the amplifier's signal and hit the button. What this does is send a spike of extremely high voltage back to the amp. And it's cooked."

"Wow. That's fantastic," said Waterhouse. "You could sell them, I bet."

"Yeah," nodded Grant, "except they're illegal. I can zap anything. I can stop cars, boats, cell phones. I have a radar zapper on my car. It'll kill anything."

"I'll be damned," said Waterhouse approvingly. "I didn't know you were *that* good. I guess you really are a genius."

"Yeah, except I got 550 on my SATs."

The waitress suddenly appeared with a small pad.

"Need more time?"

"No, that's OK," said Waterhouse, and he ordered scrambled eggs well done, home fries, rye toast, and coffee.

"Same for me," said Grant, folding his menu. "I'd like a small tomato juice also. Please."

The waitress turned and moved away. As she entered the kitchen, Grant and Waterhouse heard her bellow, "*What happened to the music?*" Waterhouse looked down and shook his head, smiling. Grant was one fun dude.

Twenty minutes later, they had finished their breakfasts. Grant lit a cigarette and said, "What's our destination? I have to file a flight plan."

"Pittsburgh," said Waterhouse, taking a sip of his coffee.

"What's in Pittsburgh?"

"Nothing special. Just a place for me to blend in, rent a car, and take off. And that is all I can tell you, my friend."

"OK," nodded Grant. "You're not the only one with secrets, you know."

"I should hope not. But once I'm settled, I'll give you a buzz."

"You know what you oughta do?" smiled Grant.

"What?"

"Get one of those keyboards. They're really great."

Waterhouse replied thoughtfully, "Maybe I will. Maybe it's time for a little music."

An hour later, they were aboard the sleek Cessna, high above the clouds, heading due east. Speaking through headsets,

Waterhouse and Grant reminisced about the old days when both were soldiers during the Vietnam conflict. Waterhouse had been a platoon leader in the Special Forces, and he had set himself apart with his uncanny ability to perceive the enemy position prior to an assault. He did this by running his fingers lightly over a map. If they detected heat, that is where the enemy was. This had helped the U.S. military accomplish stunning victories; lives were saved, and Waterhouse had become a valuable asset.

When his second tour ended in 1969, he reenlisted, was promoted, and got reassigned to a top secret base in Thailand. He then "disappeared" to a base known as Club Sand, which provided intelligence support for Task Force Alpha.

It was at Club Sand that he had met Grant, a wisecracking Air Force pilot who played guitar and was a whiz with electronics. Typical of sky jockeys, Grant had a wild streak. He liked to drink and entertain ladies with his music and crazy stories. During his tour in Vietnam, Grant had flown recon until he was shot down not far from Pleiku. As he lay in a rice paddy, wounded and helpless, he was less concerned about being captured than about the giant tigers, which had attacked—and eaten—humans. But thankfully, Grant was rescued by a medevac helicopter and was quickly taken to the nearby 71st Evac Hospital. It was there he had met Waterhouse, who was visiting a wounded friend.

Grant had serious injuries, and during his convalescence, he met some intelligence personnel who ran the "big ears" listening post. They were always looking for guys who could fix the gear, which was frequently hit by enemy fire. Because Grant was skilled with electronics and knew about radio transmitters, he was able to help keep the equipment working and the listening post active.

Waterhouse, meanwhile, was providing invaluable intel about the enemy's position and movements around Southeast Asia. He was a one-man recon unit; within the course of two days, he had pinpointed twenty enemy strongholds. The next day, B-52 sorties cleared out more than a dozen.

Grant was fascinated by Waterhouse's psychic ability. At first he didn't believe it, and he gave Waterhouse a test. Waterhouse obliged, and was able to psychically describe Grant's boyhood home in Arizona perfectly, even down to the broken metal flag on the mailbox. Grant had never met anyone who was psychic and was mightily impressed.

Off hours, and with Grant's encouragement, Waterhouse began to view non-assigned targets. The procedure was this: Waterhouse never knew what the "target" was. Grant would simply write coordinates—latitude and longitude—on a piece of paper, place it into an envelope, and put the envelope into his footlocker. Then Waterhouse would "acquire" the target and draw, or describe, what he saw. It took time, but if Waterhouse started to sketch or write, that meant he "had" something. Grant targeted the Oval Office one day, and Waterhouse learned of Nixon's secret plan to bomb Cambodia. This was not especially comforting.

Grant had grown up near Phoenix, Arizona, and had maintained a never-ending fascination with the Lost Dutchman Gold Mine. Located in the Superstition Mountains near a town called Apache Junction, it was rumored to contain an enormous cache of gold. Grant told Waterhouse about the mine, but he expressed scant interest. On more than one occasion, Grant would "target" the mine, and Waterhouse would just see "a lot of rocks and dirt."

But Grant remained hopeful that maybe one day he would give Waterhouse the right coordinates, and then they'd go find the gold and become billionaires. Or, if not that, then they'd go to Las Vegas and Waterhouse would pick all the winning numbers. Waterhouse would merely smile and shake his head. Grant was hopeless.

In 1974, at the end of the Vietnam conflict, Waterhouse was enticed to continue his psychic work stateside at Fort Meade, Maryland. In an intelligence operation, jointly created by the CIA, the NSA, and the Department of Defense, Waterhouse—and five other "highly perceptive" individuals—were called upon to locate and describe various targets within the Soviet Union. These targets were often sites from which long-range nuclear missiles could be launched or sites that housed mobile transport, such as large trucks or railroad cars; also included were radar installations and other sites of top-level importance. They also tracked movements of ground personnel and new construction projects in Siberia, the Balkans, and the Urals. This new super-secret unit was called the Office of Special Intelligence, or OSI. The psychics were called "remote viewers."

Waterhouse's superior was Nathan Miller, a distinguished professor of neurological research at George Mason University in Fairfax, Virginia, who, in addition to his ties to academia, was a civilian employee of both the CIA and the NSA. It was Miller who had first recruited Patrick Waterhouse. Miller also recruited a short, highly intuitive young man from Alabama named Dick Petit. Petit was small in stature and spoke with a high-pitched drawl. Some found Petit a bit overbearing, but Miller could care less: the guy was good. Miller had also recruited a bright U.S.

Army officer named Fred Kent. Kent had short, sandy hair, and a sunny disposition. He was one of the few OSI members who was married, and, because he was still an officer in the U.S. Army, he lived on a nearby base with his wife Maria.

Waterhouse liked Kent; but he didn't especially care for Petit. Kent was open and affable; Petit was guarded and secretive.

In a phone conversation, Grant had expressed surprise when Waterhouse had said he was going to "stay in." But Waterhouse explained, "I have to do something, and I'm pretty good at this." Grant remarked that it might be fun to get back to their old activities, and Waterhouse replied, "I'd like that, but I'm under a microscope here. Maybe someday, though."

The OSI program was instituted partially in response to Russian initiatives in psychic spying and partially due to Petit and Waterhouse's spectacular achievements in the field. The Russians had a head start; they had spent millions developing a team of highly skilled psychic spies, and nobody in the United States knew what information they had already obtained.

Simply put, remote viewing means long-distance reconnaissance in which the target is outside the range of any of the five physical senses. The stellar achievements of Waterhouse and Petit provided a great deal of significant information. Petit felt he was a better viewer than Waterhouse, but he had to acknowledge that Waterhouse could "see" numbers and letters, which was beyond the ken of everyone else. Waterhouse also had the ability to see "virtual certainties" hours, even days, before events occurred. Strategically, this was most valuable where the movement of troops and weaponry was concerned. This was like a baseball outfielder knowing exactly where the ball would be hit, so he could position himself in advance.

In 1980, Waterhouse and Bud Grant renewed their activities, which they called "skimming the pool." This meant creative targeting by Grant, and remote viewing by Waterhouse, of non-assigned targets. Grant had friends with above-top-secret clearance and he had obtained leads on interesting targets. One was a secret underground base in Alaska that was conducting research on UFOs; another was a multi-kilo cache of heroin used by a government agency to fund covert operations.

Somehow, Miller found out about Waterhouse's non-assigned viewings and was not pleased. Waterhouse had superseded his authority and it had to stop. Additionally, Miller was concerned that information about the activities of OSI were being reported off campus, and that was a huge security risk. It implied that one of the viewers was either a mole or was reckless with classified intelligence.

In a closed-door meeting, Miller explained to Waterhouse that if he valued his position at OSI, he would keep his mouth shut and immediately cease any viewing on his own initiative. Miller reminded Waterhouse that he had signed a secrecy oath and that violating it could lead to serious consequences. Miller didn't elaborate on what the consequences might be, and he didn't have to. Waterhouse apologized to Miller, assuring him that he would keep his viewing to assigned targets. This seemed to satisfy Miller. Waterhouse had a stellar record and had been highly decorated.

Waterhouse kept his word, but he stress of the daily routine and of being under a cloud of suspicion took its toll. He developed high blood pressure and often had difficulty sleeping.

One Friday morning in the hallway of the OSI facility, Waterhouse said to Miller that he was thinking of retiring. "I've been at this for a long time, and I'm tired."

"Well," said Miller, "can't say I'm surprised. Why not take two weeks, see how you feel? Go someplace nice and relax. If you want out, I won't stand in your way."

This answer surprised Waterhouse, but he did not show it. He merely said, "Thanks for understanding."

Waterhouse had been feeling less like a suspect and more like a target. He could be wrong; maybe it was just paranoia. Such feelings were common in top-secret work: someone was always looking over his shoulder. Waterhouse was stuck with uncertainty. Maybe if he took a break, he would come to some clarity.

The following day, he had sent Miller an e-mail saying that he'd take the two weeks starting Monday. Waterhouse had also been thinking about contingency plans. Two months before, he had felt a strong intuitive feeling that something was up. As a precaution, he had rented a storage garage and had begun to fill it with nonessentials: furniture, books, recordings, memorabilia, and sporting gear.

Waterhouse visited the public library to research possible cities to which he might relocate should the need arise. He could have done this on his home computer, but he suspected his PC was being monitored, as well as his phone and fax lines. There could have been bugs in his apartment also, though the last sweep turned up nothing.

Sitting at the computer in the library, Waterhouse looked at potential places to live—places he had admired but had never visited, places where he could disappear. He made a short list: the Adirondacks; Brattleboro, Vermont; Sedona, Arizona; and Marietta, Ohio. He loved the Adirondacks; it was a beautiful area with majestic mountains covered with pine trees, crystal blue lakes perfect for fishing, and friendly people. But it was sparsely populated and often snowed in, and that was a liability. The same was true for Vermont. Sedona, Arizona, had many positive attributes: good weather, fairly well populated, lots of things to see and do, and the area housed an interesting mix of the old west and the New Age. But Sedona was also surrounded by vast tracts of desert, and that didn't appeal to him. Marietta, Ohio, was a good mix of cultures and people, and was a beautiful little town with things to do and places to golf and fish. That would be his destination.

By late afternoon, Bud Grant and Patrick Waterhouse had landed at Pittsburgh International Airport. Grant's plan was to refuel and make the final hop to Westchester.

"I need one more favor from you," Waterhouse said.

"Oh?" smiled Grant.

"I need you to rent a car for me. I'll pay you back."

"Man, you are pushing your luck."

"Don't I always?"

Ten minutes later, Grant had rented a car: one-way to Marietta, Ohio. He drove the white Lincoln Town Car into the parking lot, got out, and motioned for Waterhouse to take over.

JILL MESSENGER: OUT OF BODY

"Why'd you rent such an expensive car?"

"I like my friends to be comfortable."

Waterhouse laughed and said, "I'll send you a check for the rental."

"Forget about it. Once we find the gold mine . . ."

Waterhouse smiled, shook his head, waved, and drove away.

It was about three hours to Marietta from Pittsburgh. He had printed out a *Yahoo!* Map, and now it lay on the passenger seat. He decided to cut over to Route 7 from Wheeling, West Virginia, and to follow the pretty Ohio River south into Marietta. It was a clear day, good for driving, and there was not much traffic on the road. He liked this car and wished he had brought some CDs along.

On the open road, he thought about what he was leaving behind. The guys at OSI would be curious at his sudden departure, but he was pretty sure that some CIA spooks were behind the hit. He would have to take a look, but not right away. They were probably still trying to locate him somewhere in Nevada. *They overreacted,* he thought. Yes, Waterhouse had seen some disturbing things, things that made his flesh creep, things he never should have viewed. But was that a reason to take him out? The world of spooks had its share of backstabbing, and now Waterhouse had experienced it firsthand.

As he approached Marietta, he saw the massive steel bridge that spanned the Ohio River to West Virginia. It was like night and day: pretty Marietta on the west, and grimy West Virginia on the east. Consulting his map, Waterhouse drove up Seventh Street and made a series of turns that brought him exactly where he wanted to be: his new home.

Ridgewood Court was an apartment complex behind the Oak Grove Cemetery on the north side of Marietta. It was composed of a long row of three-story, rust-colored brick buildings. There was only one road in, which Waterhouse didn't much like—he would have preferred more access—but its remoteness appealed to him. If anyone from OSI tried to view him, they would see a lot of bodies, either in the apartment complex or in the nearby graveyard.

He had sent a deposit for a two-bedroom apartment and had later struck up a conversation with Debbie Becker, the rental agent who had been in the service during Desert Storm. Now that he had arrived, he signed a year's lease and bought a 1999 white Chevrolet pickup for $2,000 from Debbie's brother Glenn.

Within the first week, Waterhouse had painted the kitchen and bathroom light blue; the living room, hallways, bedroom, and office a deep green; and the trim on the door frames and windows white. The white ceilings were OK. He bought sturdy, second-hand furniture—his needs were modest—but he got a new double bed, without a frame, at Mattress Max, which he laid flat on the floor.

Although he still had personal effects stored in Maryland, he had the essentials: his laptop, a stereo, a portable MP3 player, clothes, toiletries, a few books, notebooks, and a shoebox of memorabilia.

He set up some bookshelves in his second-bedroom office and bought books he had always wanted—but rarely had time—to read: Tom Clancy, John Grisham, books about history and naval warfare, books about religion and spirituality, and a volume of Yukon ballads by Robert W. Service. He also planned to visit the local library.

Ridgewood Court was within walking distance of the Giant Eagle supermarket and a couple of fast-food restaurants. Convenient.

Long before his arrival in Ohio, Waterhouse had created a second identity, just in case. He had all the proper documents: a Social Security number, a driver's license, and a bank card. He was now James Lee Harper; Patrick Waterhouse was dead. That, he hoped, would be the report from Las Vegas. However, to be cautious, he had asked Bud Grant to rent the Lincoln.

The real James Lee Harper—from New Orleans and a year younger than Waterhouse—was a soldier who had died in Vietnam. He been shot dead as he was "walking point." Waterhouse, as his commanding officer, had the biographical background information on Harper, so assuming his identity was fairly straightforward. Harper had no family. He was an only child who was reared by nuns when his parents were killed in an automobile accident. If Harper had other relatives, then they remained undiscovered and, frankly, Waterhouse didn't care to look. But getting used to being called James Harper would be another matter.

Once his apartment was squared away, Harper took himself out on a tour of Washington County; he walked the broad streets of Marietta, sampling the restaurants, visiting the shops. He was glad to see a martial arts place on Front Street. Maybe now he would have the opportunity to get back in shape. Or at least try. He walked over the old, rusty railroad bridge to the west side, to an area known as Harmar. There were nice little stores here, too, and he smiled when he saw a ladies' hairdressing establishment named The Beauty Barn, not far from a coffee shop, The Busy Bee.

A few days later, Harper bought some fishing gear and set out for a drive along the Muskingum River, slightly west of Marietta. The man at the sporting goods shop was helpful and made a few suggestions. Harper drove out along the River Road, which followed the circuitous course of the river. As he came around a bend, he saw a small beige-and-brown, cinder-block building: The Edgewater Bar. He might have driven right past, but the black-and-white POW/MIA flag over the door caught his attention. The Edgewater had the look of a place for ex-military and working-class guys, and he was glad to see the flag. He knew the identities of several MIAs and a few POWs. He still wondered about those guys and what had happened to them.

Harper steered his pickup into the small parking lot, got out, and went in for a beer. The Edgewater was dark, even in daytime, and it immediately reminded him of bars near military bases: not exactly spotless, but with solid food and bottled beer. It was nearly lunchtime, and there were about half a dozen guys at the bar and at tables, all kidding around and enjoying themselves. Within ten minutes, he was among other vets, talking shop and enjoying a pizza burger, chips, and a beer. As they swapped war stories, he noticed that one of the guys wore white sneakers with black laces, something that Fred Kent had also done. Harper hadn't thought about Kent for a while, and now seeing the sneakers brought him right back. The last Harper had heard from Kent was when he had sent Harper an e-mail about the new place where he was working: The Madison Institute. Kent wrote to say that if Harper were ever interested in some "really interesting higher-consciousness stuff," he should look into it. "The things they do here are right up your alley," he'd said.

As Harper finished his burger, he wondered if he still had Kent's e-mail on his computer. He'd have to check.

He said goodbye to the guys in the bar and walked back to his truck. There would be fishing another day.

Later, at home, he checked his laptop for Kent's home e-mail. Harper found the old one at NSA.gov, but he knew that Kent was no longer there. He decided to visit the Web site of the Madison Institute. Maybe he would find Kent's name.

The Institute had a vast Web site with detailed descriptions of the various residential programs for the study of higher consciousness and out-of-body techniques. Harper was interested. He had heard about out-of-body recon, but Miller was dismissive of its use as a form of intelligence. "There are some risks to it," he had said, without adding what those risks might be.

On The Madison Institute's products page, Harper saw a ten-CD set: *The Discovery Experience*. It was the home version of a residential program at the Institute, *The Discovery Voyage*. It would familiarize the participant with various states of higher consciousness and how to function within these states. Harper clicked the *buy* button and entered his name, address, and credit card number at the prompt. He was excited at the prospect of learning this new technique.

Over the next six weeks, Harper put himself through *The Discovery Experience*. The CDs were to be used in sequence, with each lesson building on the next; there were two lessons on each disc, each about thirty minutes long. The participant was to lie down and use headphones for listening. Harper already was using similar brainwave sounds he had downloaded from an Internet site. He found that he could focus better and that he had more accurate remote viewing results with his brain coaxed into an alpha brain state.

Some of the skills that could be acquired included enhancing intuitive abilities, manifesting abundance, exploring nonphysical realities, and having out-of-body experiences. Because there was no one "right" way, there were several techniques for achieving an out-of-body state; each person's experience was different. As the little booklet in the CD box stated, many people experienced fear on first separation.

But something was wrong.

Try as he may, Harper was unable to "lift out" and achieve an out-of-body state. He could get to the point of departure, but then suddenly had the feeling that brakes were being applied, like an airplane gathering speed for takeoff but then shutting down. Harper was doing something wrong and wasn't sure what it was. He decided to visit the Washington County Library to see if they had any of Robert Madison's books. They might fill in some gaps in his understanding.

He called the library and learned it was a not far from where he lived.

When Harper entered the venerable brick building, he saw a woman he would come to know as Sara Hopkins at the main information desk. As he approached her, he took off his cap and asked if the library had any books by Robert Madison. Sara checked her computer, making pleasant conversation about the upcoming Sternwheel Festival and the Washington County Fair in the fall. Harper liked her easy manner. She was also attractive, if a little over done.

"Yep," she said, "We've got a couple by Madison. Here, I'll show you where they are."

Sara led him to the shelf, pulled out the books, and handed them to Harper. He smiled and said, "I'll take them."

"You must be new here," said Sara. "I'm pretty good with faces, and I don't think I've seen yours before."

"Yes, I am fairly new," smiled Harper.

"Well, I hope you have a great time," said Sara. "The people are nice."

"So I'm discovering."

Harper got a library card and checked out *Astral Journeys* and *Far Out* by Robert L. Madison.

Within an hour, Harper was stretched out on his couch, reading. He learned that Madison was an ordinary businessman with no interest in psychic occurrences who had suddenly gone out of his body one night as he was trying to go to sleep. That event was the first of many, an event that was to change the course of Madison's life and, eventually, the lives of many others.

By the next afternoon, as Harper read Madison's books, he came to the conclusion that it *was* fear that was keeping him back. But fear of what? He had been close to getting killed a couple of times in Vietnam and considered himself to be pretty much fearless. But this was something deeper. Well, he would keep at it. Madison wrote that persistence would result in achieving an out-of-body state.

One benefit of using the CDs and achieving higher levels of consciousness, Harper found, was that his intuitive sensing abilities had taken a quantum leap. Although he was fairly adept before, now he had a "knowingness" that bordered on the eerie. He found he could "read" people and situations and know what was going on.

But one thing he did not know for certain was what Miller, Petit, and the others were up to. He dared not view them; they would be expecting that. He had to stay off the radar and out of reach.

CHAPTER THREE

Jill decided to not cash the winning ticket while she was still with Robert at the track. Call it woman's intuition. Instead, she sat patiently with him through the rest of the races, making modest two dollar bets and hitting one show bet for $4.80. Robert was a gentleman, but there was something about him she couldn't quite figure out. He was friendly all right, but there was a kind of formality, a stiffness, that made her think he couldn't ever relax and have fun.

Maybe it was just image maintenance.

Robert offered to take her to dinner at the golf club, but Jill begged off, saying, "I'd love to, but it's been a long day, and I have to call my daughter. Maybe another time."

Robert took the small turndown graciously and drove Jill home. As he pulled his sedan in front of her house, he asked, "May I call you sometime?"

"Sure, *Bob*," smiled Jill. "We'll be seeing each other. Thanks for a lovely afternoon."

Robert waited until Jill was inside her house, then he drove away.

Jill went upstairs to change. She was excited about winning at the track, but she knew she'd have to keep a cool head. And yet, with this ability to go out of body and into the future, she could maybe pick the winning Powerball numbers. Wouldn't a few million be a kick? But that would only cast her into a spotlight, and that is something she would never want. Nor would Dave have approved. Whatever wild streak Jill had when she first met Dave, his quiet sensibility had prevailed, and she was glad.

But maybe she could win a *little*, so she wouldn't have to get a job. She'd have to figure all that out.

The most annoying part about winning seven thousand dollars was that she couldn't tell anybody. Could she? Dr. Singh had advised her to keep quiet about her ability, and that was smart. Maybe she could tell *him*? She thought that would be OK, but it was the weekend, and he wouldn't be available until Monday. Maybe she'd change her mind by then. Yes, secrecy was better.

She put away her necklace and earrings and pulled on gray sweatpants, a green mock turtleneck, and thick cotton socks. Then she went downstairs, heading to the kitchen. She wasn't hungry, but felt she should eat something. She could always order a pizza or Chinese; she hadn't done that for a while.

As she entered the kitchen, she saw that she had a message on her answering machine. She pressed the button; it was Cathy.

"Hi, Mom, just checking in. It's Saturday around 5:00. Call back if you get a chance. I might be at the library tonight though. Love ya. Bye."

The library on a Saturday night? thought Jill. *Right.*

Jill had the Chinese restaurant on speed dial, and she ordered wonton soup, an egg roll, and pork lo mein. "Twenty minis, OK?" the woman said.

"Great, thanks."

She poured herself a vodka and tonic and went into the living room to catch the 6:00 news. The top story was about the Brownie troop and their jamboree at the Marietta Fairgrounds. One of the girls, Katie Hodge, age eight, was missing, and the local police were combing the area near the river. Divers had been brought in; the other Brownies had been sent home.

How awful, thought Jill. *Katie's parents must be beside themselves.*

The Chinese food arrived, and Jill carried the plastic bag back to the kitchen. She poured the soup into a bowl and scooped some of the lo mein onto a plate. She removed the egg roll from the little pouch and put that on the plate also. She put everything on a tray and carried it back to the living room so she could watch a movie on TV and have a quiet dinner.

It had been an eventful day: seeing the winning horses the night before, then having them come in for a lot of money. And, perhaps best of all, the likelihood that she could do that any time she wished. That was exciting. In fact, the whole realm of discovery while out of body thrilled her: she could do *anything.*

Around 10:30, Jill went upstairs. She had barely touched her vodka and tonic, but that was probably a good thing. She wanted to go "out" again and, if she was drunk . . . well, who knew what might happen?

She lay on her bed, put on the headphones, and pressed the play button.

You are going on a voyage of discovery . . .

Within a few minutes, Jill was floating on the ceiling. She liked it now. She held the intention of standing in her room and was suddenly standing at the foot of her bed as she had the night before. She felt free and good.

Where would she go?

She thought of Cathy, hundreds of miles away in Virginia.

Suddenly, Jill was in a strange place. It appeared to be an apartment, and it was dark. Before her were two people on a bed, kissing passionately.

Cathy?

Jill yelled, *"So you're at the library, huh?"*

Cathy and the guy heard nothing.

"Who is this weasel?"

Jill approached the bed and tried to touch Cathy, but her hand passed right through her. It gave her the creeps.

The young man stopped kissing Cathy and said, "What was that?"

"What was what?" asked Cathy.

"I just felt something cold, like a wind," the young man said, slightly alarmed.

Cathy moved slightly and looked around.

"Oh, it's nothing. C'mere, you."

Jill was suddenly back on her bed, hearing the CD on her headphones. She took a deep breath, turned, and glanced at the clock. 10:45 p.m.

She reached for the phone and dialed Cathy's number. It rang a long time before Cathy said, quietly, "Hello?"

"Hey, who's that guy in your apartment?"

"What? There's no guy here!" said Cathy awkwardly.

How could Mom know?

"Well, try not to get yourself pregnant, OK?" asked Jill.

She hung up, leaving a baffled daughter at the end of the line. Then she chuckled; glad Cathy was finding a little romance.

She was suddenly hungry. She went downstairs for a dish of pistachio ice cream and to watch the 11:00 news. Katie Hodge, the missing Brownie, was the top story, and there was still no sign of her. As Jill sat crossed legged on the sofa, eating ice cream, she wondered if she could find Katie. But how?

Well, she could *look.* She remembered how she felt when Jamie got lost at the Washington County Fair—they had become separated, and she was terrified that he had been abducted. He was only six years old and had walked over to watch "the man make cotton candy." In the twenty minutes he was missing, Jill and Dave were panic stricken. So she could well imagine what Katie Hodge's parents were going through.

She took the empty dish to the kitchen, poured some water into it, and set it on the bottom of the sink. Then she went upstairs, unsure of what she would do, but hopeful nonetheless.

Jill put on the headphones and pushed the play button. The swirling tones had barely begun when she was out of her body, floating above her bed. She was nervous and excited; she wanted to find the missing girl.

She floated through the outside wall and was soon over Sixth Street. She extended her arms, like Superman, and thought of Katie. Soon she was in a dark, desolate area, over the Fairgrounds, next to the murky Muskingum River.

From high above, Jill could see wide yellow tape surrounding the search area. She dropped down so she was flying about ten feet over it. She flew back and forth, looking for the little girl.

Nothing.

She floated over the river and tried to see the underside of the riverbank, but it was dark, and the thick scrabble of brush along the riverbank made viewing nearly impossible. She moved in closer so she was at the edge of the riverbank, moving slowly through the thick brush. She could feel the small branches as they passed through her; they felt like tiny gusts of wind, not unpleasant.

No wonder they had a hard time searching; this is a mile of birds' nests.

Then Jill saw her: the limp form of a girl wearing shorts and a T-shirt, under a ledge next to the river, her foot wedged between large rocks. Jill sensed that Katie was alive, but weak and not fully conscious.

Don't worry honey,—I'll be right back!

She didn't think Katie could hear her, but the girl moaned. At least she was alive. If she could just hang on for another few minutes . . .

Jill floated up, trying to familiarize herself with landmarks so she would be able to find the spot later. She would call the police; they would surely come to get her.

Back in her body, Jill stirred herself to normal consciousness. She was groggy. She got up, walked unsteadily to the bathroom, and splashed cold water on her face. Then she returned to the bedroom, picked up the phone and dialed 911.

"Marietta Police Department, this is Kevin," said the quiet voice on the phone.

"Hello," began Jill, unsure of what to say next.

"Can I help you?" asked Kevin.

"Yes. I . . . I think I know where that missing girl is," said Jill, her voice trembling.

"May I have your name, please?"

"She's caught between two rocks in the Muskingum River, under a ledge, out behind the fairgrounds."

"Lady, we combed that area several times. Who is this?"

Jill quickly set the receiver down.

Within a few minutes, Jill was in her car heading west on Seventh Street. Marietta was dark and quiet and looked abandoned, particularly on this stretch of road. She turned into the fairgrounds and drove to the far corner. It was deserted except for a white pickup.

Jill got out of the car and ran toward the riverbank, trying to recall the memories of her earlier vision. It looked different now, but she was on the ground, in physical reality, and not hovering above the river.

She walked to the edge of the bank and looked down. It was so dark she could barely see.

Why didn't I bring a flashlight?

She knelt down and leaned over the edge of the riverbank. She saw nothing.

Suddenly she heard a male voice: "Excuse me, can you give me a hand?"

Startled, she righted herself and looked around.

"Over here!"

Jill looked to her right and saw something about twenty yards down the river, a dark form; it was difficult to make out.

"Yes! Hold on!" yelled Jill.

Kevin *had* taken her seriously, thank goodness. She got up and ran down the riverbank to where the voice came from. She stopped and leaned over. She saw a man, holding the limp form of Katie Hodge.

"I can't get her up to the top of the bank!" said the man. "Can you hold her?"

Jill bent down and grabbed Katie from under the shoulders, then lifted her up so that the girl was now lying on the soft grass of the riverbank. The man climbed up and moved next to Jill, who was smoothing Katie's hair and saying, "You're going to be fine, Katie."

"I think she's OK, just unconscious. Are you Kevin?"

"No. I'm . . . James Harper."

Jill looked at the rugged face and smiled.

"I'll call 911," said Harper, standing up and fishing a cell phone from a leather holster on the side of his belt. He punched three numbers and moved away.

A few minutes later, a boxy white EMS paramedic unit lumbered into the fairgrounds, its bright blue lights popping eerily in the darkness. Harper waved a flashlight, and the wagon stopped a few feet from where he was standing. By now Katie was alert but dazed, talking with Jill. Two EMS technicians rushed to where

Katie lay. One of them said, "Just be still, Katie. We're going to check you before taking you to the hospital. You'll be OK. Your mom and dad will meet you there."

"OK," sighed Katie wearily.

Jill stood up and moved next to Harper. They watched in silence as the paramedics checked the girl's vital signs. There were no external injuries, and the girl was very much alive.

"So. Do you come here often?" quipped Harper.

Jill laughed. "No. I just felt so bad for the girl's parents . . . I had to do something."

"Me, too," said Harper.

Harper moved to where the technicians were securing Katie to a gurney and putting an oxygen mask on her face. "Which hospital?"

"Marietta Memorial. It's the closest," came the reply. "It would be good if you followed us. We've called the girl's parents, and they would like to meet you."

"No problem. How is she?"

"In mild shock but stable. Blood pressure is way down. You saved her life."

Twenty minutes later, Jill was seated in the hospital cafeteria, drinking coffee from a white Styrofoam cup. The cafeteria had long since closed, but the vending machines worked, and that was good enough. The coffee was pretty decent, considering. Being in a hospital again brought back memories of which she was not especially fond. Still, she felt good, relieved that Katie was OK.

Harper appeared and walked to where Jill was sitting. He sat in a chair opposite Jill and sighed, nodding.

"Katie's parents are here. I think they just want to . . . well, I don't know yet. Where'd you get the coffee?"

Jill motioned with her thumb, over her shoulder, toward a hallway. "Vending machine."

"Right. You want anything? Candy bar?"

"No thanks. All set."

As Harper went to get a cup of coffee, Jill thought about Dr. Singh, about the CDs, and about how her life had changed so utterly in the space of a week. Her drinking binges seemed to be a thing of the past; she had found a new source of adventure. And now she had helped save a little girl.

Harper returned with a steaming cup of black coffee and sat down across from Jill. He smiled, and she smiled back.

"Well, I think we did our good deeds for the day," he said.

"Yes, we did," replied Jill, sipping her coffee.

"Isn't it strange that we both turned up in the right place at the right time," Harper, a sly smile on his face.

Jill didn't know what to say.

"If you hadn't been there, I don't know how I would have gotten the girl over the ledge," said Harper, somewhat pensively. "How did you know where to go?"

"Oh," began Jill. "I didn't, really. Just a woman's intuition."

Harper sensed there was more to the story, but let it go.

"OK," he said.

"She'll be all right? Katie?" asked Jill.

"Oh yeah. Nothing major. Her parents will probably take her home tonight."

"That's good," nodded Jill. "Hospitals can be scary places, especially for kids."

"Yeah," said Harper.

There was an awkward silence; then Jill spoke.

"Good thing we were there."

"Yes," nodded Harper, looking down.

"So what do you, Mr. Harper?" asked Jill.

Harper smiled and chuckled once, "James. I'm . . . retired."

"From?" asked Jill.

"Oh, consulting for the government. That's probably the easiest way to put it. Now I'm a man of leisure." He smiled and sipped his coffee.

"I would have guessed you were in the military," said Jill.

Why did I say that?

Harper smiled and looked at Jill, somewhat surprised. Then he nodded and said, "I was, long ago. Why? Were you in the service?"

Jill laughed and shook her head.

"No, I went to college, met my husband, and then we moved here."

"What does he do?" smiled Harper.

"Well," began Jill slowly, "he and my son Jamie, were killed this past January in an accident. I have a daughter in college."

"I'm sorry about your husband and son," said Harper.

"Yeah," said Jill, distantly. "I'm moving through it. So. What about you—wife and kids?"

"No wife and no kids that I know of . . ." smiled Harper, and Jill laughed. "I guess it was, well, a combination of things. But no. No wife or kids."

Jill stirred her coffee with a thin red plastic stick and asked, "So how did you find the girl?"

James Harper looked down and said, "Ahhh . . ." There was a long pause before he spoke again. He leaned forward and said quietly, "A long time ago, I learned how to locate things and people. I don't talk about it much."

"I understand," nodded Jill. "Well, can you give me a hint? There's a reason I'm asking."

"I'll tell you what motivated me to find that little girl Katie. About eight years ago, I was living in Maryland. And one night I got a call from a friend who lives in upstate New York. Dobbs Ferry. He called to say that a young kid, a boy, who had wandered away from his family's campsite had gotten lost in the woods. The local law enforcement couldn't find him. He'd been gone six hours, and it was hunting season, and it was cold. I used to do something called remote viewing, and I was able to 'see' the boy. I could see where he was. That is what I did with Katie. I *saw* where she was."

Jill nodded and said, "Did you find the boy?"

"Sort of," Harper said. "I flew up there, and I met with the local law enforcement. I told them that I knew where the boy was. They didn't believe me. It took me three hours to convince the sheriff because the kid was outside the boundaries of his search grid. By the time he finally dispatched a team to locate him, the kid was dead, curled up under a log. Died of hypothermia. They were an hour late. That has haunted me to this day. Finding Katie tonight was a kind of . . . redemption."

"I bet the sheriff felt terrible that he hadn't listened to you sooner," said Jill quietly.

"I would have thought so too, but all he said was, 'Don't talk to the press.'"

Jill shook her head. "So he was more concerned about his image than the dead boy?"

Harper nodded. "Yup. But I learned a few things. Not just about law enforcement, but about people in general. They don't trust psychic ability, even if it works. When I did that kind of work for the government, they were pleased with the results, but didn't want to know about anything psychic. It was just too 'woo-woo' for them, and they would lose credibility if they were associated with me. I had to live with that. I need you to keep what I told you confidential. As far as Katie Hodge is concerned, I will say I just got lucky. OK?"

"Absolutely," nodded Jill.

"Thank you," said Harper quietly.

"I have something to tell you, too," said Jill, nervously. Harper looked around quickly, then into Jill's eyes, and nodded. "OK."

"I found her the same way. Almost."

Harper blinked and cocked his head slightly. "*Really.*"

"Yeah," said Jill, "and I am keeping my mouth shut."

"Sounds like we have some things in common," smiled Harper.

"I think so," replied Jill.

"So how'd you find her?" asked Harper.

Jill looked down, wondering what to say. Then she began speaking.

"About a week ago I had an out-of-body experience. It was my first one. Know what that is?"

Harper nodded, "Uh-huh."

"That's how I found Katie. I went out of my body and flew around the site until I saw her, trapped by some rocks. Then I returned to the physical and drove out to the fairgrounds. This is all new to me. This is an amazing . . . gift. And I've just started."

"So who's Kevin?" asked Harper.

"Oh," laughed Jill. "Before I drove out, I called the Marietta police station, to tell them I found Katie. Kevin was the guy who answered."

"You know," began Harper. "If anybody asks, we're going to have to say that we just got lucky. I can't mention what I did, and you probably don't want to either."

"Right, right," said Jill.

"But I would like to talk with you more about that," Harper said earnestly.

"Well, OK," replied Jill. "I haven't told many people about it."

"I tried to have an OBE myself, but I never got anywhere. I bet I tried for six weeks, every day," said Harper. "So what's your protocol?"

Jill looked puzzled. "Protocol?"

Harper smiled and said, "I mean . . . how do you do it? What's the procedure?"

"Well the first time it happened, I was in the hospital, recovering from a head injury. I had fallen. So when it happened, the out-of-body thing, I thought I was dying. I think the injury kind of scrambled my brains, so I was just . . . there . . . on the ceiling of the hospital room. It really scared me."

94

"But then, after I got home, I found I could do it pretty easily. I have some special CDs that I use. I think part of it for me now is just to hold the intention. And then I'm out."

Harper smiled quizzically and cocked his head.

"What kind of CDs?" he asked, leaning slightly forward.

"They're from . . . ah . . . The Madison Institute. My neighbor Sara gave them to me."

Harper shook his head and smiled.

"They were mine. I gave them to Sara Hopkins a while ago. I thought she'd put them on the library shelves. Guess I was wrong."

"Well, well. Small world," said Jill, her eyes dancing.

"Isn't it?" said Harper, smiling.

On Monday afternoon, Jill drove out to the Mid-Ohio race track, the winning trifecta ticket in her purse. It was a clear day, and the parking lot of the track showed few cars.

She walked up to the gate and said, "I'm not here to wager, I just want to cash a ticket from Saturday."

"Well, you'll still have to pay for admission," said the man in the booth.

"How much?" asked Jill.

"Three dollars for the grandstand," the man replied.

"Here you go."

She walked up the sidewalk and into the lower level of the grandstand. The concrete floor was littered with paper. A few people milled about; individuals stood behind makeshift booths, selling the day's racing forms and tip sheets. Just beyond was an elevator that led to the mid-grandstand level from which one could see the racetrack from a slightly elevated level, and to reach the cheap seats. Above this level was the clubhouse, where she and Robert had sat.

At this hour, the stadium was nearly empty even though two races had gone off. Jill got the feeling she was in a kind of movie as she moved around characters who glanced up from their racing forms to give her a quick once-over. She looked around for the cashier windows and saw them at the back wall. In a long row of a dozen windows, only three were open. She looked at the faces of the cashiers, eerily illuminated under a row of harsh fluorescents, deciding which one to approach. There was one middle-aged woman cashier; she would be the one. Jill was slightly nervous, but walked steadily up to the window. She opened her purse and took out the ticket. She slid it through the window toward the cashier.

As the cashier inspected the ticket, Jill noticed that the woman was wearing too much makeup and had a teased, flipped platinum blond hairdo that was a throwback to the '70s. Her face was ruddy, as though she either worked outdoors or drank too much.

"I'll have to get you a tax form for the payout on this, and I'll need to see some ID," said the woman flatly.

"OK."

The woman moved away and called for a supervisor. Jill could not hear their conversation. They returned to the window together, and the woman with platinum hair reached below the counter and found a tax form. She handed it to Jill.

"You need to fill this out."

96

"Looks like you hit the jackpot," the supervisor said as he smiled. He was portly and unshaven, but wore a fresh white shirt.

"Yes, sir. I sure got lucky," Jill replied as she fished a pen out of her purse.

Jill quickly filled out her name, address, date of birth, and Social Security number.

"We take a one percent cut," said the man. "And we report all earnings over one thousand dollars to the IRS and the state of Ohio, so you will have to declare any winnings as income."

"Right," said Jill. She opened her wallet and took out her driver's license.

"Got a Social Security card?" asked the woman with blond hair.

"Yup," said Jill. She fished it out and slid it to the woman.

The portly man and the blond scrutinized the card, Jill's license, and the form she had filled out. Then the man nodded to her, as if to say, *Pay her.*

"Well, OK, then," said the woman.

The cashier counted out seventy-one hundred-dollar bills and the remaining twenty-eight dollars in odd bills. It made quite a wad.

"Do you have an envelope?" asked Jill.

"Sure don't. There's a stationery store in Marietta," the cashier said flatly.

"So . . . if I win less than a thousand dollars, there isn't any paperwork?" asked Jill.

"That's correct," said the man.

"But what if I were to . . . say, win more than one race . . . and each race paid a thousand dollars?"

"It's the ticket value that matters," smiled the man. "Why? Feeling lucky?"

"Wouldn't you?" asked Jill, as she waved the cash.

The man made no reply.

Jill tucked the wad of bills into her purse. Then she said thanks, turned, and moved toward the elevators. As she moved away, the pudgy man also moved to the far end of the cashier's line and spoke to another man. The other man picked up the phone as Jill descended on the escalator.

As she made her way to her car, Jill wondered what she would do with all the cash. If she took it to the bank, Robert would certainly find out, and she didn't want that. She could always go to another bank. Or she could just put it in a sock. She liked having seven grand in her purse. *Maybe I have a new career as a gambler*, she smiled to herself.

Her mood changed as she suddenly thought of Dave. She would love to be able to tell him what she did. He would think it was clever of her and advise her to "spend a little and save the rest." He had always been sensible about money.

On the drive home, Jill thought about some of the things Dr. Singh had said. Maybe she would try to see Dave again. She wondered how she would handle it, if she would panic when the time came. *Well,* she thought, *there is only one way to find out.*

CHAPTER FOUR

Terry Buckman was a scary-looking dude. A veteran of Desert Storm, he was forty-five, 6'3", muscular, and imposing. He had tattoos, scars from numerous battles, and a gold tooth. His long gray hair was usually in a ponytail, and his grizzly beard and mustache completed the look. In short, he looked like a mix of Willie Nelson and Hulk Hogan. And yet, Terry was thoughtful and highly perceptive, a side few ever saw. He rode a 1986 Harley-Davidson motorcycle and wore a WWI German infantry helmet. Terry was the weekend bouncer at the Edgewater Bar and was supremely effective when some of the younger patrons got unruly. He would simply pick them up and fling them out the door . . . or over the fence of the back pavilion.

Terry did not drink or use drugs. He had in the past, however, not long after his return to the States. He was nearly killed in a Columbus brawl and, after being patched up, was obliged to enter rehab. It was either that or jail time. Terry wisely chose the former. Now, years later, he was a faithful member of AA and had ten years' sobriety, of which he was proud.

Terry's friend in AA was another motorcycle-riding vet— of the Vietnam era—an equally large black man named Preston Caldwell. Preston would stop in at the Edgewater for a bottle of water and a sandwich, either before or after a day of fishing on the river. If he caught a lot of fish, he would keep two and give the rest away. He lived on the Muskingum River, upstream from the Edgewater, with his wife Grace.

Preston, 63, was in top physical shape; he had short-cropped, salt-and-pepper hair and freckles. While in Vietnam, Preston had begun to study martial arts and had attained a high degree of proficiency in karate and aikido. Though he no longer practiced, he was able to dispatch any assailant with ease. These were usually young jerks at the Edgewater who had consumed too many beers and who didn't like black people. Sometimes Preston assisted Terry with crowd control. But mostly, Terry and Preston went fishing in Preston's little boat.

Many mornings, Preston would go out the little patch of lawn between his modest house and the Muskingum River and practice tai chi while in a meditative state. He rarely spoke of his interest in Asian pursuits.

Having met Terry and Preston a week earlier at the Edge-water, Harper felt an immediate bond with the two men. They shared a love of the military, women, and fishing. They were also older than some of the other guys at the Edgewater, especially the weekend crowd. They talked a lot about their military lives, although Harper did not say what his true role was, only that he was a platoon leader and had seen combat.

Preston had a battered, 14-foot aluminum boat with a 25 horsepower Evinrude outboard motor. It was all he needed for fishing, and he and Grace would frequently "catch supper" in the river.

This morning, Harper and Terry were on Preston's boat, trolling for whatever might swim by: catfish, walleye, sauger, perch, or bass. At 7:30, the Muskingum was quiet, and the haze of morning was beginning to lift. The three men sat quietly in the bobbing boat; the only sound with the soft *tic-tic-tic* of the fishing reels.

"You guys know anything about the martial arts place in town?" asked Harper.

Terry and Preston thought for a moment, then Terry spoke.

"I think you mean the Dojo, on Front Street. Yeah, it's good. I went there to learn tae kwon do a couple years ago. I went there a couple times a week, before I got steady work," said Terry softly.

"Any good?" asked Harper.

"Oh yes, the Dojo is good. They have everything; the guy is a good teacher. I forget his name," replied Terry.

"That would be John," said Preston. "Why? You thinking of takin' it up?"

"Well, I'm getting out of shape," said Harper. "And I think it might be good to do."

"We *all* out of shape, my brother," observed Preston.

"They sell a lot of hippie stuff in the front. Tie-dyed shirts, incense, and whatnot," said Terry, disapprovingly.

"Gotta make a living," replied Preston.

Harper's reel suddenly went taught, and the reel made a

zzzzz sound as the line played out.

"Got one?" asked Preston.

"Got something," said Harper intently.

Harper began to reel the line, flexing the pole and reeling fast. Within a minute, Harper was lifting a catfish out of the water as Terry netted it, its mouth and whiskers twitching.

"That'll make good eating," observed Preston.

"Maybe so," smiled Harper. "I was hoping for a bass."

"Well, you may get what you wish for," said Preston.

Terry was looking at the far side of the river, squinting to see something.

"What is that over there?" murmured Terry.

Harper squinted to see what Terry was looking at. It was fairly large, bobbing near the edge of the river.

"I don't know. There's some cloth on it. Could be a log."

"Doesn't look like a log to me," said Preston. "Let's go take a look."

Preston gave a sharp yank on the Evinrude's worn gray rope, and the old motor sputtered to life. He then steered the boat slightly upstream so the boat would gently come down to whatever was in the water.

As they approached, the three men suddenly realized it was no log: it was a body of a young man, face down and floating, dead. He wore a red T-shirt, jeans, and one sneaker.

"Holy shit," said Terry. "He's *dead*."

"Wonder who it is?" said Preston.

"Let's turn him over."

"I wouldn't do that," said Harper. "If there was foul play,

then this would be a crime scene."

"Oh, I doubt that," said Preston. "Poor kid probably just drowned."

Terry thought for a moment, "Yeah, maybe we should just leave him be."

"I'll call 911," said Harper as he reached for his cell phone. He intuitively sensed that the young man had been murdered.

The Marietta police soon arrived and immediately referred the matter to the Ohio State Police, who had better resources for determining the time and cause of death.

Within twenty minutes, the OSP had a medical examiner, a photographer, and a CSU detective on the riverbank. They had a tricky time because the underbrush along the riverbank was thick.

When the young man's face was revealed, Harper and the others were unable to identify him. He looked like a nice kid, with one earring and blond highlights on his short brown hair. His skin was pale, and his lips were purple.

After the photographer had taken several photos, the ME and the detective checked the body for a wallet or ID. The young man's pockets were empty. There were no visible marks or bruises. The only thing out of place was the missing sneaker.

"You did the right thing by calling," said the detective. "It may be an accident, but an autopsy will be necessary."

"Can we find out the results?" asked Harper.

"Not unless you're family or a guardian. Are you?"

"No," said Harper quietly. "Just a . . . concerned citizen."

"We will need your names and addresses."

"We'll run his prints and maybe DNA to see if we can figure out who this kid is. He'll probably turn up."

Harper didn't think so.

Returning from the racetrack, Jill walked up the steps that led to the front door of her house, picking up the mail that was lying, bundled, on the top. She paused to look around. The house needed painting. Its soft, gray tone was beginning to flake off. The wrought-iron railings beside the steps needed paint. The sorry excuse for a lawn never seemed to grow, and there were conspicuous bare patches of dirt, starved for lack of water and attention. The only bright spot was the American flag, which bravely waved from a flagpole on one of the front porch pillars. Jill liked the porch, and she reflected that it had been a long time since she had sat on her glider and watched the goings-on of Sixth Street.

Well, there's time for that now, maybe.

Her house was dark, cool, and quiet. She walked straight back to the kitchen and checked to see if there was any coffee left. There was just a little, which she poured into her tan stoneware mug. Then she sat down at the table, opened her purse, and took out the wad of bills. It was a comforting sight. She thought she might return to the racetrack some day and win some more races, but for now she was all set. She stuffed the cash back into her purse, got up, and walked toward the staircase at the front of the house.

Thoughts of Dave and Jamie filled her head as she slowly climbed the stairs, slightly anxious about what might happen. She had never tried to go "out" during daylight hours. Somehow, the night seemed more suited to it, more appropriate.

The little player and headphones were on the floor beside the bed. She picked them up, set them on top of the bed, and took off her shoes. She crawled onto the bed and got herself settled, ready for takeoff. Then she thought of her sleep mask. That might help. She opened the drawer on her bedside table and fished it out. Then she put it around her head so the patch was resting on her forehead.

She put on the headphones, pushed the button, adjusted the sleep mask to cover her eyes, and settled back on her pillow.

There was the familiar voice and the tones; within a minute, she was on the ceiling, looking down at herself. It felt odd in daylight, but she was fine. She hovered around a little, then found herself standing at the foot of her bed. She floated toward the front bedroom window and stuck her head through it.

Man, this is fun.

With her head still sticking through the window, she could see the shabby roof of the porch.

I should have that fixed.

Then she thought about winning at the racetrack and immediately found herself there, floating near its entrance. The man at the gate was reading his newspaper as Jill floated past him and into the large pavilion.

You're not getting three bucks today, Spud.

She then floated inside, among the gamblers near the betting windows, oblivious to her presence. She floated out, behind the grandstand, to the paddock area where the horses and jockeys waited before the race. The horses immediately sensed her presence and began to whinny and stamp. The trainers noticed that something spooked their horses, and they looked at each other quizzically. Jill did not want to bother the horses and suddenly thought about Cathy.

Jill was now transported to a modern classroom, somewhere in Charlottesville, Virginia. Cathy was seated at a student's desk, which had been turned to face a student in another desk. Both were looking at a book. Cathy was trying to make a point, and the student was trying to understand.

That's my girl.

Then she thought of Dave and said his name aloud, as though she were calling him.

"Dave?"

There was a loud whooshing sound, and Jill was suddenly in blackness, traveling fast. It was as though she were on an amusement park ride, but in a tunnel without an end. She did not like the feeling; she did not feel safe. Still, she thought of Dave and held the intention, as Dr. Singh had suggested. The thought of seeing her dead husband and son made the blackness bearable.

Suddenly she heard a familiar voice.

"Jill! Is that *you*?" asked Dave.

Jill was now in the garden she had glimpsed a couple of days previously. It was a breathtakingly beautiful place bursting with abundant flower gardens, warm sunshine, a babbling brook, and smiling people. Dave, looking much younger, stood in the middle of a path. He smiled at Jill.

"Have you crossed over so soon?" asked Dave.

"Oh, Dave," said Jill, overjoyed to see him looking so radiant, "No, I haven't. I learned how to separate my consciousness from the physical. I had to see you. I had to know how you were, and Jamie."

"We're just fine. I had so many things to tell you, but I couldn't. Once you're over here, you can't have contact with people in physical density. I hovered around you and called your name, but you couldn't hear me."

"You did? You were in the house?"

"I was there, Jamie was there, the previous owners . . . I saw you getting drunk, and we all felt such compassion for you. But of course we were powerless to say or do anything."

"Well, that's over. I hope," said Jill.

"I think it is. You have a completely different energy now; you're like the girl I married."

Jill beamed. Dave wasn't one to give compliments, but this one was great.

"I won a lot of money at the racetrack!" blurted Jill. "Seven thousand dollars!"

"That's fantastic! I know how resourceful you are."

"Oh, Dave, what the heck am I saying? Are *you* OK?"

"I am just fine, terrific. And so are you, but you may not realize it. It's beautiful here! I have seen people I haven't seen for a long time, for lifetimes."

"Lifetimes?" asked Jill.

"You and I go way back, Jill. This last incarnation in Ohio was the most recent, but you and I have been together through countless lifetimes together."

"We have?" asked Jill. "How many?"

"I don't know. Maybe dozens. I did a partial life review—

everyone goes through that here. I was able to see my past lives, and you were in just about every one. Sometimes you were a man, and sometimes I was a woman. We experience almost everything in the physical plane—that is where we get our soul work done. But between lifetimes, here, we take stock of who we are, what we have done, and what we need to do the next time."

"Is this true?" asked Jill. "What about Jamie?"

The image of a strapping young man with curly brown hair came into Jill's view. She gasped.

"You've grown up?"

Jamie smiled, "Not exactly. But I am just fine, Mom."

Dave continued speaking, "Oh yes, we all have been through this before—many times. We have to go, but we will see you again . . ."

"Dave, wait! Don't go! Please! Jamie!"

But their images faded, and now Jill saw a brief glimpse of people she knew from her past in upstate New York: Dr. Hawley, the pharmacist; Mildred Henty, her grandmother's aide; old Mr. McEvoy, her elementary school principal. They all looked younger and more radiant, but she knew who they were. Then she saw her grandmother as a young woman in Scotland, laughing and nodding. She saw her father, Ronald, looking fit and hardy, talking with a group of people she didn't recognize. They were in a kind of woodland clearing. She called out to him, "*Dad!*" But he didn't hear her.

It was reassuring and yet heartbreaking.

Then a beautiful woman suddenly appeared. She had straight black hair and was wearing a plain, light blue dress cinched at the waist.

"Hello, Jill," the woman said with a smile.

"Uh, hi," replied Jill.

The woman smiled and bowed, blinking slowly.

"You may not recognize me, but we have been companions for a long time."

"We have?"

"Yes."

"I'm sorry, but I don't recognize you."

"You will." The woman continued to smile gently.

"What's your name?"

"My name is Mata, and I am your guide. I have been with you since the beginning. There are other guides who are also with you. Please know that you are guided and you are loved . . . by many."

"Guides?" asked Jill.

"Spirit guides. The others are appearing now before you . . ."

Jill saw what appeared to be a group of fireflies hovering around Mata. They sparkled and danced.

"Are you, like, a guardian angel?" asked Jill.

"No, but you have a guardian angel. She rarely reveals herself, but she is with you also, for guidance and protection. Your soul knows her."

"I don't mean to be disrespectful, but I don't recognize you . . . Mata."

"I was only in the earth plane once, long ago. Here, see if you recognize me."

Mata was instantly transformed into another woman, with different physical features, but with the same energy. She sat under an old tree, somewhere in Asia. A vast expanse of woodland surrounded the small clearing. The woman wore a beautiful orange silk sari, and her dark eyes sparked with warmth and compassion.

"Do you recognize me now?"

The vision of the woman stirred something within Jill's memory. She felt she knew the woman, but how? When?

The woman read Jill's thoughts and gently said, "It was long ago. You were a young boy, and I taught you to fly. Do you remember?"

Jill saw herself as a young Indian boy standing near the tree. The tree! She recognized the tree, and it kindled a memory from a long-distant past.

"Do not be concerned if you do not remember everything all at once. It will take time. This was the only time I appeared in physical density. I was called Mataji."

Jill tried to remember. This was overwhelming: past lifetimes, learning to fly . . . as a *boy*?

"You are a lucky woman," said Mataji, her dark eyes sparkling. "Few have the ability you have to leave the physical world and move about in time and space. You will be of great service to many."

"I will? How?" asked Jill.

"Opportunities will present themselves to you."

Suddenly the vision began to fade, and Mataji slowly blinked to say farewell.

Jill dimly became aware of the whooshing sounds within her headphone as she awoke on her bed.

She took off the headset and sleep mask, sat up slowly, and

blinked. She felt disoriented. She took a deep breath, then a sip of water from the glass on the bedside table.

Holy smoke.

She had the inclination to immediately go back out and find out more answers, but for now, she had enough to think about. She was pretty sure it wasn't a dream—or was it? Either way, it sure seemed real. Real confusing.

Back in Ridgewood Court, Harper thought about the young man that he, Terry, and Preston had found floating in the river. Seated at his desk, he took out a piece of paper and a soft lead pencil. Then he put on his headphones and pushed the button on his little MP3 player. It contained a dozen 45-minute sound files he had downloaded and modified. Most were alpha-wave generating tones, but others were high beta, which would maximize his concentrative abilities.

He sat for a few minutes with eyes closed, breathing slowly and deeply. Then he opened his eyes and started to draw. He first drew two graceful lines that came to a point; then he drew other lines. As he drew, a picture of a boat emerged: a cabin cruiser. Harper paused for a moment. Then he took in a deep breath, exhaled, and resumed his viewing.

He sketched trees and bushes behind the boat. He filled in more details. He couldn't tell the exact length of the boat, only that it had a hard top and an inboard-outboard motor.

He began to draw little rectangles in the middle of the boat. He didn't know what they were at first, but then he realized that they were probably drugs: many kilos of cocaine or heroin. He

JILL MESSENGER: OUT OF BODY

drew small, rectangular bricks, stacks of them, in a compartment aft of the cabin.

There were three people on board in addition to the young man who had been found dead in the river. Harper could not see their faces, but he got the impression that a woman was with them. Her energetic signature was different from the others.

He suddenly thought of Jill Messenger. He wondered if he should call her to ask her to take a look.

It's too soon for that, Harper thought. *I can do this.*

But maybe he would call her anyway. She was interesting.

As he studied the drawing, Harper knew this had been no accident: the young man been drugged and dumped overboard, or maybe he had taken the drugs himself, or maybe it was drugs and alcohol. As Harper read it, the young man was pretty far gone before he hit the water. It was night when he was dumped over the side. Then the boat wheeled around and glided back toward Marietta. Harper tried to see the numbers on the front of the boat, but it was too dark. He might be able to recognize the boat if he saw it in daylight, but there were too many marinas along the Muskingum and Ohio rivers, and searching for it could take weeks. He briefly thought about calling the police but then reconsidered. How could he possibly explain what he saw? Still, he was curious and wanted to figure it out. This was something new, trying to solve a crime.

The next morning, Harper walked over to the Giant Eagle and bought a copy of the *Marietta Times*. He got an Egg McMuffin and a black coffee to go from the nearby McDonald's and ambled back down Ridgewood Court to his apartment.

It was a perfect summer's day. Kids were playing in the street, and crickets chirped from the grassy hillside.

112

Back in his apartment, Harper unwrapped the sandwich and uncapped the coffee. He poured the coffee into a mug and spread the paper out on his kitchen table. He scanned it for a report about the young man found in the river, but there was nothing. The big story was about the annual Sternwheel Festival that was starting in a week or so. This piqued his curiosity: in any other city, a murder would have been big news.

Maybe they're covering this thing up?

He moved back to his desk, quietly became focused, and then viewed the scene again. It took several minutes to acquire the target, but the only new information he gleaned was that the woman had red hair, and one of the men was fat. He could not see the numbers on the boat, and this baffled him because it ought to have been easy.

He then tried to locate the boat based on the scant information he had acquired, but it was gone. He was coming up empty, and he didn't like it.

The River House, a venerable, redbrick dining establishment in downtown Marietta, faced the scenic Ohio River. Built in 1815, the River House had once been an inn, then a dry goods store, and now was a restaurant. Harper, wearing the navy blazer and tan slacks that he wore in Las Vegas, was waiting out front when Jill walked up. She looked great—her hair had a new cut and was now a lighter shade of brown, almost a honey blond—and her baby blue tank top, white shorts, and bright green Crocs made her look years younger.

They smiled at each other and shook hands like old friends.

"Perfect day," Harper said.

"Yes it is," replied Jill.

As they entered the River House, Jill remarked, "I heard that Abraham Lincoln was once in this building."

"Really?" replied Harper. "Interesting."

"Could be a local legend, though," said Jill.

"He's one of the presidents I most admire."

"Don't say that too loudly," she cautioned. "There are still quite a few 'Rebs' around here."

They were immediately shown to a table, but then they waited a long time for a waitress. They heard angry voices from the kitchen. Eventually, a harried-looking young woman approached their table with menus and glasses of water.

"Sorry for the delay," said the waitress, whose mind was clearly elsewhere. "Can I get you a drink to start?"

"Looks like you could use one," smiled Harper.

"Yeah," said the waitress, scratching her nose.

"Ginger ale," Jill said.

"Bottle of Beck's for me."

"Sorry, no Beck's. We have Sam Adams, Bud, Bud Light, and Yeungling."

"Yeungling then."

"OK," the waitress said as she moved off toward the bar.

"I have to tell you," said Harper, looking into Jill's eyes, "that you look terrific."

"Thank you, James. You look pretty good yourself."

Harper wasn't sure what to say, but Jill continued.

114

"So, whatcha been up to?"

"Oh, a few things. Went fishing the other day," replied Harper.

"Catch anything?" asked Jill.

"I caught a catfish," replied Harper, "and the body of a young man floating in the river."

Jill looked up, startled. "For real?"

"Yeah," replied Harper. "I was in a little fishing boat with a couple of friends and we saw this . . . kid, facedown in the water. He was very dead."

"Yikes. What happened?"

Harper leaned in and clasped his hands together.

"Officially, I don't know. But, unofficially, I was able to see the scene, later, kind of the way you see things . . .?"

"Yes, I remember," Jill said. "So?"

"So when I viewed the scene, I knew the kid had been murdered. Drugged or something and dumped off the boat, late at night."

"Oh wow. What a way to go," Jill whispered, looking down. "And that's all you could see?"

"Yeah," said Harper quietly. "I got a few details about the boat, and that there were some other people on board. It was a cabin cruiser. But I couldn't get the number or much intel about it. And there were drugs on the boat also. So my thought is that this is a pretty heavy-duty criminal thing."

The waitress glided up and set the ginger ale in front of Harper and a Bud Light in front of Jill.

"Ready to order?"

"Just another couple of minutes, please," requested Jill.

The waitress sniffed and moved off.

Jill continued. "So. What did you do when you found the body?"

"I called Kevin."

Jill gave a quizzical smile and cocked her head.

"Well, the Marietta police. Then they called the Ohio State Police, and they arrived and took over, and that was it. I checked the paper this morning to see if there was anything about it, but there wasn't."

"There's probably a reason for that," began Jill. "Here's your beer, by the way. Cheers."

They clinked glasses and took sips.

"Happy days," Harper said with a smile. "So what's the reason?"

"There'll be a lot of tourists in town for the Sternwheel Festival, and a story about someone being murdered is not good for the tourist industry. They like to keep everything upbeat and . . . positive."

"Geez. Well, so much for the news," murmured Harper.

Jill continued, "Ever see the local news on Channel 10? The anchors are high school girls."

"Really? I gotta watch," laughed Harper.

The waitress returned with a basket of rolls and tiny pats of butter. She set it between Jill and Harper.

"I can tell you the special today."

"Please do," smiled Jill.

"It's salmon with rum sauce and onions. It's really good."

"OK," said Jill. "I'll have that."

"Ya want a salad?"

"Sure. Bleu cheese dressing on the side and no tomatoes."

"I'll have the burger, rare, and coleslaw," said Harper, handing the waitress his spotted menu.

"Fries?"

"No, but I would like Swiss cheese on the burger."

"No problem. Swiss burger rare with slaw."

"That's it."

When the waitress had departed, Jill leaned toward Harper.

"So. What about this kid? Do you want me to . . . do something?"

"Well, maybe. If you're interested," nodded Harper. "When I saw it, I got a bad feeling and felt that whoever did this . . . was probably going to get away with it. Nobody saw anything, but I saw a little. Now, if the boat were still there, then I could paint you a complete picture. But I am trying to look at a shadow, and shadows don't have enough information."

"Well, I don't know," said Jill. "When did this happen?"

"Sunday night or early Monday morning."

Jill thought this over. Then she said, "For me to see it, I would have to go back in time, to a specific point and then . . . well, maybe. I can't promise you anything, obviously. I am still pretty new at this."

"I know," replied Harper. "But I thought you might like a challenge."

"I would."

They sat in silence for a few moments. Jill unfolded the napkin on top of the basket of rolls and took one. It was cold.

"This thing just came out of the refrigerator!" chuckled Jill.

"Well, you could ask them to heat it up."

Jill made a face.

"Really, they'd do that. They have ovens."

"Nah. I don't want any bread anyway. So. Where were you before you came to Marietta?"

Harper paused for a moment.

"Maryland, Fort Meade area. I was part of a team that gathered intelligence for various agencies."

"Oh right. I think you said something about that the other night. Like the CIA," said Jill.

"They were one. We did some work for them."

"So . . . ?" asked Jill, and Harper laughed.

"I can't tell you the specifics, but it involved remote viewing for the government. I saw a lot of things, including some things I wasn't supposed to see."

"Really? Like what?" asked Jill.

"I *really* can't tell you. Some of it involved our government, other governments, weaponry, troop movements . . . various kinds of secret installations. Stuff like that. I'm no longer with them, but if I told you, then you could be in some danger with that information."

"Ohhh," said Jill. "Then you'd have to kill me?"

Harper laughed, "I don't think so."

He studied Jill's face and guessed her age to be somewhere around 45. She looked younger because of her youthful bearing and sharp mind; he could tell by the way she spoke and the things she said.

"So what happened after your son and husband died in the accident?"

"Oh," said Jill.

Harper's question caught her off guard.

"I don't know if I'm over it. My world ended, and I didn't handle it well. I drank a lot. I have a daughter—she's in college—and she's been a great help. And my neighbors have been supportive, and Sara Hopkins, whom you know. She lives right across the street from me. She's been great. And, ah, her giving me those CDs, the ones you had, they have been kind of a lifesaver."

"Really? In what way?" asked Harper.

"To be honest with you . . . at one point, I didn't care if I lived or died. I was that depressed, distraught. I got hammered one night and fell down the stairs. I really hurt myself. Sara found me the next day, and that's how I ended up in the hospital. She brought me the CDs . . . and then I started having the out-of-body experiences."

"Interesting," said Harper.

"I was terrified, but . . . I got over it. Now I . . . it's funny that you asked about my husband and son. When I was out of body, just last night, I saw them, and they are all right. I talked with them."

"Really?" asked Harper, interested.

"Well I wasn't in normal physical reality, so I can't tell you. But it sure seemed real."

"I envy you," Harper said earnestly.

The waitress returned with a tray of lukewarm food. She set the salmon in front of Harper, and a well-done burger and fries in front of Jill.

"Anything else?"

CHAPTER FIVE

In the wee hours of the morning, Jill was flying low over the dark river, looking for the death boat. She had successfully gone back to the time frame Harper had given her, but so far, she had been unable to figure out how to locate the boat or the young man. Her thought had been to start with the young man's body and work back in time. She held the intention of 3:00 a.m. and soon was hovering just over the river, in the approximate area Harper had described: a half mile north of the Edgewater Bar.

It was quiet, and the earth seemed to glow with an inner radiance; the trees looked alive. Even the river seemed to sing a happy, murky song as Jill glided west, skimming a few feet over its surface.

Then she saw it: a body of a young man, face down, gently bobbing ten feet from the riverbank. He had lost a sneaker. He did not radiate any energy. She moved underneath the body and came up to see his face. It was peaceful and white. His eyes were open. Jill was not frightened—whoever he was, he was in a better place now. Maybe she could find him . . . out there, somewhere.

Then she remembered that Harper said the boat headed back toward Marietta after dumping the young man. Maybe if she placed herself at the *Becky Thatcher* riverboat, near the center of town, and then came back up, she might run into the cruiser.

As soon as she had thought of the *Becky*, she was hovering over its white prow in the moonlight. Beneath her were white tables with red umbrellas.

Nice place for lunch.

It was quiet; only the sounds of summer crickets could be heard. She held the intention of moving up the river and, as before, was immediately flying a few feet off its surface. She glided under the Putnam Street bridge, then the Washington Street bridge, greatly enjoying the experience.

She skimmed along for a few minutes, passing houses on the river's edge: some with docks and boats, some with nice lawns, and some with pretty pavilions. Then, about 100 yards ahead, she saw a boat approaching with its running lights off.

It was as Harper described: a cabin cruiser with a hard white top. As it chugged toward her, she noticed the top had an overhang in the front and along the sides. She also noticed a shiny metal railing that extended around the front and down the sides. The cabin windows looked like rectangles that had been flared out at the bottom.

As the boat began to glide past her, she turned and moved into it, placing herself in the interior cabin. She gasped in surprise

122

to see there were two other people right next to her. But they did not see her; they were engrossed in a conversation. Seated at a small cabin table was a woman in her thirties with red hair. She was beautiful but looked tired. A balding fat man sat across from her, drinking wine from a spotted plastic tumbler. He looked vaguely familiar, but Jill couldn't place him.

As they spoke, it was difficult to make out what they were saying. Something about how no one would be able to connect them to Tim. Tim must have been the body she had seen.

Jill remembered what Harper had said about drugs and tentatively moved her head through the aft part of the cabin, behind a wooden staircase. Sure enough, there were bricks—maybe thirty or so—of what looked like flour. The only sounds were the conversation from the cabin and the low chugging of the motor. For the first time, Jill felt a panicky rush; she felt trapped. With an upward intention, she moved straight up and into the helm at the back of the cruiser.

The helm was fairly open under an expansive roof, with a small table and opposing bench seats on the left, and a pilot's chair and wheel in the front right. Two small louvered doors opened to the cabin below.

She turned to look aft, but the back deck of the boat was empty, except for a coil of rope and something dark lying on the floor near the starboard side: a sneaker.

Jill suddenly sensed a man's cologne, one she vaguely recognized. She looked at the man piloting the boat and moved to see his face.

Robert Guerra!

She peered into his face. He held a steely expression of grim determination; it alarmed her.

Robert looked right at her, or seemed to, and she froze in fear. Then his face faded into the distance, as though she were being pulled backwards, away, very fast.

When she stirred back to normal consciousness, Jill sat up slowly and took a drink of water from a glass on the bedside table. Her hand trembled as she held it.

Then she set the glass down on the nightstand, opened the top drawer, and took out a notepad and a pen. Jill shifted her position and began to write down the things she remembered: where the body was located, what the boat looked like, descriptions of the people in the cabin, the sneaker, and Robert.

Would she tell James about Robert? He had helped her when she needed some money, and had taken her to the racetrack. And yet, if he was mixed up in something criminal . . .

She decided that before telling James about Robert, she needed to do some more investigating. But she would fill him in about everything else.

Harper's number was downstairs, held to the front of a refrigerator by a little magnet. She was soon dialing his number, but his line was busy.

She paced anxiously around the kitchen, hitting the redial button every thirty seconds. No luck.

Harper was on the phone with Bud Grant. Grant breezily said that he had a vacation coming up and wondered if "Patrick" would like some company.

"You bet. Except I'm not Patrick these days. Call me James. It's important. Patrick died in Vegas."

"OK. I'll practice all the way."

"You gonna fly down?"

"No, probably drive. You got room for me at your place?"

"Yeah, if you don't mind a couch."

"Not a problem. I have an air mattress, so I can bring that," said Grant.

"Whatever suits you," said Harper. "When do you think you might arrive?"

"Probably Sunday, late afternoon."

"Need directions?" asked Harper.

"Just the street address. The GPS unit will do the rest."

"How are those things?" asked Harper.

"I'd be lost without it," replied Grant.

"Oh, funny. OK, buddy. Listen, when you come, bring your fishing pole."

"Really? Good fishing around there?" asked Grant.

"Pretty fair. There's perch, bass, catfish. I know a guy with a boat, and there's a few docks and bridges . . . there's a lot of places."

"OK, OK, we'll fish," chortled Grant.

"Oh, bring some of your cool electronic gear, too. I know a couple of restaurants that are pretty noisy."

"I always have my goodie bag with me. You never know . . ." smiled Grant.

After he hung up the phone, Harper stood up, stretched, and went into the kitchen. The phone rang again, this time it was Jill.

"James, Jill. Got a minute?"

"Sure. What's up?"

"I took your advice and . . . went *out*, you know? And I

saw the body and the boat. I was there. I was *there*. I found out a lot. I saw everything," she said.

"That's just fantastic Jill. Wow!" exclaimed Harper, impressed. "What did you see?"

"I . . . don't feel comfortable telling you over the phone."

"Sure. Where do you want to meet?" Harper asked.

"Why don't you come over here? It's not far from where you live. I'll make some coffee. Do you know how to get to Cutler Street?"

"Ahh, no," replied Harper.

"Um, you walk over to Seventh Street, by the little park there, and you'll see a stairway across the street. It's in the trees. Take the steps up and it will bring you to the end of Cutler Street. My street, Sixth Street, is a little ways down on your left. Number 617. Gray house with a flag out front. And my black Honda is out front, too."

"OK, that's easy. Be there in a bit."

Fifteen minutes later, Harper was seated in a large armchair across from Jill; he was leaning forward, his hands clasped together. Before him, a steaming mug of coffee rested on the coffee table. Jill perched on the edge of the couch, her notes before her. She was still nervous and anxious about what she had seen.

In a hesitant manner, Jill related what she knew about the boat, the young man in the water, and where she had seen it. Then she suddenly added, "And . . . it turns out . . . I know one of the people on the boat, the guy who was driving it."

Why did I say that?

"Really?" exclaimed Harper.

Might as well spill the beans.

"Yeah, a guy at the Frontier Bank. I know him. And I can't believe he'd be mixed up in something like this."

"You're sure they didn't see you?"

"I don't think so. How could they?"

"Were you able to see the guy actually being dumped overboard?"

"No. I tried to, but I was a few minutes late. I just saw the body and the boat on the way back. It had its running lights off, and the cabin was blacked out with curtains."

"Did you get the number on the boat?" asked Harper.

Jill shook her head, not understanding the question.

"Yeah, it's on the bow, both sides. It's a registration number. Every boat has one."

"Oh. Sorry, no. I didn't know about that," said Jill.

"Do you think you would recognize the boat if you saw it again?"

"I think so."

"OK. Then what we need to do is to find the boat," said Harper.

"Should we call the police?"

Harper took a sip of coffee and shook his head.

"What would we tell them? There are drugs aboard a cabin cruiser, somewhere, and a guy from one of the banks is involved?"

Jill nodded grimly; Harper was right.

"We need evidence. And besides, if we call the police,

they would figure I was in on it, especially with my being nearby when the body was found. No. I think the better way is to find the boat. And then once we do that, then I can track it, and you can too. Because . . . if they have a lot of drugs on board, they're not only dealing, they're connected to something a lot bigger."

"You mean like . . . the Mafia?"

"Could be. It could be them, it could be the Russians, it could be the CIA . . ."

"The CIA? Do they do that?"

"Oh yeah. They're a money pit. Never have enough."

"Wow. Well, I was going to go out, you know, and see what I could find out about the guy from the bank."

"You don't want to tell me his name?"

"Not yet. I want to check him out first. If he's mixed up in criminal stuff, then of course I'll tell you."

"When can you do that?" asked Harper.

"Tonight probably."

Harper nodded.

"So. How do we find the boat?" asked Jill.

"Well, one way is to visit local marinas. Know of any?"

"Well . . . there's one near the *Becky Thatcher*. There's maybe 20 boats there. There are some private marinas in the area . . . a few on the Ohio River. There's a big one on the Muskingum, halfway to Zanesville."

"I suppose plenty of people have private docks, too?" asked Harper.

"Oh yeah, all along the river . . . you know what?"

Harper shook his head. "What?"

128

"*I* have a boat," exclaimed Jill.

"You do?" replied Harper. "Where is it?"

"It's in storage," said Jill, waving her hand, "Out on Pike Street. I forget the name of the place, but I could find it."

"Does it float?"

"Oh yeah. Dave and I took excellent care of it. It's a cabin cruiser."

"Well, that's nice, but it probably wouldn't hurt to visit the marina downtown. Whaddya think?"

"Sure, when?"

"How's right now?"

"I want to see the boat first, if you don't mind," said Jill.

"That's fine. I'd like to see it, too. Might come in handy."

Chester Hamblet was a sour, squat little man of 73. He was standing outside his warehouse, smoking a grimy corncob pipe when Jill and Harper drove up.

"Good morning, Chester," yelled Jill as she got out of the car.

Chester spat on the ground. "What's good about it?"

"Well, it's a nice day, and the sun is shining. Remember me? Dave Messenger's wife? I think our boat is here."

"Yer kinda late. Season's 'bout over."

"Well, you probably don't know what happened. Dave and our son were killed last January," Jill said matter-of-factly.

"Oh. Didn't know. Well, gee now, that's too bad," said Chester. "Anyways, your boat's here. You wanna get it?"

"Not today," said Jill. "Do we owe you anything on it?"

"No. I think you're paid up through October."

"Can I see it?" asked Jill.

"I guess so," said Chester as he spat on the ground again and turned to enter the cavernous entrance to the warehouse.

It was dark and cool, with enormous racks on the left and right walls. Each rack had a space for a boat, and it reminded Jill of a mammoth Hollywood Squares. Harper walked beside her.

"Who're you?" asked Buster.

"Friend of the family," smiled Harper, as he noticed a tattoo on Buster's forearm.

"Looks like you were in the service," observed Harper.

"Korea. Three lousy years."

He stopped and pointed to the prow of a boat sticking out from one of the bays in the rack.

"There she is."

The sight of the boat caught Jill off guard, and she was momentarily filled with emotion. Dave's boat, *Keuka Maiden*, quietly perched eight feet off the ground.

"Nice looking boat," said Harper approvingly. "What is it?"

"It's a Carver," said Jill. "Spent a lot of time on her."

"Looks pretty nice," said Harper approvingly.

"She's 26 feet long. Has a full galley, sleeps four . . . has an enclosed head. I think the motors are MerCruisers? Is that right?"

"Yep," said Chester.

"The tank holds a lot, so there's good range. We made it to Cincinnati once without refueling. It's basically a fishing boat, but Jamie water-skied behind it once. Took a lot of gas!"

"Very nice," said Harper.

Jill looked at Chester Hamblet.

"How much notice do you need to get the boat down?"

"Same day, unless I'm busy."

Jill thought for a moment.

"I don't know if we have a trailer."

Chester sniffed. "I don't think ya do. Dave used to rent one."

"How much is that?" asked Jill.

"Sixty for the day, fifty-five to get the boat down."

"OK. Thanks," said Jill. "It'll probably be a few days. I have to find out if there's dock space."

"I wouldn't know about that."

There was an awkward pause. Then Jill spoke.

"Good seeing you again, Chester. I'll give you a call about the boat."

"I'll be here."

As Jill steered the Honda out of Hamblet's parking lot, its tires crunching on the gravel, Harper said, "Interesting man."

"Very active in the Presbyterian church. You wouldn't think so to listen to him."

"No, I wouldn't," said Harper.

A few minutes later, Jill turned her car onto Front Street, in downtown Marietta. One thing she liked was that there were parking spaces when she needed one. Usually. She parked across from the entrance to the *Becky Thatcher*; the marina was next door.

She and Harper crossed the street, walked together under some shady trees, and soon were descending on the long aluminum ramp that led down to the gray, wooden dock. Harper noticed that the posts on the dock were extremely tall and resembled telephone poles.

"Why are the posts so high?"

"'Cause the river floods and the docks float up."

"Wow," Harper said as he stepped onto the dock behind Jill. "*That* high?"

"Oh yeah. This whole area, Front Street, Harmar; they've all been underwater. If you go into the Lafayette Hotel—down there on the corner—you can see the high-water mark on the wall of the lobby. Pretty scary when that happens."

"How often do you get floods?" asked Harper.

"There's high water every spring, and some years it's bad. According to local legend, if the river floods and leaves ice behind, then the river will come back to reclaim it. That's when the fun starts."

"Wow," Harper said, shaking his head.

"In the years I've been in Marietta, there have been two bad floods. The one in 2004 was the worst."

Jill began to move down the dock. There were a wide assortment of boats: a Carver weekender, a Chaparral, a SunDancer, a Stamas, and some houseboats. There was a Penn Yan speedboat tied up to the dock of the *Becky Thatcher*, about fifty yards downriver. Jill smiled; she had once lived in Penn Yan, when the boats were still being made. Now, she reflected, Penn Yan boats were much prized.

She stopped beside one cabin cruiser.

"This one is close, but I don't think it's the one I saw. The windows have the same shape, though."

Harper nodded. It wasn't the boat he saw either.

Jill turned and walked down to the other end of the dock. Harper trailed leisurely behind, pausing to look into the various boats.

"Jill?" said a man's voice.

Jill looked up; it was Willie Pindar, and old friend from church. He was standing on the back deck of his houseboat, holding a fishing pole. He wore a tattered plaid shirt, paint-spattered khaki shorts, and a baseball cap. Beside him was a metal pail with three perch in it. Next to the pail lay a weary old border collie. He looked up with baleful eyes, then settled back down.

"Willie!" exclaimed Jill. "How ya doin'?"

"Oh the same: a day late and a dollar short," smiled Willie.

"How they bitin'?" asked Harper.

"Got a lotta babies. Had to throw 'em back," muttered Willie. "Hey, Jill, I heard about Dave, but I didn't know where you guys lived or I woulda sent a card or something."

"It's all right," said Jill, "Thanks for thinking of us."

She motioned to Harper.

"This is James Harper. James, Willie Pindar."

They shook hands.

"This here is Flash," said Willie, rubbing the dogs head. "Flash, play dead. Good dog."

"I remember Flash." Jill smiled.

Willie smiled at Harper and said, "From out of town?"

"Sort of. I just moved here, and Jill was kind enough to show me around. I'm thinking of buying a boat. So I'm looking into dock space."

"Geez, I could sell you this thing, but then I wouldn't have any place to live," grinned Willie. "And neither would Flash, would ya boy?"

"No, well, I was going to try to find a used Bayliner cruiser. I had one a long time ago and I like 'em."

"They're pretty good. A little too much power for around here, but they're nice boats," observed Willie. "I don't think we have any Bayliner boats here. I think that guy . . . Ernie T. has one. You know, he's related to the guy at the bank, that Guerra guy. They use to go out quite a bit when Ernie docked here."

"Where does he dock now?" asked Jill.

"I think he's up in Newport. You know, when they opened that marina up there, a bunch of guys went up because the rental fees are about half what they are here. But I don't think he's got it for sale. Now, if you wanted to buy a boat, the Sunday paper has a list at the back of the want ads. I always read 'em 'cause you never know. I always dream about getting something fancy, you know, then go on a long trip, down the Mississippi . . ."

"That'd be a great adventure," Jill said.

"Yeah, if you got the money."

As Harper and Jill returned to her car, Harper spotted a little restaurant named Cafénated.

"Hey, let me get a couple coffees to go."

"You read my mind."

"Ya think?" laughed Harper.

"I'd like an iced coffee, light, no sugar, please," Jill said as she got into the car.

Soon they were again heading out on Pike Street, north

toward Newport. They passed a beautiful tree farm, then some auto body shops. The further out they got, the more impoverished the surroundings. They passed several trailer parks.

"You know," said Jill. "There's a young kid, lives in one of these trailer parks. He's an Elvis impersonator."

"Yeah?" smiled Harper.

"The kid is just unbelievable. I don't know what he does, but he just morphs into Elvis."

Harper smiled. "Does he wear the white leather suit?"

"Oh no, this kid does the young Elvis, the Elvis of the fifties."

"I'd love to see that."

"He performs around town. He'll probably do a spot at the Sternwheel Festival and the Washington County Fair."

"Sounds like fun."

Jill followed Route 7 and was soon in Newport. There wasn't much to see; this was farmland, scrub brush, and trailer parks. She pulled into a dilapidated Mobil gas station across from an old IGA grocery store and looked toward the river to see if she could spot the marina.

"It's gotta be around here somewhere."

"I'll find out," said Harper as he got out and walked toward the gas station.

A few minutes later, Harper and Jill were driving down a rutted gravel road that led to the Ohio River. As they came around a bend, they saw a labyrinth of docks and boats. It was twice the size of the Marietta marina. Jill was impressed.

She stopped the car. Then she and Harper got out and moved toward a gate, breezing by a sign that read "Boat Owners and Guests Only."

As they began to move down a winding path, a man's voice said sternly, "Can I help you?"

Jill turned to see a large, balding man who was coming out of a little shed to intercept them.

"Yes, you can," said Jill. "I'm here to see about renting some dock space."

"There's nobody here now," he grumbled. "I'll give you Dave Lawrence's number. He'll give you all the info."

"OK," Jill said as the man returned to the shed. Harper was intuiting some info about the man, which was coming through clearly.

The man returned and gave a card to Jill. Then she spoke.

"So you don't know how much the spaces rent for?"

"I'm just security, ma'am. Can't help you."

"Well, can we just take a look at the docks?"

"Call Mr. Lawrence. He'll be able to help you. I have my orders."

"I just want to see if there's fuel and A/C power out to the boats."

"Just come back when Mr. Lawrence's here," the man said tersely.

Jill looked stumped. She turned to Harper.

"How long were you at the monastery?" asked Harper quietly.

The man looked stricken.

"Uh. Do I know you?" he asked uneasily.

"Why don't you give us two minutes to check out the docks?"

The man shifted slightly. Then silently, embarrassed, gave a quick nod of his head toward the boats.

Jill and Harper moved quickly down the path that led to the entrance ramp.

"What was that all about? Do you know the guy?"

"Tell you later."

On the gray wooden planks, Jill began to walk around, searching for the boat she saw in her out-of-body state. Harper merely closed his eyes.

Then he said, "There," and pointed to a middle dock. They moved quickly toward it. It was the Bayliner, the one each had seen. Harper made a quick mental note of the registration number and noted the boat's name painted in gold-and-white letters on the transom: *Salty Dog*.

"Got it. Let's go," said Harper.

"Oh wait, I want to see if they have gas pumps.

"Yeah, down at the far end. Gas and diesel. See?"

As they moved back up the ramp toward the man and the shed, Jill whispered to Harper, "So, who is that guy?"

"Once we're out of here, I'll tell you."

As they approached the shed, the man motioned for Harper to come over. Harper signaled for Jill to wait and she stopped.

The man leaned into Harper's face and said, with a mixture of anxiety and worry, "Were you there?"

Harper said, "Sort of. Don't worry. Nobody knows."

"Yeah," said the man, not quite believing him. "OK."

Back in the car, Jill was perplexed at what Harper had said to the man.

"So?" she insisted, holding her hand out.

"I got a strong vibe from the guy and did a viewing on him. Strong emotional content; kicked out of a monastery—I think Kentucky—for homosexual behavior."

"Really?" said Jill as she started the motor. "I thought that was an entrance requirement."

Harper laughed and said, "You're bad."

"I try," said Jill glibly. "Well, now we know where the boat is."

"I have a feeling it's not going to stay there long," said Harper.

"What makes you say that?"

"Because I saw it, and then I didn't see it. Now, that guy you saw, at the helm, the guy from the bank . . . I can't view him because I have no target, but I think you need to check him out."

"I was planning on doing that, checking out his house, the bank. This whole thing is weird," said Jill.

"You can say that again," said Harper.

"This whole thing is weird."

As they drove back down Route 7, Jill asked Harper, "This is probably none of my business, but . . . have you ever viewed me?"

Harper reflected for a moment, then spoke.

"Yes. Nothing bad, but I needed to check you out."

Jill pursed her lips, wondering what he saw.

"I saw you drinking, I saw you fall, I saw you recover. I got a good sense of you. And I'll tell you this: you are pretty remarkable."

Jill was not comfortable with this disclosure.

"How 'bout you?" asked Harper. "Visited me yet?"

"I thought about it, but I had to see my husband and son first. I needed to make sure they were all right," she said crisply.

"Are they?"

"Oh yeah. They are more than all right."

"Good," nodded Harper.

"I feel kind of violated," Jill said.

"It was really for your own protection. Nothing bad or improper. I check out everybody I'm in contact with. It's for my protection, too. You got an A plus, Jill. And, if it makes you feel any better, you can check me out. I would expect no less."

"Well, maybe I will."

"You can't read minds, can you?" asked Harper.

"Not yet."

"That's a relief."

They laughed.

Later that night, Jill was high over Marietta, flying northeast, skimming over the treetops, the Ohio River sparkling silently below. Her destination was Highland Drive, in a section of Marietta known as Reno. It was a well-to-do neighborhood filled with gracious homes set back from the road, overlooking valleys of trees and rolling hills.

Robert Guerra was at home; his car was in the driveway, and some house lights glowed from within. Jill floated in through the back, into the semidark kitchen. A large, half-empty bottle of Chardonnay sat on the counter next to the refrigerator. She heard the sound of a television and floated toward it. In the back den was Robert, his arm around the beautiful woman with red hair Jill had seen on the boat. The were watching a porn video and obviously enjoying it. The redhead looked up, directly at Jill.

"What's that?" she said.

"What's what?" replied Robert.

"It looked like smoke or something right there . . ."

"I don't see anything."

But Jill had withdrawn, floating lightly through the rooms on the ground floor.

Nicely decorated.

Then she floated upstairs and began to look through the rooms. There was nothing of interest. She moved up to the third floor, to what had been a kid's room; there were pictures of rock stars on the wall and a Jim Morrison poster. There was some junk stored, an old stereo, a box of CDs. Not much.

All that was left was the basement.

As she descended into the lowest level, she noticed that it, too, had been decorated. There was paneling on the walls, a drop ceiling, and linoleum on the floor. There was also the standard basement stuff: furnace, hot water heater, old furniture, a couple of old lamps, and a dusty ping-pong table.

There was an area toward the back that had a heavy lock on a paneled door.

Like that's gonna stop me, thought Jill, as she floated through it.

Once past the door, Jill gasped.

There were stacks of white bricks—more than 100—like

the ones she had seen on the boat, and they certainly weren't flour. There were many blocks of dark brown hashish, cases of pharmaceuticals, and other paraphernalia. She noticed a little hatch, high up on the basement wall, which led to the outside.

Probably easier to get the drugs in and out that way.

There was a closet with louvered doors, secured by a padlock and hasp. She stuck her head in to see what was inside.

Jill gasped.

Porn, all kinds: VHS tapes, DVDs, magazines. It was stacked from the floor to halfway up the wall. Above the porn, on a clothing rack, were suits and jackets in plastic dry-cleaner's bags. There were several official-looking black suits, an FBI jacket, and a set of green army fatigues with Guerra, R., sewn over the left pocket.

She withdrew from the closet and was moving back through the basement when she suddenly noticed an odor. It was flowery and beautiful. She was baffled.

Then someone spoke to her:

"There's more you must know . . ."

Jill froze.

She tried to move but was immediately swept into a long, black void, and she began to accelerate. She was helplessly accelerating, moving faster and faster. She was helplessly moving faster and faster, headlong into a dizzying blackness, and she screamed! But there was no sound.

Then it instantly stopped.

She was now in an elegant, spacious, old-world conference room. The walls were exquisitely paneled with dark, figured walnut. An ornate gold and crystal chandelier hung over an antique rosewood table. Venerable tufted leather chairs were arranged around the table, and old masters' paintings adorned the walls: Rembrandt, Vermeer, Raphael, and others she did not recognize.

At one end of the room was a massive stone fireplace. Over it was a heraldic shield with a Latin inscription: *Ordo Ab Chao.*

Four distinguished-looking men sat around one end of the highly polished table. They were impeccably dressed in conservative suits, and they represented untold wealth and power.

One of the men spoke in a soft, deep voice. His voice had an accent—what was it—*German? Dutch?*

"We are on schedule. The West will be unified in two years. That is the forecast I have received. The African nations will be decimated by disease and their populations reduced by more than three hundred million . . ."

"Will there be enough laborers left to work the mines? The crops?"

"Yes. There will be enough."

"What about AIDS?"

"We have vaccines for the essential people. All non-essential personnel will be allowed to expire."

One of the other gentlemen spoke. "There is still the problem of China."

"The Council is not concerned with China at this time. Our present objectives are the unification of the West under one central government and the subjugation of the African nations. None of this will happen tomorrow, as you know. Remember, this has been moving forward for more than a century. I am not concerned. If we do as required, we will meet our objectives."

"So you see no obstacles?"

"Nothing significant. As I said, we on schedule."

The old gentlemen nodded to each other.

Who are these people? What are they talking about?

Jill heard a ringing, far off.

It got louder and louder.

Then she was back on her bed, and her bedside phone was ringing loudly. She went to reach for it, but felt disoriented and lay back down. The machine would pick it up. Or, if it was important, whoever it was would call back. Then the ringing stopped, and Jill fell into a deep sleep.

The next morning, Harper was at his desk in Ridgewood Court, pencil in hand, targeting the Bayliner. After a few minutes, he caught something and began to sketch. He wasn't sure what he was getting, but it was something connected with the boat. The impressions momentarily faded, and Harper looked at what he had drawn. He was not always accurate at interpretation, but the images were of the boat, and it was on the water. This was in the upper part of the page. But there were other, curving lines he could not quite understand. Lines that looped around the page, from upper right to lower left.

He looked at it in perplexity, not quite understanding. Then it dawned on him: he had sketched the Ohio River, from Pittsburgh, down to Marietta, and then had followed it to Cairo, Illinois, where it joined the Mississippi.

The Ohio river was being used to ferry drugs using ordinary pleasure craft. And if there was one boat, there may be more.

There may be many more. If so, who was behind it? If it were the Mafia, then the money would go back to the operation. And if it were the CIA, God knows what it could be used for. Millions of dollars were involved, all of it in cash.

During his tour in Southeast Asia, Harper had learned about the vast amounts of heroin that came from the Golden Triangle area of Thailand; he discovered that their sales were used to fund Black Ops by the CIA and their subsidiary organizations. Many good soldiers got hooked on the stuff, too. The CIA used their Mafia associates to sell the drugs, and all made enormous sums. Later, during the Reagan presidency, the CIA continued its drug-running operations and introduced cocaine and later crack. This, to the CIA Black Ops personnel, served two purposes. First, it generated untraceable, unaccountable wealth; second, it eliminated undesirables because many died of overdoses or ended up in prison. To the Black Ops mindset, they were performing a public service. Morality and decency were off the table; only the missions mattered.

Harper got up, stretched, and moved into the kitchen to make a fresh pot of coffee. A box containing several bags of coffee beans had just arrived from New York City, and he was eager to try them. Harper had only a few indulgences, and freshly ground coffee was one of them. He opened a bag of mocha supreme and scooped some of the beans into his electric coffee grinder. In a few minutes, his Melitta coffeemaker was making happy *pop-pop* sounds as the steaming water began to trickle onto the fresh grounds.

While the coffee was brewing, Harper switched on his laptop to check his e-mail. Bud Grant was due to arrive the next day, and he would certainly notify Harper if there were any deviations from the plan.

Sure enough, there was a message from Grant.

Hey Bro, as it turns out I may be staying longer than I originally said. Please see if you can find me some digs in your part of the world. ETA: 6 p.m. tomorrow. Peace Out, Sherman. (I signed it Sherman so they wouldn't know who sent it. Pretty smart, huh? Hugs and kisses, General Cluck)

Harper smiled and shook his head. Was Grant serious? What could he possibly mean? Was he quitting IBM and the AI group? Had he run into difficulty? Or maybe he had zapped one too many radar units and run afoul of the law?

Grant would fill him in; there were few secrets between them.

Jill awoke at 9:00 a.m., refreshed from a long sleep. The day looked overcast, and the house was dark and quiet. She got up and moved downstairs to the kitchen, wondering about the distinguished men she had seen. What could that possibly mean? And why was this scene shown to her?

Her answering machine was flashing: one new message. She pressed the button. Maybe it was Cath?

"Hello, Jill," said the voice. "This is Robert Guerra at the Frontier Bank. I wonder if you might give me a buzz tomorrow. My home phone number is 370-7734. Look forward to talking with you, Jill."

Now this was interesting. What could he want?

She dialed his number, and he answered immediately.

"Hello?"

"Hi, Robert, this is Jill Messenger."

"Jill! How ya doin'?"

"Pretty good, thanks. You?"

"No complaints . . ." There was a pause before he spoke again. "Hey, Jill. I don't want to pry, but . . . you keeping secrets from me?"

Jill felt a prickly flush of fear.

"I . . . don't think so," said Jill. "Why do you ask?"

She could feel the anxiety in her throat as she waited for a response.

"You never told me about hitting the trifecta at the track."

How did he know about that?

"Oh! Well, that was just a lucky bet. I didn't even realize I had won until I got home and looked at the program! Remember? I asked you what a trifecta was."

There was a brief pause. Then Robert said, "So you did."

"And I just had a . . . hunch and I went with it. Kind of stupid, I know, but it paid off—just when I needed it most."

Robert didn't completely buy her story, but he had no other information. People just did not hit the trifecta with a twenty dollar bet. Especially first timers. The odds were just too astronomical. This was something he had better look into. Then Jill spoke.

"So, Robert, how are things with you?"

Getting your jollies with porn, Stud?

"Oh same old, same old. Not much going on. Things are slow in the summertime. Everybody's away."

"I guess," said Jill.

"So . . . how about dinner sometime?"

The guy was a criminal, but maybe she could pry loose some information. She'd have to be careful, though. If she did go out with Robert, she'd want James to be nearby, just in case.

"Well, yeah, sure."

"What kind of food you like?

"Let's see . . ." began Jill. "There's that natural foods place on Third Street. I forget the name, but I like it."

"Brighter Day? Good choice. It's right around the corner from the bank, and I'm there quite a bit. How about Italian?"

"I like Italian," said Jill, wondering what he had in mind.

"Casa Palermo, just over the bridge in West Virginia."

"Sounds like a dress-up place?"

"Oh no, you can go casual. I know the people there, so we won't have to wait in line."

"When's a good night for you?"

"Ah, let me check my calendar," Jill said, looking out the back window. "How's Tuesday, around six?"

"Sounds good. I'll pick you up at six," said Robert. The smile was back in his voice.

No way.

"How 'bout I meet you there? I'm going to be doing errands most of the day, and that would just make things easier."

"No problem. See you Tuesday at Palermo's then."

"OK, Robert. Thanks for thinking of me. Bye now."

"Bye, Jill."

As she hung up the phone, she suddenly thought of Dr. Singh. She didn't know why, but she felt a closeness to him.

Maybe it was because of his warmth and caring, or because of the fact that he wanted nothing from her. And, of perhaps all the people in the world, he alone knew what she was experiencing. James had a sense of it, but he didn't understand completely.

Then she realized it was Saturday, and Dr. Singh would not be at the college. What would she do? She was up for a little fun, and had some money to burn. Talking about food made her hungry. It would soon be time for lunch . . .

She picked up the phone and dialed Sara's number.

"Hello?"

"Hey, Sara, it's Jill."

Jill could hear the clatter of pots and pans being washed in the background. They made a racket.

"Hey, how ya doin'? What's cookin'?" yelled Sara.

"Oh just getting some stuff squared away. I went to see the boat yesterday," said Jill in a loud voice.

"Uh, huh," said Sara. "Out at Hamblet's?"

Now water was running. Seems every time she talked with Sara on the phone, she was doing the dishes.

"Yep. Still there."

"You gonna put it in the water? I have *such* great memories of that boat."

More pans clattered in the background.

"Hey, Sara, can you stop washing dishes for a minute?"

"Bother you?"

"Yeah, sorry!" said Jill.

"OK," said Sara, and suddenly it became quiet. Then she continued, "So you're getting your boat out? That's good. That guy Hamblet, what an ornery SOB!" exclaimed Sara.

"Hey, listen, can I buy you lunch? It's a nice day, maybe we could walk into town."

"The first part sounds good. But walk into town? I'd have to get new feet, honey, 'cause these dogs won't make it. Where were you thinking of going?"

"Well . . . I don't know. The Marietta Brewing Company?"

"*Fab*-ulous," replied Sara. "Love the place."

"Meet you by the car around 1:00. How's that?"

"Sounds like a plan," Sara replied. "See you then."

Jill had a little time to herself before she had to meet Sara, and she thought maybe she should go out again, to find her guide, Mata. She had a million questions, and Mata seemed to know the answers. She thought of Dave, too. But he and Jamie were OK, and that was the main thing. Cathy was also OK and would be calling the next evening. No, Jill needed some answers. Especially about those men she saw. Maybe Mata could give her some help. She thought about James Harper. A nice guy . . . with a mysterious past. Maybe she *would* take a look.

Her routine was familiar now. She moved quickly through the living room, and then went up the stairs and into her bedroom. The gray light of an overcast sky shone dimly through the windows. She knelt on the bed and crawled into position. Then she grabbed the headphones, settled herself, and started the CD player.

You are going on a voyage of discovery . . .

Soon Jill was hovering over the floor at the foot of her bed. She thought of James Harper and was soon beside him as he walked down Ridgewood Court, heading toward the stores. He was happy and whistling; he looked especially handsome today. Jill smiled.

"Hey, James!" she yelled.

Harper suddenly stopped and cocked his head.

"Can you hear me?"

James blinked and looked around. He was clearly sensing something, but couldn't quite get a fix on it. He put his head down and closed his eyes, ambling toward the side of the road.

"James Harper . . . I am calling you!"

He knitted his brow and pulled his head back.

Then Jill had an impression of someone else: a man in a uniform, younger, a bit more dashing. He was in a jungle clearing with other soldiers, near some grass huts. She got a clear image of him. His name tag read, "Waterhouse."

"*Waterhouse?*" she blurted.

Harper jerked his head up in response.

"Who is it?" he said, anxiously. "Who's there?"

"*Jill!* Jill Messenger!"

"Who?"

He spun around and headed back toward his apartment, moving quickly. This was not what he expected.

Jill watched him go, feeling sorry for causing him some anxiety. Well, a little payback is a good thing sometimes. As he climbed the short steps into his building, she followed briefly, then turned away and thought of Mata.

Nothing happened.

Once again she held the vision and intention of Mata, but

150

it was a dead end.

Maybe her line's busy.

She floated up, over Ridgewood Court, and then down toward the Giant Eagle supermarket. She flew in through the wall and noticed how high the ceilings were. She coasted above the aisles of food, noticing a woman in a blue coat stuffing cans of tuna into her pocket.

Hey! No fair!

But the woman, obviously poor, pocketed two more cans before moving down the aisle.

I could make a living as a store detective.

Then Jill heard a sound like a giant windstorm. It began quietly and then grew in volume and intensity.

What is that?

No sooner had she perceived the sound, then a giant force picked her up like a rag doll and propelled her forward into blackness at dizzying speed.

Oh God, not again!

She hated it, *hated* it! But she had been through it before and knew it would not last long. She was right.

She found herself enveloped in a gray, misty fog. Then it cleared and Jill saw that she was once again standing by the old tree. Mata stood near her, smiling in a friendly, comforting way. Jill smelled beautiful flowers. What were they—gardenias? Lilacs?

"I heard you call," she smiled.

"I . . . didn't think you . . ." began Jill.

"I know. It takes a few moments of your time for me to fully respond, but I am here. How may I help you?"

"Mata, it seems as though I am being drawn into a situation, or maybe several situations . . . that I don't quite understand. The boat, the dead boy in the water, then those men in . . . The Netherlands? Is that where they were? Were they real? Why did I see them?"

Mata smiled calmly and began to speak.

"Sit down, Jill. I am going to give you some information."

Jill sat on the soft grass and crossed her legs. Mata sat opposite her, her back to the tree.

"Long ago, you were chosen. And you were given some very special gifts, gifts that are given to only a few. You are now beginning to use some of the gifts you have. You must understand that they have been given to you as a sacred trust; you can be a force for good during this present earth-life experience. You are needed, you are guided, and you are loved. This is the time of your awakening, and it was necessary for Dave and Jamie to leave the physical plane. It was necessary for you to drink yourself into a stupor. It was necessary for you to fall, to make friends with Sara, and to find the tools—the CDs—which would help lead you out of your body and into No Time, where all exists."

"But, why?" said Jill. "I didn't ask for any of this."

"Oh but you did. Not consciously, but before you entered the physical reality of this lifetime, your *soul* agreed. In fact, your soul *insisted* that you reincarnate as a being who could do much good in the world."

"My *soul* insisted? I don't understand."

"Come with me," said Mata. She stood up, extended her forearm, and motioned for Jill to take it.

152

As soon as Jill touched Mata's forearm, they were suddenly in the clouds under a bright blue sky. They floated quickly forward, the bright wisps of water vapor gently tickling their feet as they flew.

An enormous marble building appeared before them as they approached. It was gold and pink, and people moved in and out on its massive steps, though gigantic entryways. Mata and Jill were suddenly on the top area, a few feet from the entry.

"What is this place?" asked Jill, impressed.

"The Hall of Records," whispered Mata as they glided inside.

The interior was quiet, and it glowed with its own inner light, softly illuminating everything. In front of Mata and Jill were massive shelves holding vast numbers of large books.

"Wow," said Jill softly. "What are all the books?"

"Each soul has a record of his or her lifetimes," explained Mata. "New pages are continually added, chronicling every moment of existence. Everything is recorded, nothing is lost. Every word, deed, action, thought . . . it's *all* here."

Jill shook her head in disbelief.

"There is something I want you to see, Jill," said Mata as they approached a lectern. On it was a large book, edged in gold.

"Here. This is your book, your experiences, over many lifetimes."

"Really?" exclaimed Jill, barely believing what Mata was saying.

"I will show you a little first, so you can understand."

She opened the book near the back, and went through its

pages until she found one she thought appropriate. She pointed to it and said, "Look."

Jill looked at the page, which had cryptic writing on it. But then the script quickly dissolved and the entire page became a viewing screen . . .

There was Jill as a young girl, happily playing with a new puppy. They were in the backyard of an upstate New York home, and Jill, about eight years old, was squealing with delight. She wore dusty blue corduroy overalls and a pink T-shirt underneath. Her shiny hair was cut with straight bangs. The puppy, a yellow lab, scampered around happily, pushing its wet nose into the little girl.

"Oh my God, *Barney* . . . My little pal," she said, choked with emotion. "I loved him so much."

"Yes, and he loved you, too," said Mata. "But there is something else, something more."

She opened the book to the middle—representing centuries of lifetimes—and pointed to a page.

"Look," said Mata.

Jill watched a voluptuous woman with dark wavy hair, having her way with a several men in a large bedroom with marble walls. The woman made them each satisfy her wanton sexual desires and then, when they had finished, she slit their throats with a razor-sharp dagger. They were powerless under her and they cried out—first in ecstasy, then in profound agony—as they slowly bled to death. As each lay, twitching and tormented, the woman laughed, then drank from a silver goblet. When the last man had expired, the woman moved toward the doorway, spitting on their lifeless bodies.

Jill was filled with revulsion.

"That was . . . me?"

"Yes," began Mata. "You had several lifetimes when your extreme greed and lust led you into perversity and wickedness. Many thousands of people suffered and died because of your insatiable needs. The more you got, the more you wanted. No one was able to stop you, until . . ."

Mata turned a page and pointed.

Now Jill saw a scene similar to the previous one. Men were brought in for the woman's insatiable pleasures and she began to take the men on, one by one. Then, after they had pleasured her, she repeatedly stabbed their helpless forms as they cried out and crumpled to the floor. When she reached the last man, something unexpected happened: he defiantly slapped her face.

No one had ever struck her before, nor had anyone caused her pain. She reeled back, confused.

He struck her again, harder, and she fell, mouth open, eyes wide.

"How *dare* you strike me!"

The man knelt beside the woman and put his hand on her throat, holding her down.

"Because you are evil. You are *wicked*. You were given powers to help others, but instead, you choose to satisfy yourself."

"Take your hands off me!"

The man struck her again, and the force of the blow caused a reverberation in the chamber.

"You stupid, selfish cow. You have two choices . . . either quit your present ways or you will suffer a horror far greater than the men whom you abused."

"You are disgusting!" she cried hotly.

"Your powers were a gift because you were worthy. And you betrayed them! You spat upon the hand of the Giver. So you have a choice now: either change . . . or lose *everything*."

"Here's my answer, fool," hissed the woman, as she spat into the man's face.

He withdrew his hand, stood up, and moved from where the woman lay. He nodded and backed away.

A wasp entered. It buzzed around in the air for a moment, and then flew toward the woman. She waved a hand at it, but the wasp would not be deterred. Soon, another wasp entered the room, then another, then another. Then there were thousands of wasps descending on the woman in a noisy, hideous swarm.

She screamed in horror . . . again and again, as the wasps hovered, landed, and stung her face and eyes.

Jill couldn't bear to watch any more. She turned away as Mata closed the book.

Then Jill looked at Mata, not knowing what to say.

"You were rendered powerless for centuries. You had lost everything. You endured hardships most people could never have withstood. You saw your children slaughtered; you were branded as a witch and burned at the stake; you suffered scathing cruelty through many incarnations. Now your debt is nearly paid; the scales are being righted, and your power has been restored—temporarily. It is our hope that you will use it—this time—for the greater good. This is your opportunity for redemption."

"But I don't know what I'm supposed to do!" cried Jill.

"Follow your instincts, your conscience, and your heart. You will be guided. Now we are through for the present."

"Wait! One question!" yelled Jill.

Mata nodded.

"Who was the man? The one who . . . struck me."

Mata smiled and said, "When the time is right, his identity will be revealed."

CHAPTER SIX

Back in Ridgewood Court, James Harper was pacing anxiously. He had been targeted. Or, rather, Waterhouse had been targeted. But by whom? He heard a woman's voice say *Waterhouse*, and that had been unnerving. It couldn't have been Jill; she knew nothing about his past. Well, not much. She certainly didn't know his real name.

If some of the spooks from OSI had found him then he would have to move to a new location. But where? No matter where he went, they could find him. Maybe they saw through the ruse in Las Vegas. Maybe they "read" the situation and figured out it was all a setup. There were too many possibilities, all of them unsettling.

In his past experiences, from Vietnam through the various remote viewing tasks, he had never lost his composure. But this was different. He had never been so obviously targeted, and it rattled him.

He went into the kitchen and opened a cabinet where he kept his vitamins. Among the little bottles was one containing an amino acid that calms anxiety and promotes relaxation. The normal dose was two 100mg capsules, but Harper took three. As he was swallowing them, the phone rang.

He stepped to his desk and glanced at the clock. 12:15 p.m. Then he picked up the phone and quietly said hello.

"Hey, James, it's Jill."

"Jill! Ah . . . hi," stammered Harper. "I'm glad you called. Listen, I found out quite a bit, about the boat and what's going on."

"Really? That's great. Listen, I'm having lunch with Sara. Want to come along?"

"Well, ah, I guess," said Harper. "When?"

"Can you come over here first? I have some info for you too. Then we'll go to the Marietta Brewery. Ever been there?"

"Oh, you mean like *now*?" said Harper.

"Yup. We do things fast around here," smiled Jill.

"Sure. That's good. No, I don't know the Marietta Brewery."

"You'll like it. It's kind of a guy place."

"OK," said Harper. "So, you want me to come over to your place right now?"

"If you can, yeah," said Jill.

"OK, I'll be there in ten minutes."

"Oh by the way," began Jill, "I hope I didn't scare you when I saw you on the road. You seemed kind of upset."

"What do you mean?"

"You seemed pretty freaked out."

"When?"

"A little while ago. I was out of body, flying around. I saw you, and I called to you."

"That was *you*?"

"Yeah, sorry. It was kind of dumb I know, but I wanted to see if I could get your attention."

Harper sighed with relief.

"Oh you got my attention all right."

"Oh, I really am sorry, James. That was a stupid thing to do."

"Actually, it wasn't," said Harper.

"By the way," said Jill. "Who's Waterhouse?"

Harper flinched.

"He was a soldier I knew long ago," he whispered. "I'll tell you when I see you. Give me a couple minutes."

"OK, then. I'll make some coffee. Or would you prefer iced tea?"

"I don't care. You pick."

Harper hung up the phone, feeling greatly relieved.

Jill was something else.

He went into his bedroom and looked for a nice aftershave to put on. Wouldn't hurt to smell good, and he had a pretty decent collection, not that he ever got to use them much. Other guys used Old Spice, but not Harper, not since his sister had started sending him fragrances from Filenes in Boston. He grabbed a bottle of Hermès and splashed some on; it was citrusy and good.

Whistling, he bounced down the steps and out into the sunshine of Ridgewood Court.

While Harper was walking toward Sixth Street, Jill was upstairs in her bedroom deciding what to wear. She liked this guy

161

and couldn't help but wonder if he was the man from long ago who held her down. She put on a pair of khaki shorts, a pink T-shirt, and white canvas Keds. Then she moved happily out of the room, down the stairs, and into the kitchen to make iced tea.

Ever since the morning's experience with Mata, she wondered what it was she was supposed to do. How could she help people? And was she being greedy by winning the money at the track? Then again, if that was a problem, Mata surely would have said something.

She thought about the woman she had seen with all of those men. Those hunks might make for a very interesting evening . . . without killing them, of course, or suffering a swarm of wasps. It had been a long time since she had been intimate with a man. Dave had been her man and, frankly, he wasn't much of a lothario. But if he was quick, he was also sincere.

As Harper walked up the steps to Jill's house, he could hear music playing from inside. He rapped on the metal door frame and, hearing no response, moved into the entryway.

"Jill!"

"Back here—come on in!"

The stereo was cranked, and Etta James was blaring from the speakers.

Harper walked back to the kitchen where he found Jill putting a pitcher of iced tea on the kitchen table.

She really keeps a clean house. That's good, thought Harper.

"So you're an Etta James fan?"

"Oh yeah. You like her?"

"She's great."

"I better turn it down; I have things to tell you."

"OK."

After Jill had switched off the music, she and Harper sat at her kitchen table, sipping sweet tea and trading information. She was fascinated to learn about the boat and the Ohio River, and that there seemed to be some massive drug trade on the waterways.

"The guy driving the boat, the guy from my bank, his name is Robert Guerra. He's definitely mixed up in this somehow, and he's in pretty deep."

She explained what she had found out: the drugs and the porn stored in his basement. Then Jill added that Guerra had invited her to dinner on Tuesday, to an Italian place in Williamstown, across the Ohio River.

"Gonna go?" asked Harper.

"Yeah. I just don't know how much I should say. What do you think?"

"I think," began Harper, "that you should play it cool; not let on anything you know. Once you reveal information, you can't get it back."

Jill nodded and sipped her tea.

"Maybe you should hint that you'd like a boat trip. That might be a good step."

"Hmm," said Jill. "Let me think about that. I don't know if I'd feel safe on a boat with that creep."

"I also think you should get your boat in the water, and put it in at the marina in Newport."

"I thought about that, too," said Jill, "I have the guy's card. I'll call him later. I'll call Chester and make arrangements.

I'll need your help."

"Sure thing. Tell you what," began Harper. "I have a friend arriving tomorrow. I don't know how long he's going to stay, but he can help, too. If the motor needs a fix up, Bud Grant is the guy to do it. I think it might be a good idea to follow that cruiser and see where it goes."

"But what if it's gone for a few days?"

"Then we'll have a real adventure, won't we?"

Jill looked down and thought for a moment. She barely knew this guy, and now he was suggesting they go on a boat trip together?

"Would it be just you and me?"

"No," began Harper. "If we were just going fishing, sure, that would be fun. But if we're tailing some criminals, mafia types, then I think we could use some extra help."

"Such as . . .?"

"Such as Sara Hopkins and Bud Grant."

"I don't even know Bud Grant," said Jill.

"And I don't really know Sara," said Harper. "Tell you what. You'll meet him; he'll be here tomorrow. If you don't like him, or the idea, then we'll just drop it."

"When is he arriving?"

"Late afternoon. He's driving down from New York and that's about eight hours, give or take," said Harper.

"OK, here's an idea," said Jill. "I'll have a little cookout in the backyard. Hamburgers and hot dogs. I'll invite Sara, and you bring your friend. We'll see how it goes. How's that?"

"Good," smiled Harper. "Maybe Bud will bring his guitar."

"Well, that'll be festive," said Jill warily. "Actually, Sara plays too. She's pretty good."

"OK, then we'll have a cookout and a folk festival. I'll bring some beer. Any kind you like?"

"I'm sticking to ginger ale. Sara might have a beer though." Jill paused, then asked, "So who's Waterhouse?"

Harper stirred his tea.

"Hmm. I have to be careful with that."

Jill nodded.

"There are people who would kill for that information, and I mean that. It's been tried."

"Yikes," said Jill, wondering if she was in danger.

"Years ago," began Harper, "my name was Patrick Waterhouse. That's my real name. I'm from Rhode Island, originally—a little town called Warren—and my sister Joanne still lives there. Well, in Barrington, which is next door. She's married and has two grown kids. Our parents are both dead now. Anyhow, I was attending college in Boston . . ."

"Where?" asked Jill.

"Boston University. I was a sophomore in communications, and then I got drafted and sent overseas. I was on active duty in Vietnam, and that's where I met Bud. Anyhow, it was Patrick Waterhouse who did top secret spying for the government, and who saw things that were usually concealed from view. So. I ended up here, with a new identity. I am trying to keep a low profile. So far so good. Same old face, though."

Jill nodded.

So the guy is on the run.

"Been back home?" asked Jill, changing the subject.

"No, not for a while. I visited Joanne a few years ago. But not since then. What about you? Where are you from?"

"I'm from Penn Yan, New York. It's in upstate. It's a nice place in the middle of farm country."

"Isn't there a lake there?" asked Harper.

"Yup, Keuka Lake. It's one of the Finger Lakes. That's how the *Keuka Maiden* got her name."

Jill glanced at the clock on the stove: 12:55.

"Listen, James. Since we're being honest with each other, I need to tell you some of the things I've learned. I don't know if they're real or not, but I think they are."

"Like what?" said Harper, leaning forward.

"Well," began Jill. "As you know, I've been going out of body almost every day."

"Yeah. You're lucky," smiled Harper.

"Maybe you will do it; I don't know. But the thing is, I've been shown some things, things I could never have imagined in my wildest dreams."

"Such as . . ."

Jill explained about seeing Dave and Jamie, meeting Mata and visiting the Hall of Records, and seeing some of her past. She did not mention the men or the sex or the wasps.

Harper nodded, impressed. He had heard similar things previously. His early readings of Edgar Cayce made him familiar with the Akashic Records; Jill was now confirming them.

"You're doing things I've only read about."

"I think you'll be able to do it, too," Jill encouraged.

"Well, maybe I'll try again sometime. Or go down to The Madison Institute and take one of their programs," he said reflectively. "Did you see anything else of interest?"

She told him about the group of wealthy men in The Netherlands who were planning to subjugate and rule the world. Even more alarming, it appeared they had the means to accomplish their goals. She described the men and the room in detail, and she tried to explain the ominous feeling she had gotten while she was there.

When she had finished, she leaned back in her chair and said, "I have no idea who these men are, or if they are in present-day time or are from the past. But the idea of letting millions of people die and using the world as their personal property . . . well, that's scary stuff. They mentioned something called the Council."

Harper nodded. The name meant nothing to him.

"Do you have any idea of their location?" he asked.

"No. But the building looked to be quite old, like an exquisite villa or castle."

"Do you think you could go there again?"

"I don't know. I could try."

"Tell you what. Take a look and see what you find, but I think keeping the focus on the boat and the drug trafficking might be best for now."

"OK," said Jill.

There was a banging on her front door. Startled, Jill got up to see who it was.

Sara!

"I been standing next to your damn car for ten minutes. Don't you have a clock?"

As she vented, Harper suddenly appeared in the hallway behind Jill. Sara looked up and understood: Jill had company. A man.

"Sorry, Sara! We're running just a tiny bit late. You remember James Harper?"

Sara opened the door and shook Harper's hand.

"Nice to see you again. Are you going to be joining us?"

"If you don't mind," said Harper.

"Not a bit. Well, come on. Let's get the show on the road!" she exclaimed as she bounced down the steps toward Jill's car.

At 6:00 p.m. the following day, Jill was talking on the phone with Cathy. She held the phone in the crook of her neck while she made hamburger patties for the cookout.

"So, what's up?"

Cathy explained that she had taken a position as an intern at the Charlottesville NBC affiliate and was learning various jobs in TV production. She was "rolling prompter" for the 5:00 news, and she found it a bit maddening. Her bosses had promised that she would be an associate field reporter, which meant that she and a crew would cover local stories. Then they would be broadcast back to the station from a van. Cathy liked the excitement of a busy TV station and was thinking of switching her major to communications. And no, she wasn't dating anybody seriously.

While Jill was talking with Cathy, Bud Grant was pulling his bright red Jeep up in front of Harper's apartment on Ridgewood Court. Sensing Grant's arrival, Harper moved down the steps just as his friend was easing into a parking space.

When Grant switched off the engine and got out of the Jeep, he gave Harper a heartfelt hug. Harper slapped Grant on the back and said, "Great to see you, buddy. Glad you made it in one piece."

"Yeah, one piece. Got a speeding ticket," chuckled Grant.

"With all that gear?"

"Yeah, well the guy *followed* me. No radar!" laughed Grant. "But I'll beat it. I learned a trick long ago."

"You'll have to tell me about that."

"All right."

Harper helped Grant carry his luggage up the steps and into the apartment. It took a few trips; Bud had brought along a lot of stuff.

"Wow," said Harper. "Looks like you brought everything but the kitchen sink."

"I tried. It was bolted down."

When everything had been brought in, Harper spoke.

"Well, my friend, we have a dinner appointment. A cookout with burgers and hot dogs. Need to be there by seven."

"Sounds good," smiled Grant.

"Bring the guitar," said Harper.

"OK," Grant said, looking around Harper's apartment. "Nice setup. Reminds me of your old place in Maryland."

"The colors are the same."

"Yeah. *Deep greens and blues . . .*"

"So, how long were you planning to stay?" asked Harper.

"Funny you should ask," said Grant, plopping into a chair.

"Let me get you a beer," said Harper. "If you can stick around for a couple weeks, I have a little adventure for us."

"Oh, I think I may be here longer than that."

"How come?" said Harper, as he moved to the refrigerator.

"I mean, that's great. You'd like it here."

Grant took a deep breath and let out a long sigh. "I guess I just had it. I didn't like the new work assignment. I don't like retro-engineering; I like building things."

Harper grabbed two bottles of Becks and said, "We live in an age of corporate manipulation, Bud. Want a glass?"

"Yes, I would. Anyhow, I told them I had a better offer from an outfit in Columbus. Which is true, actually. Ever hear of Battelle?"

"No," said Harper as he handed Grant the beer.

"They do high-tech stuff as well. Been after me for the last couple years, after I got a patent on a new kind of weapon. It's my patent, too. All that bullshit about IBM owning whatever I came up with—my lawyer shot that down quick, since weaponry was not part of the contract."

"Wow. Must be some weapon."

"Yep. Uses sound instead of bullets. It's pretty amazing."

"What's the range?" said Harper, impressed.

"Better than 100 meters. Remember, we're not firing a projectile, and sound dissipates relative to the square of the distance. But it's pretty effective."

"Did you bring it with you?"

"*Maybe . . .*" Grant said, and smiled as he sipped his beer. "Then the goddamn Israelis came along and made their own, in total violation of my patent."

"Can you sue?"

"Sure, and I would win, too. It would only take ten years

and about a million bucks. So, anyhow, I figured I'd take a break and come see you. Maybe do some fishing, goof off, drink a lot."

"You picked a good town."

"Yeah, looks nice. So what's happening with you?"

Harper quickly filled Grant in on the town, the guys at the Edgewater, the pretty good fishing, and the decent restaurants.

"Sounds like a nice place. Hell, I even might like to settle down here."

"You? Settle down?" asked Harper.

"It's about time, don't ya think?" said Grant seriously.

"I am the wrong person to ask."

There was a brief pause for assessment, and then Grant spoke.

"So, you working on anything?"

"Sort of. Yeah," replied Harper, as he sat on the couch across from Grant and began to explain about the goings on: the dead young man, the boat full of drugs, the marina in Newport, and Jill. He did not let on about Jill's unique abilities; that was too complicated to explain now.

Grant sat silently and nodded. Then he said, "What about law enforcement? Aren't they on this?"

"If they are, it's not evident. When I saw the boat, it was all alone, heading up the Ohio River. I didn't get the sense of it being tracked or monitored."

"Jeez," exclaimed Grant, "I don't know if I wanna play Junior G Man. I mean, this sounds dangerous."

"We're just going to tag along and see where they go, that's all. I can do recon, you know. You'd like a boat trip, I bet.

Only be a few days. If we find something bad, we can alert the authorities, and then we've done our good deeds. The goal is to keep the danger to a minimum."

"What the hell," smiled Grant. "As long as there's beer, fishing, and a couple of broads, count me in."

David B. Lawrence was a tall, fair-haired, ex-military man of 64 who owned and operated the marina at Newport, as well as three other marinas along the Ohio River. He selected Newport as his base of operations because it was nearly midway between East Liverpool—the northernmost town on the river—and Cincinnati. He ran the operation from a little wood-framed office not far from the docks, and he had constructed a small, wood-framed guardhouse to keep visitors out. He was selective about who he allowed to dock at his marina; he didn't need the money. What he needed most were boats and gullible people willing to make a few hundred dollars. And, in the low-income towns he selected, there were quite a few.

As he sat in his squeaky swivel chair, he looked out the window and watched the light begin to fade in the sky. West Virginia lay just across the river, and its grimy smokestacks disgusted him. He glanced at his watch: 6:29 p.m.

The phone rang and Lawrence answered on the first ring with a quiet, "Yes?"

A voice on the other end said, "Portsmouth delivered, got the cash."

"Did you count it?" asked Lawrence.

"Always. All there."

"Good. So when do we see you?"

"Well, I'm knocking off for the evening. Probably Monday."

"OK. See you then. Thanks."

Hanging up the phone, Lawrence hit a speed-dial number and somewhere a phone rang.

"Hello?" said a pleasant voice.

"The lucky number is twenty-six," Lawrence said.

"Very well. Thank you," said the voice, and the line went dead.

On the walk over to Jill's house, Harper went into the Giant Eagle and bought a 12-pack of cold beer while Grant waited outside with his guitar and smoked a cigarette. Then they resumed their journey. After crossing the street, Harper and Grant were soon at Jill's front door.

Harper led the way up the porch steps and entered through the front door, yelling, "*Hello!*" as he stepped into the foyer.

"Back here!" yelled Jill from the kitchen.

Grant set his guitar case down in the living room as he and Harper walked back to meet Jill and Sara. Sara was bending over the table, stirring potato salad, and Jill was filling a tray with things to be taken outside. Grant couldn't help but notice Sara's obvious cleavage, and something inside him twitched.

"Hi, Jill, Sara," said Harper pleasantly. "This is Bud Grant, a friend who may be moving here."

Jill extended a hand and Grant shook it.

"Welcome—I've heard a lot about you," she smiled.

"Thanks, likewise," said Grant.

"This is Sara Hopkins," said Jill as Sara stood up and smiled at the two men.

"Nice to see you," she said.

"Same here," smiled Grant.

Yeah, she was a looker all right. And Jill wasn't bad, either.

They sat in folding chairs under the cool shade trees behind Jill's house. Bud and Sara played their guitars, trying to figure out songs they both knew, as Harper worked on getting the charcoal started. Jill sipped iced tea and smiled. Sara began to sing "Lonesome Traveler," and Grant quickly followed along, adding guitar licks and singing harmony. Sara smiled and nodded as he sang with her.

She was impressed with Grant's custom-made guitar. He played well, too. He sensed her interest and offered it to her. She took it like a newborn baby—gingerly, cradling it with respect. She strummed a D major chord, and her jaw dropped. The sound was rich and full, unlike her inexpensive guitar.

"Where'd you get this? This is amazing," she cooed as she started playing with a little more vigor.

"A guy made it for me," Grant said, and he smiled as he tuned Sara's elderly Epiphone. "You could use some new strings."

"Yeah, but I hate doing that. It messes up my nails," she said.

"I have an extra set in my case; I can change them for you," offered Grant, trying to be casual.

"*Would* you?" asked Sara, beaming.

Within a few minutes, Grant had removed the strings,

polished the guitar with a soft cloth, put on a new set of strings, and adjusted the truss rod; now it played much more easily and even sounded better. He handed the gleaming guitar back to Sara. She held it up approvingly.

"It looks brand new," said Sara, impressed. She strummed a G chord and exclaimed, "It even plays better!"

"If I had a workbench, I could give it a good setup. The action is still a little high," smiled Grant.

Sara was impressed.

"I would pay you for that," she offered.

"No thanks, sister," cracked Grant. "You know what I want from you?"

"What?"

Oh shit, here it comes . . .

"I want . . . a library card," cracked Grant, and Sara burst out laughing.

"*That* I can do," smiled Sara. Then she strummed the new strings and began to sing "Sweet Bonny Lee." Grant began to play along and sang harmony on the chorus:

Goodnight, you fair young maidens.

Rockabye, Sweet Bonny Lee . . .

While they were singing and exchanging glances, Jill moved to Harper and stood beside him, looking down at the grill.

"How's it comin'?"

"It'll just take a few more minutes for the coals to get hot. I don't want to use too much fluid," said Harper.

"I like your friend," whispered Jill.

Harper smiled. "Bud's a good guy."

"I can tell," said Jill.

"Listen, I want you to do me a favor," said Harper. "I want you to try to contact me again, while you're out-of-body. I want to see if I can hear you, understand what you're saying."

"Sure thing. When?" asked Jill.

"Doesn't matter. I just need to take a minute to tune in. I wasn't able to do that before. Oh. There's something else."

"What?" asked Jill. There was something in his expression that excited her.

"I think you should try to go out of body without using the CDs. See if you can do it on your own. Just repeat the mental exercises in your mind and see if you can do it."

"Oh," she nodded. "I can try that, but why?"

"I think it's the next step for you."

"Maybe it is," said Jill. "OK. I have my homework assignments. By the way, did you tell your friend about my . . ."

"Going out?" said Harper, finishing Jill's sentence. "No. Not a word."

Jill nodded, relieved.

"Does Sara know?" asked Harper.

Jill shook her head.

"Better this way. They'll find out eventually, and Bud knows I can do remote viewing, but he doesn't know a thing about what you can do."

Jill nodded, "Can he do any kind of . . ."

Harper shook his head. "No. But he's pretty intuitive, and he's a whiz with electronics. But no, nothing like the weird wacky psycho stuff we do."

CHAPTER SIX

Jill smiled at Harper, her eyes dancing.

"Yeah, weird wacky psycho—that's me!"

"But he's funny and plays guitar and is a stand-up guy."

"Yeah. He's great."

The summer evening was idyllic. The food was hearty and good, and everyone laughed a lot and enjoyed each other's company. Bud's song "Granny Got a Harley" amused everyone, and the two women exchanged glances.

Later in the evening, when the coals had faded to embers and most of the dishes had been washed and put away, the four friends drank coffee and ate thick slices of ice cream cake.

Then Harper and Jill explained the plan about the boat, the river, and what might transpire. To the best of their knowledge, they were the only ones who knew about the smuggling operation; law enforcement was not in evidence.

Sara was aghast to learn about Robert Guerra and the drugs, but the porn was no surprise. Every time she ran into him, he made some kind of suggestive comment.

Grant made a mental note to himself about Sara: *Do not act interested . . . even though you are.*

It was well past 1:00 a.m. when Harper and Grant said goodnight and began to walk back to Ridgewood Court.

"Looks like you and Sara hit it off," smiled Harper.

"She's a gem," said Grant, seriously. "I got the sense she's put up with a lot of shit over the years."

"Yeah."

"And Jill. What a sweetheart."

"She's been through a lot, too," Harper said, "but she is resilient, that woman."

"Got a sense of that," nodded Grant.

Monday morning

Jill sat at her kitchen table, reflecting on the pleasant evening with the two guys and Sara. They seemed like old friends now, and this put her mind at ease. She held the business card with David Lawrence's number on it and dialed the number.

"Hello," said the high male voice.

"David Lawrence, please."

"This is he," came the reply.

"I wonder if you might have some dock space for rent."

"Maybe," Lawrence said. "What kind of boat do you have?"

"A 26-foot Carver. It's been in storage and I want to get it into the water while there are a couple of months left."

Lawrence explained the details, the rent, and the access ramp, and then asked Jill if that was OK. She replied that it was.

"So, when do we see you?"

"I don't know yet," she explained. "I have to check with the storage place and find out when I can get the boat."

"I understand," said Lawrence. "By the way, if you pay in cash I won't charge you sales tax."

"Oh, OK. But I'll want a receipt," said Jill.

"Not a problem," he said.

"Thanks very much. I'll call to let you know when I'm coming."

"Good. Thanks a lot. Bye."

"Bye," said Jill and hung up the phone.

Harper and Grant were in Harper's pickup, driving west on their way to meet Terry and Preston for a little fishing. The plan was to go to Terry's house, pick him up, and then continue up the road to where Preston lived to get the boat. Harper wasn't sure where Terry lived, but Grant had brought the GPS unit and had punched in the address. Harper was amused at the female voice on the unit: *Turn left in one point seven miles.*

"That's some voice—an electronic woman!"

"Yeah," smiled Grant. "If I knew how to reprogram the voice commands, I'd have her say 'Turn left, *baby.*'"

"I bet you could do it," said Harper.

"Yeah, but why? I'd get all excited at a GPS unit, and they don't put out. Did you bring any beer?"

Harper replied that Terry and Preston didn't drink, but there would be a cooler of soda.

"No problemo," said Grant. "I like soda. Once a year."

Harper smiled and shook his head.

As they approached the address, Harper slowed down. Then they saw it: a beautiful two-story redbrick house from the 1800s, with green shutters and crisp white trim, set back from the road. It was surrounded by tall, stately trees whose leaves stirred in the morning breeze.

"Wow, this looks like something from *Colonial Home*," said Grant.

"Who knew?" said Harper. "Man, it's just gorgeous."

"Looks like an authentic Georgian house," observed Grant.

As they turned into the driveway, Terry came out from around the back, a brown-and-white Springer spaniel tagging happily along. Terry was dressed in cutoff jeans, flip-flops, and a baggy red T-shirt.

Harper got out of the truck, walked over to Terry, and shook his hand.

"Had no idea you lived in such a mansion," Harper said with a smile.

"Yeah, well, my mother's family built it around 1820. It's all original except for the back room. I'm redoing all the floors while I'm on vacation."

Harper introduced Grant to Terry; Terry was pleased to meet another vet. As they exchanged info about tours of duty, units, and platoons, Harper knelt down to pet the friendly dog.

"That's Daphne," said Terry. "She's a good girl. She's pretty old now." Terry watched Daphne's soulful response to Grant's attention. Terry smiled and said, "You'll fit right in around here."

"Good," smiled Grant.

Terry took them on a little tour, moving across the expanse of lawn behind the house, passing Terry's truck and Harley-Davidson, to three outbuildings. One of the buildings was a small, one-room house.

"This was a working farm for generations. My grandma was the last to work it. We had cows when I was a kid."

Grant poked his head into the tiny house, "Hey, looks like somebody lives here."

"Naw. Sometimes people need a place to stay. It's a mess right now, but it has a bed, running water, and an old potbellied stove. Tiny john. Big workbench along one wall. TV. I sometimes stay here myself, just for the hell of it. Long ago, some of the farm help used to stay here."

A few minutes later, the three men scrunched into the front seat of Harper's pickup and drove about a mile up the road to Preston Caldwell's modest home by the river. As they pulled into the short driveway, past Preston's maroon Harley XL, they saw him sitting on a bench near the dock. He raised a hand in greeting.

Soon they were all in Preston's boat, chugging up the river toward a large sweeping bend.

"They been bitin' pretty good up this way lately," Preston said. He switched off the motor and it wheezed to a stop. The boat continued to drift forward.

"This is a good spot," said Preston as the others baited their hooks.

Then they cast their lines and began to fish.

Grant turned to Harper and said, "This is good. Glad I came."

"Me, too," said Harper.

Jill was lying on her bed, trying to do what Harper suggested: to lift out without using the CD. She closed her eyes and took a deep breath, trying to imagine hearing the voice of Robert Madison. She became relaxed and went through the mental "prep" exercises.

Then something odd happened.

Her right arm lifted out, but the rest of her stayed in the body. She waved her arm around, but that was all she was able to do. She tried her left arm, thinking it might prompt her body into a full separation, but it seemed stuck.

Darn.

She returned to normal consciousness, sat up, and took a sip of water. Then she put on the headphones, lay down again, started the CD player, and soon was out of her body, floating at the foot of her bed.

She thought of Harper and held the intention of seeing him.

And there he was, with Bud Grant and two men she didn't know, sitting in an old metal boat in the middle of the Muskingum River. She wondered if she should try to reach him, as he had suggested. She decided against it; another time would be better.

She could tell by the empty pail and the expression on their faces that they had not caught any fish.

Too bad.

Then she had an idea.

She flew upstream, about 100 yards from where the men were, dipped under the water, and extended her arms. Scores of fish noticed her and, frightened, began to swim rapidly downstream. Working as a herder, Jill moved back and forth, driving the fish toward the boat. Then Jill floated out, above the river, and watched their movements.

Suddenly, Preston felt a tug on his line.

"I think I got one," he said.

Almost simultaneously, Grant, Harper, and Terry all had strikes. They looked at each other in disbelief and began to reel.

"Strangest damn thing I ever saw," Preston mused.

Harper looked up, sensing that there was something else, but said nothing. Jill, hovering over him, smiled and waved, wiggling her fingers. Then she flew skyward, arms outstretched, a radiant smile on her face.

It was a beautiful day as Jill zoomed around the sky, enjoying herself. She made a loop-the-loop, laughing; then she flew under the Washington Street Bridge and up high again. She headed toward Harmer, and flew down to the Beauty Barn, moving through a row of ladies sitting under hard-bonnet hairdryers. They were chatting and were completely oblivious to the woman flying past them.

Then Jill soared, high over the Muskingum, and flew to the Ohio River. Beneath her were boats, a guy on a Jet Ski, and two white sternwheelers arriving for the festival. She continued north until the Newport Marina came into view.

Nice-looking place.

She began to slowly descend, noticing that there were about 50 boats at various places among the large, double-F-shaped wooden docks. Some of the boats had people on them, sitting on the back deck, enjoying morning coffee. One guy was drinking beer and fishing. She looked for the Bayliner but didn't see it.

She saw the little white house and wondered if this is where David Lawrence had his office. She decided to take a look.

It was a tidy little place, almost military looking: a steel desk with an office chair behind it, two chairs of vinyl, and a green metal file cabinet. Atop the file cabinet was an old boom box, and beside it was a photograph of Lawrence standing in a campground, with his arms around the shoulders of two boys. There were broad windows that faced the docks, and a smaller one that faced the pathway in. Behind the desk, on the wall, was a large cabinet of gold-colored wood, with its doors folded in and locked together.

The lock got Jill's curiosity and she stuck her face through the doors to see what lay behind it.

What she saw piqued her curiosity.

It was a map of the midsection of the United States. The entire length of the Ohio River was highlighted, from its origin in Pittsburgh clear down to Cairo, Illinois. The map also covered Pennsylvania, Ohio, West Virginia, Kentucky, and Indiana. And at various points, colored pins were placed in the map. There were scores of them.

If the pins represented locations for the delivery of drugs, then this operation was far greater than she could have imagined.

The Missouri and Mississippi rivers were also outlined, but there were no pins along their routes. However, St. Louis, Minneapolis, and Memphis were circled.

Jill began to grasp the scope of the operation. This enterprise covered most of the United States, clear down to New Orleans. Using private boats and paying the owners in cash for a delivery was brilliant. Few boats were ever searched for drugs; it just didn't happen on American rivers. In the Gulf of Mexico and around the Florida Keys, yes, but not on the peaceful Ohio River.

Jill recalled that, a few years before, the Ohio State Police and the FBI had run a successful sting operation on Route 77, a large highway that ran from Cleveland down to Marietta and beyond. Many vans and cars had been intercepted; their passengers had been caught and booked for possession with intent to distribute. But the big guys, those supplying the drugs, were never caught. It looked like the entire operation had moved offshore.

Smart.

She had the feeling that there was contraband on some of the boats she had seen, but wasn't about to go snooping. Maybe later; or maybe Harper could take a look.

Harper, Grant, Terry, and Preston were catching fish, one after another, without effort. The pail had long since been filled, and now the freshly caught fish flapped helplessly on the bottom of the boat.

"This is a day for the record books," observed Terry, as he took a large perch off his hook and dropped it on the twitching pile.

"Never saw anything like this before," agreed Preston.

"I wonder what's doing it," said Harper.

"It's my aftershave," Grant said solemnly.

The others laughed.

Floating out of Lawrence's little office, Jill soared high, maybe a thousand feet. Below her, she could see the entire section of Washington County, looking peaceful and sweet. Cars moved along roads, boats moved slowly on the river, and the levees displayed a few sternwheelers. Very pretty, all of it.

She had never ventured very far, but made a mental note to see how high and far she could go. France? The Netherlands?

Then she thought of Robert Guerra.

Suddenly, she was traveling at a high rate of speed, moving

west. Where was she going? The Mid-Ohio racetrack came into view. As she descended, she notice that it was deserted except for a few cars in the parking lot and a couple of horses walking around the paddock circle.

Then Jill was moving through the grandstand toward the far wall, through several doors and corridors, until she was inside a small office. There he was: Robert, dressed in a tan suit and blue tie. With him was the fat man she had seen at the window when she cashed in her ticket. She now realized it was the same man who was on the boat, in the passenger compartment, talking with the redhead.

Who are these people?

On a small conference table was a black metal briefcase with its top open. Inside were stacks of hundred dollar bills.

Jill couldn't quite fit the pieces together, but maybe the racetrack laundered the money from the sales of drugs and porn, and then created fake tickets to show payouts. Was that it? Was Robert also involved in money laundering?

She recalled that she was having dinner with him the following night at Palermo's in Williamstown, West Virginia. What would she say?

She was now beginning to feel a little anxious; she had been out for about forty-five minutes—the longest she had ever been—and thought about returning home.

She flew leisurely back toward Marietta, pausing to dip down to where the men had been. She saw the boat at a dock further down the river and the men carrying great quantities of fish from the dock to a cooler. They were laughing like schoolboys.

Guess it worked!

As she ascended into the blue sky, she felt a strangely familiar tug, and soon she was in the black tunnel, traveling at a breathtaking velocity.

Oh no . . .

Suddenly, Mata stood before her, smiling serenely; the tree was nearby.

"Hello, Jill. Welcome back."

"Thank you, Mata."

"This won't take long. We have been watching your activities and admire your courage, Jill. You have done well. But you are entering a period of danger, and we want you to know two things. First, our help is always present, should you need it. Second, this is a kind of challenge—to see how well you do."

"But why?"

"You have been through much. In the past, you encountered great temptations to which you succumbed. You are not free of trials yet."

"What kind of trials?"

"Alcohol is still a temptation to you. There are others."

"I'll stop drinking. I promise I will!" exclaimed Jill.

"That isn't necessary. You need to be mindful of how it can affect you, though."

"Yes, I know. All right. What other things?"

"You sometimes act out of ego instead of spirit. This is very common, but you have the means to elevate yourself."

"How will I do that?"

"Ask yourself: is what I do, think, or say for the greater good?"

"Yes, I guess I should do that more," said Jill, feeling somewhat chastened. "This is not easy, what you're asking me to do."

"No one ever said it would be. And you always have the option to just live your life any way you like. You can set things right in the next incarnation. Only then it will be a bit more difficult. If you can, meet your demons now, and vanquish them."

"I'll do my best."

"You have a good heart. We know you are earnest in the things you do."

"Can I ask a question?"

Mata nodded.

"Well, I have quite a few, actually. But those men, wherever they were, the ones I saw the last time . . . who are they?"

Mata was silent for a few seconds before she spoke.

"They are the enemies of mankind, of humanity, of all that is right and true and good. They are delusional because they think they are saving the world, but they are only feeding their own greed. If they succeed, millions of lives will be lost. However, they can be stopped, though not in the immediate future."

"Where are they?"

Mata was silent for a moment. Then she said, "The men you saw *were* in The Netherlands. But the group they referred to has other members throughout Europe and several in the Americas."

"Why did I see them?" asked Jill.

"You are on a particular path now," Mata began. "These men are at the very end of it. You will not encounter them directly for some time, but they are ultimately connected to the endeavors you and your friends are now embarking upon."

Jill nodded and said, "The friends? You mean James and Sara and Bud?"

"Yes. They are good souls, with whom you have had contact in many previous incarnations. You and they are learning lessons now. These are important lessons for the growth of your respective souls."

"What about Bud and Sara?"

"There is information about these two I cannot reveal at this time. But I will say that they are blessed beings whom you can trust to assist you."

"Is there anything else I should know? Should I go forward and have dinner with Robert Guerra?"

"Be bold. Do not be afraid. And do not believe all that you think you perceive. You are guided; you are loved. We are through for the present. Someone is calling you . . ."

The phone was ringing beside her bedside, and Jill roused herself to normal consciousness to reach for it.

"Hello?" said Jill, faintly.

"Mrs. Messenger, this is Chester Hamblet. We can get your boat down tomorrow and put it on the trailer. How's that?"

"Oh, that's fine. What time?"

"We'll have her ready to go by 8:00 a.m. Bring a check."

"OK," said Jill. "How about cash?"

"Sure, that's good," said Chester.

"Fine. See you then, Chester," said Jill.

Jill hung up the phone and rubbed her face. There was

much to think about. She was happy that James, Sara, and Bud Grant had gotten Mata's *imprimatur*, so to speak.

David Lawrence sat in his silver Acura in the parking lot of the Newport marina, talking on a secure, scrambled satellite telephone.

A voice on the phone said, "We have to weed the garden. Weeds have a way of spreading."

Lawrence seemed distressed, "I'm not aware of any . . . weeds. I've been extremely careful."

"It's not you. This is a necessary precaution. There's too much at stake, and this can serve as a warning to others."

Tuesday

Because Grant's Jeep had a trailer hitch, they used it to haul the *Keuka Maiden* from Hamblet's storage facility to Newport. Lawrence was waiting out front as they pulled up. Jill got out and walked up to him, with six hundred dollars in her pocket.

Good thing I won that money.

Harper and Grant were out of the Jeep, looking toward the access ramp.

"You must be Mr. Lawrence," Jill said, approaching the tall, distinguished man.

"Yes, I am. Nice to meet you. Did you bring the rental fee?"

"Sure did," said Jill as she handed him six one hundred dollar bills.

He swept it into his pants pocket and said, "Come with me, and I'll show you where your berth is." As he moved toward the path leading to the docks, he nodded toward Harper and Grant, who nodded back.

"Nice morning," Harper said.

"Yes it is," replied Lawrence, and he moved down the path, Jill following.

Harper got an intuitive sense of Lawrence: a bad guy, but a good front man. He also got the similar "vibe" from him that he had gotten from the guy in the shack the other day. The other man, the outcast from the monastery, was not around this morning.

Harper turned to Grant and said, "I wonder what kind of shape the boat is in?"

"Looks OK. The guy at the storage place said he'd winterized it, so that means draining the lines and putting in some fresh fluids. Also, the motors haven't been run for a while, so it's going to take a little work to get it ready."

"How much time would you say?" asked Harper.

"Figure a day," said Grant, as he looked at the boat approvingly.

"She's been well taken care of. Not a mark on her. Even the hull got scrubbed." Then he moved close to Harper and said, "You know, since we're on a recon mission, I can put some gear aboard that might help."

"Like what?"

Grant rattled off a short list of gear he could install. Then he added, "The only thing I don't have, which might come in handy, is diving gear."

"What do you need diving gear for?" Harper asked.

"Let's say we find a boat that we want to track. I can place a GPS sensor on the outer hull. It's tiny; they'll never notice it unless they scan for it. So the best way to approach a boat undetected in the water is *from* the water. That's why we could use the diving gear."

"You couldn't just hold your breath?"

"Great idea. *You* do it," smiled Grant.

Jill and Lawrence walked along the gray planks until they came to a space on one of the F-shaped docks.

"How's this?" Lawrence asked.

"Looks OK," Jill said. "Is there electric power?"

"Right down here," said Lawrence, and pointed to an A/C outlet at the top of a gray metal pipe, a few feet from Jill's berth.

"You'll need a heavy extension chord if you run more than ten amps."

"OK, thanks," said Jill.

"Here's the contract. It's standard; same one I give to everybody. If you have a problem with any of it, then 'See ya.'"

Jill did not care for his tone, and were it not for their mission, she would have told Lawrence to cram it. But she looked it over and finally said, "Got a pen?"

Lawrence handed Jill a ballpoint pen, and she signed her name and the date on the bottom of the contract. Then she handed both back to Lawrence.

"I guess you're all set. Feel free to call if you need anything,"

"Thanks," replied Jill. "Oh, how long in the season does the marina stay open?"

"Probably mid-October. Depends on the weather," said Lawrence. "OK, then. See ya."

By mid-afternoon, Grant had gotten the MerCruisers running and had checked out the electrical system and replaced a couple of lightbulbs. Jill and Harper had washed the inside of the boat, including the vinyl seats, and checked the galley's supply of utensils and dishes. The refrigerator worked; the shower and the toilet worked. The boat was nearly ready to cruise, except for the registration renewal and Grant's installation of the gear he had mentioned.

As she polished the chrome and glass bow lights, Jill thought of Dave and had a wistful longing he were with her now. He loved the *Keuka Maiden,* and it really *was* his boat.

She suddenly felt a pang of anxiety: what if something were to happen to the boat, or to her or the others? They were up against some dangerous men, and this *la-di-dah, going-on-a-boat-trip* mindset didn't exactly sit easily or well with her. They could all be killed. And soon she was going to face a likely murderer: Robert Guerra.

Around 5:30 that evening, Jill was dressing for her dinner with Robert. She grew increasingly nervous and anxious about what might happen, and she tried to put these concerns out of her mind. She was not successful.

A drink will take the edge off, I bet.

She went quickly downstairs to the kitchen and poured herself a vodka and tonic. She sipped it. She felt better already. It was a crutch; she knew that. But she needed a crutch now. Guerra was not to be trusted; he was a lousy, rotten criminal, and she had information that could bring him down. But what if she let slip? What if she said the wrong thing? Palermo's was a mafia joint, wasn't it? Wasn't Guerra Italian? Wouldn't there be big burly guys with guns and meat hooks and an open Cadillac trunk? Would she become another floater? Or just disappear into the night—never to be found?

She took another sip of her drink and then topped it off before returning to her bedroom to dress.

She set the glass on her dresser and selected a conservative indigo cocktail dress, a simple necklace of mother of pearl shells, and matching earrings. Then she gave herself a little misting of *Fracas*, which seemed appropriate.

This may be my last night alive on earth.

She took another drink.

How could Robert have known about my winning the trifecta?

Then there was the briefcase full of money in the racetrack office and the likelihood of money laundering.

How would she behave? Mata told her to be bold, but what did that *mean*?

By the time Jill was ready to drive to Williamstown, she had finished two vodka tonics and was feeling a little more relaxed.

At 5:50, Jill turned into the parking lot of Casa Palermo. It took her a minute to find a parking space. Then she eased the Honda into the spot and switched off the motor.

She wanted another drink.

As she was walking toward the entrance, she spotted

Harper's white pickup. As there was no one in it, she assumed Harper and Grant were inside. This made her feel a little safer.

Jill walked into Casa Palermo. It was dark, with red glowing lights in the entry. The hostess, a pleasant-looking young Italian woman said, "Would you like a table?"

"Not yet. I'm meeting Robert Guerra?"

The young woman smiled and said, "That's fine. Would you care to wait in the bar? When he arrives, I'll tell him you're here. Miss . . .?"

"Jill."

"Fine, thank you," said the hostess.

As she entered the bar, she caught the eyes of several men. Then, as she slid onto a bar stool, the bartended moved quickly over and placed a cocktail napkin in front of her.

"What's your pleasure?" he asked.

"Vodka tonic, please," she replied.

The bartender nodded and said, "Right away."

When the drink arrived, Jill gave it a brief stir and then took a long swallow. It felt good. It felt really good. She took another drink, finishing half of it. Added to her earlier drinks, the warm buzz of alcohol began to tickle the neurons in Jill's brain.

The antidote to stage fright. Sorry, Mata. I need this.

"Geez, I hope I didn't keep you waiting long," Robert said as he entered the bar. "I got stuck at the bank. It's either mortgages or taxes."

"No, I'm usually early," Jill said as she smiled at him.

Guerra was nattily dressed in a dark blue suit and a silk Armani tie. He smelled good.

"What is that cologne you're wearing? It's very nice," said Jill, wobbling slightly as she stood up.

"Oh, you like it?" smiled Robert. "It's called *Zizanie*. They don't make it any more, but I managed to get a couple of bottles. Frank Sinatra wore it."

"Really," said Jill.

So now I know how Frank smelled.

The hostess showed them to a table toward the back, next to the wall. This position gave Grant a perfect line of sight, but Harper's back was to them.

"Looks like our gal is having a cocktail," observed Grant.

Harper nodded. "She's a grown-up."

Jill opened her menu and tried to read it in the dim light. The vodka had somewhat blurred her vision.

"Why don't you order for us?" said Jill. "You know the place and what's good."

Guerra smiled and nodded.

"I'd be pleased to. What do you like? Any preferences?"

"Nothing too heavy," said Jill, as her head wobbled slightly. "Not crazy about spaghetti and meatballs. Well, I *am*, but I can make that at home. Oh I don't know, maybe veal or chicken or seafood. Something light."

"They do a great chicken scaloppini. Maybe a small side of spaghetti? Their sauce is fantastic."

"Sure," said Jill, finishing her drink. Guerra noticed and said, "Would you like another drink?"

"Why not? It's been a long day."

"What have you been up to?" asked Guerra.

"Oh, I got our boat in the water finally," she said, her speech slightly slurred. "I know, the season's half over, but I figured what the hell? I have the boat, so I might as well get some use out of it, right?"

"Right," nodded Guerra.

"You like boats, Bob?" asked Jill.

"Oh yeah. If I ever retire, I am going on a long cruise."

"Like down the Ohio River?" said Jill.

Guerra smiled, and replied, "Well maybe. There are a lot of waterways for boats. But I was thinking on one of those big cruise ships."

Jill nodded.

The waitress approached and asked, "Ready to order?"

Guerra nodded and relayed their choices to the waitress.

"Do you want a salad?" asked the waitress.

"I don't care for one," said Guerra. "Jill?"

"No thanks, but I *would* like another vodka tonic."

Grant, watching Jill and Guerra, whispered: "I wish I knew what kind of car he's driving. I could put a little tracker in the wheel well."

"Oh, he's a pretty public figure from what I hear. Position of responsibility at a local bank, a pillar of the community. He can be found."

"It's always the big guys who get greedy. And the little ones, too. And some in between."

"Your logic is a marvel," cracked Harper.

"Hey, they just got their soup. We should order something."

Harper waved to the waitress, who quickly approached.

"Ready to order, gentlemen?"

"Yes we are," said Harper. "I'll have a bowl of minestrone soup, an order of clams casino, and a side order of spaghetti."

"Very good," the waitress said. Then, turning to Grant, "And you, sir?"

"Linguini with white clam sauce. Please ask the chef to add some fresh parsley."

The waitress finished taking their orders and soon returned with two bottles of Yeungling.

"What's happening—anything?" asked Harper.

"Naw, they're just schmoozing."

Jill was halfway into her second vodka tonic when the soup arrived from the kitchen. Robert, obviously hungry, picked up his spoon, smiled at Jill, and said, *"Bon appétit!"* Jill raised her glass. She was enjoying the buzz and wasn't particularly hungry.

She watched Robert as he spooned the tasty Italian wedding soup.

The guy must be starving.

As he ate, Jill casually said, "Can I ask you a question, Bob?"

"Sure," said Guerra, barely looking up.

"What were you doing driving a boat on the Muskingum in the middle of the night last week?"

Guerra visibly jolted. Then he quickly regained his composure.

"Couldn't have been me," he said.

"It *was* you. I *saw* you, Bob."

Guerra slowly shook his head and took another spoonful.

"I think you're *mistaken*, Jill."

"Who was the young man in the river?"

"I think you're asking the wrong guy," said Guerra.

"The young man who was found dead. The young man who lost a sneaker," Jill whispered intently.

"*Shhh*," said Guerra. Then he looked around and whispered intensely, "Not so loud, please. People will think you've had too much to drink!"

Then he straightened up, smiled, and said, "This soup is fantastic."

Jill leaned forward and said in a low voice, "You can play dumb if you want, but I am going to find out."

She picked up her spoon.

Guerra took a piece of focaccia from a straw basket.

"What about the drugs on the boat?"

He poured some olive oil on a small plate, smiled, and looked at Jill.

"You've got a great imagination. You should write books."

"Reality's plenty," Jill said, eyeing him evenly.

Guerra suddenly leaned back, flushed. His face was red, and he reached to loosen his tie. He took a deep breath and put one hand on his chest.

"I . . . don't feel well," he said.

"Yeah, well, maybe it's your guilty conscience," said Jill.

"I think I'm having a heart attack," said Guerra.

"Really?" asked Jill.

Time seemed to stand still as Jill watched Guerra's face grow contorted. His eyes bulged as he clutched at his necktie, gasping for breath. Then, his voice constricted, he uttered, "They put something in the soup. I . . . I've been poisoned. Don't eat the soup, Jill . . ."

Then Guerra doubled over on his side, toppled out of his chair, and landed hard on the carpet.

Some of the other patrons saw Guerra topple to the floor; there were gasps.

"Holy shit! The guy just keeled over!" whispered Grant.

Jill quickly knelt beside Guerra.

"You'll be OK, Bob," Jill soothed.

Guerra, quickly ebbing from consciousness, motioned for Jill to come close so he could tell her something. She leaned down so her ear was near his mouth.

"I'm . . . with the FBI. The boy . . . Tim . . . was my son. And now they've killed me, too."

"Who? Who killed you?" whispered Jill intently.

But it was too late. Robert Guerra was dead.

CHAPTER SEVEN

With uniformed police officers standing near the door, the patrons began to file out of Casa Palermo, whispering anxiously about what happened. As they moved out, Grant muttered to Harper, "Dang. Didn't get my linguini."

"That's the least of our worries."

"You mean, like Jill?" asked Bud.

"The whole situation," said Harper grimly. "That guy was murdered. I'm sure of it. Some kind of neurotoxin. If it was food poisoning, he would have puked his guts out."

"So . . . if he was mixed up in murdering that kid . . ."

"Yeah, this is pretty big."

As they reached Grant's truck, he said, "Well, do you want to hang around?"

"No, not a good idea. Jill can take care of herself. I'll leave a message on her machine to call us if she needs us for anything."

"OK," said Grant. "Well, I'm still hungry. Any ideas?"

"I think we should head back to the apartment, in case Jill calls. We can pick up some stuff at the Eagle."

"All right," Grant said as he started the engine.

As Grant eased the truck onto the highway, heading back to Ohio, Harper spoke.

"There's something about Jill you need to know."

"Yeah?"

"She can go out of body."

Grant whistled low in surprise. "You mean like astral projection?"

"Yep. She can do it. She's a one-woman recon unit. She can go out of body and go anywhere she wants, sight unseen. That's how we knew that Guerra was on the boat. She went back into time and she saw him."

"Wow . . . that is something," exclaimed Grant. "She can really do that?"

"She really can," nodded Harper. "She's pretty amazing."

"How'd you find this out?"

Harper explained that he met Jill on the Muskingum riverbank while locating a lost girl. And now, with their mutual psychic abilities, they were able to discern facts about the case, starting with the kid floating dead in the river.

"And since we're going on a mission together . . . well, you should be in the loop about what Jill can do."

"What a dame," smiled Grant. "What about Sara? What can she do?"

"I wouldn't know," smiled Harper.

"Well, at least there'll be a couple of normal people on this mission," laughed Grant.

Back at Ridgewood Court, Harper and Grant were finishing a pepperoni pizza. Harper had left a message for Jill, and he hoped she would call him back. "It must have been a horror to see Guerra just . . . die, right in front of her."

The phone rang, and Harper sprang to answer it.

"*Hello?*"

"James, Jill."

"How are you? Are you all right?"

"Oh yeah. I had to stay at the restaurant for a while and answer some questions, but it was nothing major. Can you and Bud come over tomorrow morning? I think we had better figure out some contingency plans. Seeing Robert die was no joke."

"I know, I know," said Harper. "Listen, there's another thing."

"What?"

"I told Bud about your ability to go out."

There was a slight pause.

"Well. I guess that's all right," she said quietly. "If he knows about the stuff you do, then it's not much of a stretch, I guess. Was he OK with it?"

"Oh yeah," said Harper. "He's been around weird wackos before."

Jill laughed. "Yeah. Weird wackos—that's us all right."

The next morning, Harper and Grant sat with Jill in her living room, the *Marietta Times* on the coffee table. The lead story was about the untimely death of Robert Guerra and it listed a few facts about his life in Marietta. It had been on the morning TV news also. Jill was nervous.

Harper spoke, leaning forward with his elbows on his knees, his hands clasped together.

"If Robert Guerra really *were* an FBI agent, then he reported to *somebody*. They'll have agents down here, if they aren't here already."

"What if he was retired and just doing this on his own?" asked Jill.

"You never retire from the Bureau," Grant said. "They always know where you are, and you can be recalled anytime they want you. Same with the military. And that could explain why his son's death was never made public. The FBI claimed jurisdiction and stopped anything further."

"Yeah," nodded Harper. "That sounds right."

"You know, I don't know if this boat trip is a good idea. I'm really not comfortable with it. If they could kill Robert like that . . . I don't think I want to go. Why ask for trouble?"

Harper looked down, gently cradling the coffee cup in his hands.

Grant spoke earnestly, "Here's what I think. If you were considered a threat, the way Guerra was, you'd be dead, too."

"Seriously?" asked Jill, astonished.

"Oh yeah. They have lots of ways to make a death look accidental. The soup was one way, but your brakes could fail, or they could hit you with an aerosol, poison your coffee. Boom— you're dead. But that hasn't happened, and I don't think it will. You're nobody to them."

Harper looked at Jill and asked, "Are you serious? You really don't want to go?"

"I'm just not comfortable with it, let's put it that way." Grant spoke again.

"Frankly, you would be safer on the boat than hanging around here. We'd be with you, and we'd all be on the water. Who's going to get aboard to hurt you? But I honestly don't think you're a target. You're just not a threat to anybody. This Guerra guy was mixed up in drugs, in money laundering, all sorts of things. Plus, he knew a lot. And he was FBI. Any one of those factors could be a good motive to bump him off. And that's just the stuff we know about, so there are very likely other things. Maybe he was trying to blackmail somebody. The possibilities are endless. You're just not a target, Jill."

"Maybe you're right," said Jill. "But it's still quite a shock to see someone just . . . die so horribly."

Harper set down his coffee cup and said, "One thing you might do is to go out and take a look at Guerra's house. You might get some info there. You can fly around and listen in on conversations. If you were a threat, you'd hear about it. Especially now, with Guerra dead."

"Right, OK, I can do that," said Jill.

"I think we should stay with the boat trip—at least to get a sense of where the Bayliner is going. Then we could always call in the Feds if we get hard intel about drug shipments. And that would be that. Then we can just . . . fish."

Jill smiled for the first time that morning. They were earnest and caring.

"You know, at some point, if we do the boat trip with Sara, sooner or later she's going to find out about me . . . and you, too."

"That's the least of our concerns," said Harper.

"I have to get the boat registered, too," said Jill, thoughtfully.

"We'll take care of that," said Harper. "I just need your old registration. Then we'll do a last check on the boat."

"When did you want to leave?" asked Jill.

"How's tomorrow morning?" replied Harper.

"So soon?" asked Jill.

"I think, in light of Guerra's murder, we'd better get moving."

"Well," Jill said, "I guess you're right. I just wish I felt a little more at ease about this."

"You'll be fine," Harper reassured. "If we thought for a second that you'd be put in danger, we'd scrub the mission. It's not worth it."

"Absolutely," nodded Grant.

"Well, that makes me feel better."

"One other thing. Well, two," Harper said. "I want you to see if you can contact me while you're out of body. You haven't done that yet, have you?"

"No. Just that one time."

"The other thing is to see if you can get out without the CD."

"I tried that," Jill said. "My right arm came out, but the rest of me was stuck.

"I can't help you with that, but just . . . try again to see if you can do it."

"All right."

"For backup, we could put the CDs on a little MP3 player. That would be easier for Jill on the boat," Grant said.

"Yeah, that's good," Harper said.

"How do we do that?" asked Jill.

"I'll take care of it," Grant said. "I just need to borrow your CDs."

"Fine. But I'll need them for a while today."

"No problem."

After Harper and Grant had left, Jill walked back to the kitchen phone and took it off the hook.

No disturbances.

As she moved upstairs, she hoped that she would be able to find out who was behind Guerra's murder. Whatever she thought of him before, she now realized he wasn't a total creep. In fact, it had all been a cover.

Hadn't it?

She crawled onto the bed, flipping off her tan espadrilles and preparing herself for departure. She thought about what Harper had said, about trying to lift out without the CD, but this wasn't the time. She had work to do.

Places to go, people to see.

She was soon flying over Marietta, headed for Reno and Guerra's house. She saw a Marietta police car in the driveway and a white Ford Taurus; no one was visible from the outside. She swooped down to take a look, moving in through the back door as she had done the other night.

Two policemen were walking around, taking notes. A man in a suit was checking to see whether anything had been disturbed. It didn't look like it.

Jill floated down to the basement, then into the back office. The drugs were gone.

She looked carefully at the floor to see if there were any footprints or traces that might suggest someone's presence.

Nothing.

She checked the window high up, but couldn't tell if it had been opened. Then she stuck her head through the closet door; the stacks of porn were still at the bottom of the closet, but the FBI jacket was gone.

Someone had sanitized the place, leaving only a few telltale items. Gee, maybe Robert really was into porn.

She moved up and out through the little window, checking to see whether there were any indications of entry from the outside. The dirt near the window had been recently raked, and the little furrows were still visible. It was impossible to tell whether anyone had walked on the grass. She looked around for clues, but, finding none, headed for the clouds.

She felt she should visit Lawrence's marina in Newport, and soon she was zipping north, high over the trees. The day was slightly overcast, with broken clouds at 500 feet. Still, flying was delightful.

As she approached the marina, she circled over it, looking at the boats. The Bayliner was back, docked a few berths down from the *Keuka Maiden*. Harper and Grant had not arrived, but it was too soon for them, anyway. The Bayliner looked deserted.

She descended and was soon hovering over its back deck. The sneaker was gone, and the boat was very quiet. She floated through the small louvered doors and down into the center cabin.

Nobody home.

She noticed a piece of paper on the galley table and looked at it closely.

In pencil, someone had written:

Grandview – 4

Sistersville – 12

Paden City – 4

She realized that the names represented towns up the Ohio River. There were five more. She went to pick the paper up, but her hand went through it.

But something odd happened: the paper *moved*. Not by much, but a little. She tried it again; the paper moved again—slightly.

Then Jill moved away from the table and looked through the bulkhead.

There were the drugs. Maybe not all that she had seen at Guerra's house, but more than the last time.

Ah ha, so they're moving along the river and making deliveries. That's what the paper is: a list of delivery stops.

Next she flew to the little white house where Lawrence had his office. It, too, was empty. She looked through the panels behind the desk, and the map was unchanged—as least, as far as she could tell.

She moved up and out, toward the little guardhouse. In it sat the disagreeable man whom she and Harper had first seen. He sat, his back to the window, looking at a men's magazine.

Now Jill looked toward the cars in the parking lot. She noticed a man sitting in one of them. Because of the distance, she couldn't make out much; she decided to have a look.

As she moved toward the parking lot, she saw that the car was the silver Acura. Seated behind the wheel was David Lawrence, talking on his secure phone. He looked tense.

Jill stuck her head through the rear passenger door and listened to what Lawrence was saying.

"No, I don't think there's any connection to the woman. Remember, this is a small town. There aren't many single people, and Bob was something of a ladies' man. I tell you, if I weren't queer, I'd ask her out myself."

Jill smiled.

There was a brief pause and then Lawrence spoke again, "Yes, there were two guys with her, but so what? We can't suspect everybody. They were just helping her. Probably just guys who like boating and fishing. That's not unusual around here."

Lawrence listened again and his mouth tightened into a grimace.

"You say you don't want to attract attention? Robert Guerra is bringing some attention, and it's a damn good thing he didn't have a boat here. But this woman, this Messenger woman, she's not a risk. If she were, Guerra would have said something. He was very cautious, that guy."

Well, that's a relief.

She remembered the Williamstown police who had immediately arrived at the restaurant after Robert had died. After getting all the patrons' contact information, the cops cleared the restaurant, including Grant and Harper. Then an unshaven detective in a cheap gray suit began to ask Jill questions.

What was her relationship to Robert Guerra?

"Just a friend. We were having dinner."

Witnesses said that he spoke to you just before he died. What did he say?

"He said, 'I'm dying. Call a doctor.'"

Was that it? Did he say anything else?

"That was it."

I guess the poor guy just had a heart attack.

"It happens."

Jill didn't let on that, while Robert was lying dead on the floor of Casa Palermo, a man with a mustache had quickly cleared the table, leaving only the glasses of water.

Her reflection was interrupted when Lawrence got out of his car, slammed the door shut, and moved quickly toward the entry path. He was not happy.

Jill thought of Harper.

This might be a good time to pay a visit.

Holding the intention of Harper, Jill suddenly was flying fast toward Ridgewood Court, over Pike Street and down and into Harper's second-floor apartment.

Grant was sitting at the kitchen table, an open tool kit before him, working on a piece of electronic gear—what *was* that? Harper was at his desk, sitting very quietly. He was holding a pencil, and a piece of paper lay before him.

Jill floated toward Harper and stopped just behind him. She put her mouth close to his ear.

"*James? James Harper?*" called Jill.

Harper heard her and cocked his head.

"Jill . . . is that you?" said Harper, smiling slowly

"What?" said Grant.

"Jill's here," said Harper. "I'm pretty sure."

"No shit," said Grant without looking up.

"*OK,* OK, you did it," said Harper, looking all around, which Jill found amusing. "Say something else."

"Dead men tell no tales," said Jill.

"Dead men tell no tales!" replied Harper. "This is good. Just one more, just to be sure."

"Lawrence knew about the hit on Robert Guerra!"

"Wow. He did?" exclaimed Harper.

"Did what?" said Grant.

"Anything else?" asked Harper.

"I'll tell you later," said Jill.

"OK. No problem. Try this: how many fingers am I holding up?"

"Two. You made a peace sign," smiled Jill.

"Very good. Perfect," said Harper. "Now, where are you, exactly?"

"I am behind you, about a foot away," said Jill.

Harper turned and looked, but saw nothing.

"I can't see you," he said.

"That's good," replied Jill. "I want to try something."

"You want to try something? What?" asked Harper.

212

"If it works, then you'll know," said Jill as she put her hand on the piece of paper on Harper's desk. She tried to move it, and it did, a tiny bit . . . less than an eighth of an inch.

"Did you see that?" asked Jill.

"I don't know what I'm supposed to be looking at," said Harper.

"'Keep your eye upon the doughnut and not upon the hole," murmured Grant.

"Look at the paper on your desk," said Jill.

Harper looked at it.

"So?"

"Be patient!" yelled Jill as she tried to move the paper again. She pushed it, but the paper failed to move. She tried again with the same results. She kept pushing the paper with her ghostly hand.

Then the paper suddenly moved, sliding an inch across the desk.

"There! See?" yelled Jill.

"Holy cow," said Harper. "How did you do that?"

"I don't know!"

"What did she do?" asked Grant, turning around.

"She was able to move the paper on the desk," said Harper.

"No shit!" exclaimed Grant as he sprang to his feet and stepped to Harper's desk. "She did that?"

"Yup!" yelled Jill.

"She did," said Harper.

There was a brief pause.

"Did you just hear her say 'yup'?" asked Harper.

"No. I didn't hear anything. But that is very cool. I

mean, going astral is pretty cool by itself, but to be able to affect something with physical density . . ."

"Pretty good, huh?" yelled Jill happily.

"Beats the hell out of me," said Harper.

"It's an energy transfer, but on a very small scale, because she doesn't have a body to move around."

"This is something," said Harper. Then he said to Jill, "You are maybe the most gifted person I ever met."

"And I can bake a cherry pie," cracked Jill.

Harper laughed. Funny girl.

"Now, Jill," began Grant, looking all around the room, "I admire your abilities, truly. But let's get one thing clear right now. When I am in the shower, or otherwise indisposed, I am going to trust you to be somewhere else, OK?"

"No problem," said Jill.

"She said, 'No problem,'" relayed Harper.

"Freak me out," exclaimed Grant.

Jill was suddenly jolted back into her body by the incessant sound of her doorbell, then pounding, and finally the voice of Sara Hopkins, yelling from the sidewalk.

"Jill! *Jill?*"

Jill, still wobbly and disoriented, got off the bed and moved to the window. She opened it, stuck her head out and yelled.

"Sara?"

"Yeah! I've been calling, but your line's been busy. Are you still on the phone?" yelled Sara from the porch.

"Hang on! I'll be right down!"

Jill moved quickly out the bedroom door, down the stairs, and then back to the kitchen. She quickly replaced the phone on the cradle and went to open the front door.

"Am I interrupting you?" Sara asked.

"No, sorry. I was just . . . taking a nap, and I took the phone off the hook. I was awake last night quite a bit. Come on in—I'll make some coffee."

Sara entered and noticed the *Marietta Times* on the coffee table, left from Grant and Harper's morning visit.

"Isn't it terrible about Mr. Guerra?"

"I was with him last night, at the restaurant," said Jill, moving toward the kitchen and starting a fresh pot of coffee. Sara followed her.

"You were? Wow. How come?"

"He asked me out to dinner. I was sitting across from the guy when he died."

"Oh, yikes," said Sara. "What a *drag*."

"It wasn't something I'd care to do again," said Jill, as she filled the coffeepot.

Sara dropped herself into a chair. "I never had a date actually *die* on me. Although it felt like it a couple times, ha ha."

Jill smiled.

"Did he say anything . . . you know, revealing?"

"No, not really. He just was eating his soup and the next thing—*boom*—he was on the floor."

"The wages of sin," Sara said.

"I guess," replied Jill.

"So are we still doing the boat trip? They're short staffed

at the library and then the Sternwheel Festival called to ask if I could sell Belgian waffles again—you know, in that little booth."

"What did you tell them?" asked Jill.

"I said I was going on a vacation, with some friends, on a boat trip. Are we still going?"

"Yes," nodded Jill, her back to Sara. "Tomorrow morning I think. That OK with you?"

"Sure thing. I'm all packed," said Sara. "I can go down to the store and get some groceries for the trip. Want to kick in?"

"Sure thing. Let me buy," said Jill, as she opened her purse and took out a hundred dollar bill.

"Wow," exclaimed Sara. "You're flush."

"I won some money at the track last week. I got lucky."

"Geez Louise!"

"Do you know what you're going to get?"

"Well, we can always stop for food along the way, but basic stuff: eggs, bread, butter, hot dogs, hamburgers, steaks, chips . . ."

"Get some paper plates, too. We have knives and forks on the boat. And trash bags."

"OK," Sara said.

"Here's what we're gonna do . . . I think," began Jill. "You and Bud will pilot the boat. James and I will be below deck, at least until we get clear of Newport. Then we can take turns at the wheel."

"I never drove a boat before . . ."

"Oh God, you just *steer* it. One lever for the throttle: forward for fast, back for slow. If I can do it, you can do it," Jill said with an encouraging smile. "We're going to meet at the boat later today, around 4:00. So maybe we can take our stuff out then. Then tomorrow morning, all we have to do is fill the tank and take off."

"This is exciting," exclaimed Sara.

"It is, isn't it?" replied Jill, still feeling slight anxiety in the pit of her stomach.

The doorbell rang again and Jill, slightly anxious, got up to see who it was.

Bud Grant.

Jill opened the door and said, "Hey, Bud, what's up?"

"I want to borrow your CDs so I can put them on an MP3 player. I tried calling, but your line was busy. I scanned it and it was off the hook."

"You can do that?" asked Jill.

"Oh yeah."

Sara emerged from the kitchen and said, "Hi, Bud. You gonna bring your guitar on the trip?"

"I'll get the CDs for you," said Jill as she ran upstairs.

"Hey, Sara," smiled Grant. "You know, I hadn't even thought about it. Why don't you bring yours? That ought to do it."

"Oh, but you have such a great instrument," smiled Sara.

"Well, maybe I can. I'll check to see if there's room. There's not much space on a boat like that."

"Too bad we don't play ukuleles," said Sara.

Grant suddenly mimicked a Hawaiian singer strumming a ukulele and sang, in a high, breathy tenor, "*Some-wah ovah da rainbow . . .*"

"Hey, that's all right!" laughed Sara.

Jill returned with the shoebox of CDs. She had remembered to remove the CD from her player and put it back into its case.

"Here you go," said Jill. "Take good care of them."

"I'll have them back to you later today. We're meeting at the boat around 4:00?"

"Sounds good," Jill replied. "Sara will stop off at the supermarket and get some food for the trip."

"Need any money?" asked Grant.

"No. We'll buy the food. You guys pay for the gas. How's that?"

"Sounds fair," said Grant. "See you later."

Sara accompanied Grant down the steps, taking his arm as they left.

"No kidding, you sounded just like that guy . . ."

As Jill closed and locked the door behind them, she thought about trying, once again, to lift out without the help of the CD. It might come in handy.

She quickly moved up the stairs and into her bedroom. As she approached her bed, she opened a drawer in the bedside table and took out her sleep mask. She settled herself on the bed, put on the sleep mask, took a deep breath, and settled back.

As she began to relax, she imagined the soothing voice of Robert Madison, telling her to put things into the strong box with the heavy lid. That done, she began to vocalize *ahhh* in a low voice. She was becoming more relaxed. She breathed deeply and waited for the vibrations to start. Nothing happened.

She tried to lift out without success. She tried to separate her right arm from the body, as she had done previously. Nothing worked. Maybe she was too keyed up? Maybe she wasn't in the proper mental state? Funny how the CDs always managed to get her into the right state for separation.

I'll just have to practice.

Then Jill fell asleep and slept soundly for a delicious twenty minutes.

Sara, always compulsively early, pulled her minivan in front of Jill's door at 3:00. Jill heard the slam of the car door and moved to the window to look out. Yes, it was Sara. Jill quickly finished putting a few extra things into her duffel bag and zipped it up. She couldn't quite shake the feeling that they were putting themselves in danger. But then, life was a series of risks, wasn't it?

A few moments later, Jill appeared through the front door and flopped the duffel on the porch, locking the door behind her. Then she lugged the duffel down to the van, through the open side door, and set it behind the passenger seat. She noticed several bags of groceries.

"Wow. Looks like you got a lot of stuff." Jill smiled at Sara.

"Well, I started thinkin'. No sense being on a boat with handsome men and just eating burgers and hot dogs. So I got us some chips, some onion dip, and little burritos and pizza rolls to heat up in the microwave. You do have a microwave on the boat, right?"

"Toaster oven. That'll work."

"And then of course I wanted to make sure we had some desserts, like Eskimo Pies and cupcakes."

"You think of everything," said Jill, as she closed the side door and opened the passenger door.

As Sara began to drive down Sixth Street, Jill said, "Sara, there's something I have to tell you."

"What?"

"Remember those CDs you gave me a while ago, when I was in the hospital?"

"Yeah."

"Well, I started using them," said Jill.

"Oh good. Glad you got some use out of them."

"Well, it's a little more than that . . ."

As Sara drove toward the Newport Marina, Jill explained about her ability to go out of body. Sara was surprised and intrigued. She had never heard about anybody going *out* before. She said that Harper had given her the CDs, but she didn't know much about them. Jill then explained that Harper could do something called remote viewing, he could see things that were far away.

"For real?" asked Sara. "Oh wait, you're kidding me."

"Not this time. He really does it: he can see things far away and then draw pictures of what he has seen. He used to do it for the military. Honest. And, for me, being able to go out of body . . . well, it's just the most fantastic thing you can imagine."

Sara sat with this information for a moment. Then she said, "You guys are weird."

"Well. Hope it doesn't bother you," said Jill.

"Why should it? It's not like . . ." Sara paused. "You guys aren't Peeping Toms are you?"

Jill laughed.

At 3:45, as the red minivan pulled into the Newport marina, Jill saw Grant's Jeep in the parking lot. As she got out, she looked around at the other vehicles. The Acura was nowhere to be seen.

Guess Lawrence isn't here. Good.

As they began to lug their bags down the path, the man she and Harper had seen previously emerged unsteadily from the little booth.

"Hold it," he said ominously.

"Yes?" said Jill.

"You got a boat here?" he slurred. "I need to check your names."

He drunkenly eyed Jill, then Sara.

"Jill Messenger. I'm all paid up. Call Mr. Lawrence if you want. Besides, my two friends are already here."

"Oh yeah, OK. Sorry," said the man, wiping his nose and taking a step back. Then he ogled Sara and said, "Are they . . . uh, *real?*"

"No, they're inflated," said Sara. "I use a bicycle pump."

"No shit?" said the man as Jill and Sara moved down the path to the dock.

"Well, that was a new one," laughed Jill.

"Usually they just stare," said Sara.

On board the *Keuka Maiden*, Harper was looking at a chart and Grant was laying on his back, under the dashboard, with some wires dangling above him. He was oblivious to the rocking of the boat as the women stepped aboard.

"How's it going?" asked Jill.

"Good," said Harper. "Got the new registration and we're ready to go. Or will be."

"Hey, Bud," Sara called. "What're you doing?"

Bud Grant sat up and rubbed his face. "Oh, installing a few gadgets. Just in case."

"Like what?" asked Jill.

"Remember the James Bond movies?"

The women nodded.

"Same thing, almost."

"That's great," said Jill. "Where's the rocket launcher?"

"The rocket launcher!" moaned Grant. "I must have left it in my other pants."

Sara grinned and shot a glance at Jill. This guy was too much.

The women carried their bags through the deck, down the little steps, through the galley, and stowed them in the forward berth.

"Gee," said Sara. "Looks like we're going to have an old-fashioned slumber party."

"Yeah," said Jill, with palpable anxiety. There was still time to cancel the trip. But she'd wait and see; she trusted Harper and Grant, and now Sara was here. She didn't want to be a wet blanket, not when so many preparations had been made.

"I shoulda brought a little stereo," said Sara.

"Oh, it'll be fine. We better get the groceries," said Jill. "Come on."

"I could bring one tomorrow morning. I really like music on a boat."

As the women went back up to the deck, Sara said to Grant, "Can you give us a hand with the food?"

"Sure thing," Grant said, scrambling to his feet as the women climbed out of the boat. The three headed toward the parking lot.

222

As they approached Sara's minivan, a man was watching them, unseen, from one of the cars. He was skinny, with blond hair and a narrow face.

Within twenty minutes, all of the food and the gear had been stowed.

"Guess you didn't bring your guitar, did you?" said Sara, faking a pout.

"Got something almost as good," said Grant as he quickly descended into the cabin, and reemerged with a tube.

"Check this out," he said as Sara and Jill looked on with interest.

He opened one end of the tube and slid something out: a keyboard that was rolled up. He put it on the floor of the helm and smoothed it out.

"Wow," said Jill.

"Is it any good?" Sara asked.

"You bet. I have a little amp and it just plugs in. Sounds pretty darn good for a toy. Plus it doesn't take up any space."

Harper watched, amused.

"Can't wait for the first recital," smiled Harper, glancing at his watch. "Whaddya say we get some dinner and make it an early night? That way we can leave first thing tomorrow."

"How early?" asked Sara.

"How's seven?" Harper said.

"How's eight?" Sara hedged.

Harper smiled and said, "Fine."

"We need to cover the boat before we go," said Grant.

"Why?" said Jill. "Do you think someone would steal it?"

"Not steal," said Grant. "I just don't want anybody snooping around. Besides, the tarp can't be secured very well. Just zippers and snaps."

While the women waited on the dock, Grant adjusted some of his electronic gear, and then he and Harper snapped down the nylon canvas on the *Keuka Maiden*.

When the boat was secure, the four friends moved up the dock, got into their respective cars, and headed toward Marietta.

It was around 7:00 p.m. when they pulled up in front of Tampico's Mexican restaurant. They were looking forward to the adventure they were about to embark upon. Jill, Harper, and Grant were well aware of the potential danger that lay before them, but now, sitting in the Mexican restaurant, the cruise seemed like a festive outing.

A pitcher of Margaritas and a bowl of fresh chips and salsa were brought to the table.

"How long do you think we'll be gone?" asked Jill, trying to conceal her nervousness.

"I don't know," replied Harper. "A few days? Can you get me that list you saw?"

"I'll have to go back and look for it," said Jill. Then she said to Grant, "Oh, my CDs. Do you have them?"

"Yep," he said, munching on a toasted corn chip. "They're in the Jeep. You're all set. I put them all on a little player for you. I have some pretty good earbuds too. But you can use your own headphones. They drain the battery faster, but they might sound better than the buds."

"Does it matter?" asked Jill.

"Not really," replied Grant, taking a sip of his drink.

"Jill tells me that you and I will drive the boat?" said Sara, looking at Grant.

"Just for a little while, until . . . " began Grant.

His cell phone chirped. He took it from the holster on his belt and flipped it open.

"Goddamn it. Somebody's on the boat."

The others shared looks of disbelief.

Oh crap. Here we go, thought Jill.

Grant punched a few numbers and a ghostly image appeared on screen. Someone was on the back deck of the *Keuka Maiden*.

"What's happening? Can you tell from that?" asked Jill, incredulous.

"Shhh."

Grant watched the shadowy figure pull the cover back in place, so the boat was closed, and move forward toward the wheel. The intruder—whoever he was—was looking for something. But what?

Grant waited. Then he put the phone up to his mouth and held down one of the buttons on the keypad.

"You are being watched. Leave this boat immediately," said Grant.

The figure jumped back and looked around.

Who was that?

The person waited for a few seconds. The boat was dark and still.

"You have five seconds to leave this boat."

"Yeah, you gonna make me?" said the intruder. He had an English accent.

"Oh, I think so," said Grant.

"Yeah, right. Good luck, asshole."

"Aw, gee," said Grant to the others. "He just hurt my feelings."

He pushed another button on the keypad, and the boat was suddenly filled with a strange, wavering sound. The intruder was stunned. Then, wracked with pain, he fell to his knees. Grant let the sound continue for a few seconds, completely crippling the intruder, who was now convulsing on the deck floor.

Grant pushed another button and the sound stopped.

Harper, Jill, and Sara looked on breathlessly.

"I could kill you if I wanted to," said Grant. "Is that what you want?"

"No! No!" came the piteous reply. "I'm leaving. Wrong boat! Wrong boat!"

The intruder struggled to stand up, then staggered to the back of the boat. He reopened the cover and began to climb out.

"Seal it up, just like you found it!" Grant thundered.

The others looked on with awe and admiration. "General" Grant had taken command and thwarted the intruder.

Jill's eyes were wide with disbelief.

"What the heck was that?" she asked.

Grant turned the cell phone around so she and Sara could see the screen. Then he pushed another button and suddenly the entire scene—all 30 seconds of it—was replayed for the women. When the wavering tone incapacitated the intruder, their jaws dropped.

"That is just fantastic," said Sara. "And you taped it somehow, too."

"That *is* pretty amazing, Bud," said Harper. "How did you manage the replay?"

"There's a little computer server in the Jeep. It picks up the signal from the boat and then relays it here. It also records any of the cameras if the sensors are activated."

"Wow," said Harper. "What's the range?"

"Maybe ten miles if the weather's good. I could use a satellite, but that would cost me. But then the range would be anywhere on the planet. If we get into a tough situation, I can access a satellite for recon also."

"Wow, that really *is* James Bond stuff," Jill said.

Grant smiled modestly, "Well, it's fun for me. I've been messing around with electronics since I was a kid. All this stuff is really pretty simple."

"I better watch my step around you, Bud," Sara joked.

"That's right, Sister," said Grant, winking at her.

"I wonder who that guy was," Jill said, tension in her voice. "And what was he looking for?"

"Unfortunately, it was too dark to get any kind of resolution on his face. But I don't think he'll be back. He's going to be walking funny for a couple of hours, though."

The rest of the evening at Tampico's was fun but subdued. The intruder aboard the *Keuka Maiden* had put them on notice.

Around ten, Sara dropped Jill off in front of her house. Carrying the box of CDs, she opened the front door and stepped inside. Something was wrong. She had left a light on in the living room, but now the living room was completely dark. She nervously retreated to the sidewalk, pulled out her cell phone, and called Harper's number.

"I think someone's in my house," she said.

"Stay on the sidewalk, or go over to Sara's. We'll be right there," said Harper.

First my boat, and now my house. This is no good. This is no good.

She paced the sidewalk, looking around, wondering what would happen next. Sara noticed Jill on the sidewalk and crossed the street to join her friend. "What's the matter?"

"I think someone's in my house," Jill replied tensely.

"Oh shit," Sara said softly. No sooner had she said this than they heard Bud Grant's jeep roaring the wrong way up Sixth Street, squealing to a stop in front of Jill's house. She was standing on the sidewalk, with Sara, waiting for them.

"You OK?" asked Harper.

"Yeah, fine," said Jill. "I left a light on in the living room, and when I got here, there was no light."

"Front door unlocked?" asked Grant.

"Uh, yeah," said Jill. "I mean, I unlocked it. You can go in."

Harper and Grant moved up the steps and in through the front door. A full minute passed while the women waited anxiously on the sidewalk.

"Wonder what's going on," Sara whispered.

"Me, too."

Suddenly they heard a large thump coming from inside the house and a man's voice crying out.

"Oh, *shit*," exclaimed Sara, and Jill's eyes grew wide with anxiety.

Harper appeared at the front door and stepped out on the porch. He held a lightbulb in his hand.

"Dead," said Harper, smiling. "Dead lightbulb in your lamp."

"What was the thump we heard?"

Grant emerged through the front door, saying, "That was me, tripping on your goddamn *coffee table!*"

Sara and Jill laughed.

Grant limped down the steps and rubbed his leg.

"Your house is clean, electronically speaking. No bad guys, no bogeys, no hidden mics or cameras," said Grant, who held up a small electronic device.

"The bulb just burned out," said Harper.

"Oh gosh. I had you guys come over here for nothing," said Jill. "Never occurred to me, considering . . ."

"You did the right thing," said Harper.

"You're really a Mr. Wizard, aren't you?" said Sara, looking admiringly at Grant.

"Not only that," began Grant, "I'm also a lousy cook."

"Well, I happen to be a very good cook," said Sara.

"Really?" said Grant.

"Yes, really. What do you like to eat best?"

"Oh . . . pie," smiled Grant.

Jill was tired, but she felt she had better go *out* before the trip. If she were sailing into danger, maybe Mata could advise her—one way or the other.

The guys had been terrific, coming over to help her like that. She reflected on the fact that she didn't have many friends. She knew a lot of people, but they had their own lives and families. When she was with Dave, that had been different; they were a couple, and they did things together. They saw other couples in town, sometimes for cards, sometimes for a boat ride, sometimes just to hang out on someone's back deck and have cocktails. Dave had a couple of friends from Chevrol, but they didn't socialize with them, except for the blowout Christmas party every year at the Lafayette.

But now, as a single woman, Jill was often the third wheel at social gatherings, and there were precious few single men around Marietta. She remembered Sara's ongoing complaint: there were no decent single men in Marietta. She hoped that Harper and Grant would stick around, too. It was maybe the most comfortable relationship she'd ever had—no strings, no sex, no demands, no laundry. They all had their own lives, and she liked it that way. She loved her solitude, now that she was sober enough to appreciate it.

That was another thing. She had wasted months of her life in an alcoholic stupor. The house had gone to hell, and she was near death herself. But thank God for Sara and Cathy. They got her back on her feet again.

Then she thought of Dr. Singh. She hadn't seen him, and he was probably wondering what happened to her. Well, maybe she would call him when she got back; *if* she got back.

In her bedroom, Jill lowered the blinds and put the box of CDs on the bed. Then she went into the bathroom to wash her face, brush her teeth and hair, and change into her old cotton flannel

230

CHAPTER SEVEN

nightgown. Cathy had given it to her two Christmases ago and had worried that maybe Jill wouldn't like it, that it was too dowdy. But Jill liked it for that very reason; it had little flowers and ribbons on the top and around the neck, and little embroidered daisies of pink, yellow, and white. It made her feel more feminine than the black lacy teddy that Dave had given her. They had seen *Working Girl* with Melanie Griffith and Dave had been quite taken with the lingerie Melanie wore. And, Jill remembered, in the movie, Melanie's character made the observation that only men want women to wear lingerie and see-through underwear. Most women, at least the women Jill knew, preferred cotton. And once a woman has passed forty, see-through *anything* is a liability.

But Jill was in good shape for her age. She didn't know why; she sure didn't exercise or go to the Y like a lot of women she knew. She just managed to stay an even 120 lbs. which, for her 5'5" frame, gave her a nice proportion.

She padded back to the bedroom, locking the door behind her, and crawled onto the bed. The bedside clock read 11:04 p.m. She took the *Discovery* CD out of its case and popped open the CD player. She inserted the disc and reached for the headphones.

She lay back, pushed the button, and relaxed completely as she heard the avuncular voice of Robert Madison beginning the preparatory process.

She had barely managed to get to the *ahhh* part of the recording when the vibrations took hold and she floated right out of her sleeping form.

I love this.

Jill ascended straight up through the ceiling of her bedroom,

231

out through the roof, and floated over the twinkling lights of Sixth Street. The sky had cleared, and the stars and moon were in bright evidence. She stretched her arms out and zoomed skyward. Up, up! *High!*

She was far above southern Ohio, able to perceive the curvature of the earth, and the towns in the surrounding counties. It all looked so peaceful and sweet to her.

Then she heard a sound—what was that?

Approaching her from the southeast was a commercial airliner and, as it drew near, Jill flew right alongside, waving at the passengers, but they obviously didn't know she was there. As the landing gear swung down, Jill gracefully turned and headed southeast.

Flying is the only way to fly.

She thought of Mata and wondered if she might shed some light or offer some advice before they all set sail the next day.

Then it happened again: the black tunnel, the dizzying speed. She was getting used to it now, but she still didn't like it.

It seemed to last an unusually long time, adding to Jill's discomfort. Then the vista brightened, and Jill saw swirling clouds or vapors, similar to an airplane traveling through fog.

Then the vista cleared and she saw Mata standing by some old stone buildings on the edge of a desert. Mata didn't look quite the same, but Jill knew it was her.

"Hello, Jill," Mata said, nodding her head and smiling in greeting.

"Hello, Mata. I was hoping to see you. Where are we? What is this place?"

"This is a very old land; this is where much of what is recorded in your Bible occurred. The Dead Sea is just beyond."

"I see," said Jill. "So are we back in the early times?"

"Something like that," Mata answered. "There is an old friend who would like to see you."

From a nearby low stone building emerged a pleasant-looking man with long, wavy chestnut hair and a beard. He wore a light blue robe and sandals. Around his waist was a tied rope. He had an open, happy face, and he smiled warmly at Jill.

"Do I know you?" said Jill.

The man smiled and said, "Oh, yes. You and I have been together many times, though you may not remember it now. You and I have had many names and faces over the centuries. We were never related as family, but we knew each other and profited by the comfort and friendship we gave to each other. And here we are again. I remember you very well; I remember your spirit."

Jill looked down, not sure what to say.

The man looked around at the surrounding vista.

"During this historical period, Mata was known as Mary. I was called Yeshua. You were Rebecca. But those are just names. Inside, each of us is the same. The outer expressions change, but the soul remains ever constant and united with everything and everyone."

"It does?" asked Jill.

The man smiled and nodded, "Yes. But most people can't perceive this. They think that their little lives on the earth plane are all there is, so they miss the larger picture of creation. But things are changing, as people become more aware, more connected. There has been tremendous progress recently, and this has been good."

"Is this about religion? I don't go to church very much," said Jill, slightly nervous.

"No," the man said. "This is not about religion. Religions can sometimes be helpful in alleviating the suffering of others, but the best religious leaders are actually *spiritual* leaders, because they can show others how to find their connection to . . . *everything*. But many people do this on their own."

"How do they do that?"

"There are different ways. For some, meditation can be useful. In your case, the recordings you use can accelerate this process. And, with your ability to temporarily separate from the physical, you are learning a great deal. You are doing this now. Others have also done this. That is one of the reasons Mata brought you to the Hall of Records, so that you might get a glimpse into your previous lifetimes and the progress you have made."

"Is there anything I am supposed to do?" asked Jill.

"What you are learning now is to remember who you *are*. This may seem a little obvious, but most people have no idea who they are. They think their name or their physical existence on the earth defines them. But this is an error. Humanity will only progress when all persons are able to learn about their true natures for themselves and then to see that they are part of the whole of creation."

"But how does someone actually do that?" asked Jill.

"It takes time. First, they have to dig deep. This can be done through prayer and meditation. Then they have to notice what is happening to them on a spiritual level. Information sometimes comes through in the form of coincidences—which are *not* random occurrences. Then they have to *pay attention* to the information and act on it. Fortunately, though, more enlightened beings are coming into the earth plane now. These are people who are able to read the signs and get the information their souls need. You have met someone who is similarly enlightened, and you will meet more."

"Who is that?" asked Jill.

"Oh," smiled the man. "Why spoil the surprise? There is much to be said for discovery."

Jill nodded. "I guess . . . you're familiar with the situation I am in? I have met some new . . . friends, and we are about to embark on a mission on the river. Is this something we should do?"

The man looked down for a moment and then spoke.

"If one is able to see what is truly happening, in a larger sense, then your mission is important. Big tasks are accomplished with small steps. You have taken a step now, and it is important that you persevere with the others. As you progress, you will come to see the importance of your undertaking. You will be successful, but only up to a point. Then you will need new friends to help you. The friends you now have will remain as constant and good friends, but that is in the future."

"Do you mean other lifetimes?"

"No. Within this lifetime, there is much for you to accomplish. You will face quite a few challenges. But, as Mata told you, you are guided and you are loved."

"So, I should go on the boat trip tomorrow?" asked Jill. "I've been nervous about it. I'm worried that something bad might happen."

The man spoke, "If you don't go, then you will never know what might have been accomplished. It's important that you persevere, as I said."

"Can you protect me?" asked Jill.

"No. Only you can do that. We can offer guidance, encouragement, and love. But we do not interfere or intercede in someone's earth-life experience. You are likely to face some challenges, even some danger. How you handle the situations will be a test for you."

"Could I be killed?"

"Of course. That possibility always exists. But you could be killed driving your car. However, even if you are, you will come back again—with new challenges."

"That's not much comfort," said Jill. "And the others could be killed also?"

Mata spoke, "If you dwell on the negative possibilities, then you give them the energy to manifest. Stay focused on the highest possible outcome. That's the best advice we can give you: stay *positive*, Jill."

Jill reflected on what they said. It was all up to her.

"Is there anything else I should know? Or do?" asked Jill.

"Yes," smiled the man. "Get a good night's sleep."

CHAPTER EIGHT

The day dawned bright and clear—a perfect summer's morning. A light breeze stirred the trees and wafted in through Jill's open bedroom window.

Within thirty minutes, Jill had showered and changed into khaki shorts, a navy blue T-shirt, and Keds. As she brushed her hair, she reflected on Mata and the interesting man. Their words resonated within her, and she felt excited and a bit anxious: it was all up to her.

She also felt she was living in two worlds that had little to do with each other. The physical world felt real and solid, and the out-of-body world still felt like a dream. But then, she had been able to communicate with James, hadn't she? And Bud was there, too, so there had to be an intersecting reality to both worlds. If this all were a kind of test, she wasn't feeling especially prepared or even worthy. Staying positive would take some effort.

Harper and Grant were already onboard the *Keuka Maiden* when Sara and Jill walked down the dock, a few minutes before eight.

"I love to see people on time," Harper said with a smile.

"Yeah, well, I love to be seen," Sara said as she climbed into the back of the boat.

"You guys get gas?" asked Jill.

"Sure did. Didn't know the tank held 120 gallons!" laughed Harper.

Grant emerged from the cabin and said, "I put in synthetic oil and stuck a flow regulator on the gas line, so we'll get great mileage with the boat now. Also, she was running way too rich. So, I think you'll find that you won't have to fill up quite so often."

"Wow," said Jill. "Can you do that with my car?"

"*May-be*," smiled Grant.

Jill looked to see if the Bayliner was still nearby. It was gone. She had forgotten to check the list for Harper, the one she had seen when she visited the boat.

When she told him, he replied, "I was able to 'see' it this morning from home. I have the first few stops, and that's really all we need. We can track it from there. They haven't gone far."

The big MerCruiser motors roared to life, and soon the *Keuka Maiden* was easing back from the dock. Grant was at the helm, and Sara sat across from him, perched on one of the chairs. When they had cleared the dock, Grant swung the wheel and slid the throttle forward. The *Keuka Maiden's* bow raised slightly as the motors began to roar, its twin 165-horsepower engines digging into the water. Jill and Harper stood on the back deck watching

Newport recede into the distance. When the *Keuka Maiden* had reached the mid-river point, Harper and Jill moved inside and sat at the galley booth in the cabin.

On shore, watching the *Keuka Maiden* depart, was David Lawrence. When the boat had moved into open water, he set down his binoculars and picked up the telephone.

As the small group of friends moved upriver, they passed a small sternwheeler, no doubt bound for Marietta and the festival.

"Those are very interesting boats," Harper said. "I'm glad to see they still get some use. Not very efficient, though."

"Yeah," Jill replied, "but they're pretty."

Harper looked at Jill earnestly, "Are you still worried?"

"Sure, but I'm trying to stay positive."

"That's all any of us can do."

Harper picked up his paper and looked at the list of towns.

"What we have to do, I guess, is find the *Salty Dog*. Grandview, West Virginia, is the first stop, according to this. Then a place called Sistersville."

"Do you want me to . . ." Jill pointed upward.

"Not yet," smiled Harper. "I could take a look, too, but it's a nice day, and the boat doesn't have much of a lead on us. Then again, it may have changed course, so maybe I will take a look."

"Can I watch you?" said Jill.

"I don't mind. Not much to see."

Harper took out a piece of paper and a box of pencils from a cabinet; he also took out his MP3 player and his headphones. He sat comfortably at the table, the earphones sending alpha signals into his brain.

"Would you mind sitting on the couch for now?" asked Harper.

"No problem," Jill replied, and she quickly moved over from the booth seat.

Harper sat for a few minutes with his eyes closed. Then he began to draw—loopy lines as he had done before.

"It's on the east bank, farther up. In West Virginia. Just this side of a place called Grandview. I think that's the first delivery stop. I'm seeing three people on board."

He began to draw little rectangles, as before.

"It's a drug drop, I'm pretty sure."

Jill nodded.

Harper sat quietly, holding the pencil. Nothing much more was coming. Then he cocked his head and drew again.

"There's a little building—a house, a shack, a store—on the shore near the docks. This is a small marina, a little bigger than the one in Marietta. There's a gas pump, too."

Jill was impressed.

"You could see all that?"

Harper nodded, "I think it's right. But I couldn't see faces, and I can't tell the number of kilos they have stowed under the back deck. Maybe you should go take a look. You'll be able to see what's going on better than I can. And it might be a good practice run, just in case."

"In case of what?" asked Jill.

"I don't know. The unexpected."

"OK. I'll give it a try. Be interesting to see if I can do it as easily as at home. I'll use the front cabin. Wish me luck," said Jill as she moved forward.

She found the MP3 player with earbuds lying on one of the beds. She grabbed it and moved back through the boat to ask Bud how it worked.

Emerging into the daylight, Jill saw Sara sunning herself on the back deck, holding a reflective visor under her chin. Grant was at the wheel, contentedly piloting the *Keuka Maiden*.

"How do I work this thing?" Jill asked, holding up the little player.

"OK," said Grant. "First, put in the earbuds. They are marked left and right, though that may not matter. Then you hold it toward you so can see the little window."

Jill looked and there was a little window, but it was dark.

"You hold this top button down for about three seconds, and it will come on. Turn it off the same way. See if you can do it now."

Jill put in the earbuds and then held down the button. The little window began to glow with a blue light, and Jill soon heard the familiar tones of a babbling brook.

"Got it, thanks," said Jill. "This sounds good."

"Good luck, Jill."

Jill took a quick look at the river. It was pretty and serene. People were fishing off docks on the West Virginia side, and it was a peaceful morning to be on the water.

She moved quickly down the steps, through the cabin, and into the forward berth. She closed the door, took the sleep mask out of her duffel, and then settled herself.

She looked at the player and pushed one of the buttons with an arrow so it would restart the recording from the beginning. Then she settled back.

Hope this works.

She listened to the voice of Robert Madison: *You are going on a Voyage of Discovery . . .*

That's it, all right.

It was not long before Jill was floating upward through the bow deck, pausing slightly over it. It was a slightly odd sensation, knowing that her body lay beneath her, fast asleep, or "mind awake, body asleep," as Mr. Madison had said.

As she floated higher above the *Keuka Maiden*, Jill became aware of another boat behind them, maybe 600 yards astern, that was keeping an even pace with the *Keuka Maiden*. It was quite large, with a black hull, and seemed to be a very expensive yacht. It was probably just coincidence, but she decided to take a look anyway.

She flew quickly back past the boat, circled around, and approached its back deck. The name *Sea Shadow* was painted on the transom in flowing gold script. She couldn't identify the boat's make, but it was big—maybe 90 to 120 feet long—and had teak decks over its shiny black hull. The expanse of black, one-way windows prevented anyone from looking in. On top of the boat were many antennas and a revolving disc—was it radar?

She floated in through a spacious enclosed back deck into a large living room. It had exquisite tan furnishings and resembled a cozy den in an expensive home. There was a full-service bar, several comfortable chairs, a desk, bookshelves, and an impressive stereo system. On the desk was communications gear. Jill didn't know what it all was, but it looked high-tech. Behind the desk, in a rosewood wall case, was a rifle with a scope and, beneath it, a silver pistol with pearl handles.

In one of the chairs sat the woman with red hair Jill had seen previously, and two other men sat nearby. One had short-cropped gray hair; the other was a thin man with short blond hair.

The sight of the woman with red hair made Jill uneasy. The woman was obviously involved with the drugs, Robert Guerra, and the murder of his son. And now here she was, aboard the *Sea Shadow*.

The man with gray hair was G. Robert Webster, sixty-five. He was slender and wore a white shirt, open at the neck, light gray slacks, and expensive shoes. Originally from Pensacola, Florida, Webster had enlisted in the Navy during the Vietnam conflict, and had, through his various contacts, managed to be reassigned to the drug smuggling initiatives of the CIA—an association that had continued over the decades. For a time, his home base was Washington, D.C., and he had become an attorney; he was later disbarred for attempting to "unduly influence" a federal judge. But Webster didn't care; he had no interest in practicing law. The CIA and its drug business returned a comfortable living and afforded him protection from law enforcement. In short, Webster was "untouchable" . . . with vast resources and influence.

Because he was savvy and in the loop about many top-secret activities, Webster was able to travel in important circles within the intelligence communities. Though he did not have the highest, or Q-5, clearance, he was still informed of the goings-on of some highly classified activities. Among these activities were plans to undermine the stability of the United States and to help pave the way for a one-world government. For this to come to fruition, however, millions of dollars were required, and hiring trained agents to infiltrate the courts, military, and financial institutions took enormous time and patience. Webster and his associates had increased their activities during the Reagan years; these activities had continued to grow during the successive administrations.

Webster was tasked with overseeing the drug trafficking on the Ohio and other rivers. From his gleaming yacht, full of sensitive electronic gear and weaponry, Webster cruised the waterways of the United States, making sure that the operation went smoothly and that large amounts of cash continued to flow. It was Webster who had recruited David Lawrence, who oversaw the operation on the Ohio River. It was a big responsibility, but so was returning $160 million a year in cash.

As important as Webster was to the operation, there were higher-ups to whom he reported. Beyond that, his access was restricted. Once a month, he would drive from Pittsburgh to Washington with a suitcase full of money. He would meet his contact, a United States congressman, in a suite at the Willard Hotel. They would spend the evening together, dining with beautiful rented women. The next morning, the cash would leave the United States in a diplomatic pouch, destined for a London Bank. That was all Webster knew, and all he was allowed to know.

Because the covert CIA/drug operation had been so successful, much progress had been made: governments had been toppled, dictators established, the prices of various commodities had been fixed so that windfall profits would ensue. The natural resources of virtually every country had been plundered, and the locals had been given no explanation or recourse. Many of the large pharmaceutical companies were also involved—kicking back to the operation in exchange for favorable FDA rulings. It was the same with the oil companies: record gasoline prices resulted in vast amounts of cash in exchange for the rescinding of any price controls to help the consumer. In short, the world was being wantonly plundered, without regard for those who suffered. Many third-world nations were deemed to be populated by "useless eaters" who were of no value and who were, therefore, dispensable.

Overseeing these operations from a small building in The Hague was the Council. Its operation was unstoppable. There was no government or force on earth that could intimidate or oppose them. Their worldwide holdings were in the many *trillions* of dollars. There were no secrets from the Council, for, through their various intelligence networks, they knew precisely what was going on in every country, city, and locale. If there was any resistance—no matter how seemingly insignificant—it was brought to a swift, and often violent, end. But, despite their astonishing intelligence capabilities, the Council did *not* know about the four people aboard the *Keuka Maiden*.

As Jill hovered in the beautiful suite on the expensive boat, she listened to their conversation and was able to discern that they were aware of the *Keuka Maiden* and were mildly concerned.

"Probably just a pleasure cruise," said Webster, revealing large yellow teeth as he spoke. "I think Lawrence is getting a bit paranoid."

"Then why would they have that techno stuff aboard? I nearly got killed," said the thin blond man.

"Yes," said Webster slowly. "If what you say is true, then they have some pretty sophisticated gear, which is highly unusual for a pleasure craft. It might be worth a look."

The thin blond man was named Dan Heberle, a 25-year-old English national. He spoke again.

"Well, Bob, I never experienced anything like *that* before."

"What was it, exactly?" asked Webster.

"It was this . . . *sound*. I can't describe it. I couldn't stand up. It just made me fall. I lost all control."

Webster shook his head.

"OK, I'll see if we can run some kind of scan on that boat. But we'll need to get a little closer."

Webster moved to the desk and pressed a button on an intercom.

"Close the distance between us and the *Keuka Maiden*. Make it 200 meters."

"Right," came the reply from the bridge. "Five minutes."

Jill thought about returning immediately to the *Keuka Maiden* but then thought, no, she had enough time to check out the *Salty Dog* and get back to the others.

She floated up and quickly past the *Keuka Maiden*, flying up the river, keeping an eye out for the *Salty Dog*. She didn't know how far Grandview was, but she figured it wasn't terribly far. Harper said the West Virginia side, so Jill hovered just above the bank, passing houses and docks, flying fast.

She spotted the *Salty Dog* in a no-wake zone, slowing down to pull into a small marina outside Grandview. She floated down to the boat and onto the back deck, the same deck on which she had seen Robert Guerra some days before.

At the helm was the bald fat man she had seen previously when the kid was killed and again at the racetrack meeting with Robert Guerra in the office.

Who was this guy? If Guerra was truly with the FBI, then maybe he was setting them up in a sting?

In the cabin, two other men were preparing for the delivery. One was holding a small blue gym bag, as the other took four bricks from the aft compartment and placed them in the bag. Jill saw there were many more bricks—heroin? cocaine?—in the back of the boat.

Then the two young men went topside. One went along the edge to the bow to throw the front line; the other went to the line at the transom.

The boat's throttle was cut, and it glided into the dock, the pilot quickly revving the motors in reverse. The *Salty Dog* murmured into the dock near the gas pump, bumping slightly against the black cushions of old tires. A boy wearing cutoffs and a T-shirt had come out of the little house on the shore and waited for one of the men to throw him the front line. He caught it easily and cleated the boat to the dock. One of the young men from the *Salty Dog* leapt from the back of the boat and tied the back line.

"Hey, Ernie. Need gas?"

"Yeah," said the bald fat man. "Store open?"

"Yeah, she's in there. How much gas you want?"

"Fill her up," said the bald man.

Ernie? Robert Guerra's brother-in-law?

As the young man got the hose from the gas pump, Ernie climbed out of the boat, and quickly moved down the dock toward the little store, carrying the gym bag.

Jill floated behind him.

The store—typical for boaters—resembled a Nantucket shanty: gray clapboard exterior with peeling white trim and small-pane windows. Inside the creaky screen door was a small grocery store. There was a large cooler full of beer and soda along the back wall; a shelf near the door had a coffeemaker with Styrofoam cups and stirrers beside it. On the right wall was a rack of bobbers, sinkers, and other fishing gear; beneath that were shelves of T-shirts, sweatshirts, and caps. A center aisle housed a small grocery section. Near the front counter was a rack of newspapers, and behind the counter were cigarettes and used paperbacks.

A grim-faced woman of 70 stood behind the counter and nodded to Ernie as he entered. Her name was Jocelyn Menard, but everyone called her Tuffy.

"Morning," she said. "Got something for me?"

Ernie put the bag on the counter, and the woman whisked it away to a back room. While she was gone, Ernie looked around the store, hands in his pockets.

Soon the woman reemerged with the gym bag. It had been emptied of its contents and refilled with cash. She set it on the counter and said, "It's all there. You can count it if you want."

Ernie shook his head.

"We'll count it on the boat. You never stiffed me yet."

"I am an honorable person," she said grimly.

"That you are, Tuffy."

The boy entered the store and said, "You took a little over sixty gallons. That's four hundred and thirty dollars."

Ernie took a wad of bills from his pants pocket and counted out four hundred and forty dollars.

"Don't have any tens. Sorry."

"OK," Tuffy said. "You got a ten-dollar credit."

"Wait. Maybe I'll take one of your T-shirts."

"Help yourself," said Tuffy.

Ernie picked out a black tee that had a picture of a bass on the front. He held it up.

"How's this?" he asked, not smiling.

"Take it."

Then Ernie was out the door, heading back toward the *Salty Dog*, the dock creaking under his hefty weight. Soon the *Salty Dog* would be back on the river, headed for Sistersville.

I had better get back, thought Jill with a sense of urgency.

Jill stirred herself awake, the earbuds still playing the tones. She took a deep breath, smoothed off the eye mask, and held up the little player so that she could switch it off.

This thing worked pretty darn well.

Moving into the cabin, she saw Harper sitting, his arms folded across his chest, his eyes closed.

"James?" said Jill.

He breathed in sharply, opened his eyes, and looked at Jill.

"I was trying to follow you, but I couldn't," said Harper. "What did you find out?"

Jill related what she had seen in Grandview: the *Salty Dog* had made a delivery, and a woman in the store had bought four kilos.

"We ought to catch up with them pretty soon," said Jill. "But there's something else. We're being followed by another boat. It's huge, and the name is the *Sea Shadow*. They are very much aware of us and they have guns aboard. I think that the guy who broke into the *Keuka Maiden* last night—he's onboard also. I think they're planning some kind of scan. They have a lot of electronic stuff on the boat."

Harper nodded and got up, taking the binoculars.

"Hey, Bud," Harper called as he stood on the steps that lead to the helm. "Jill says that there's a boat following us that has some bad guys aboard, and they may try to scan us to see what kind of gear we have. Anyhow, they're aware of our presence."

Grant smiled.

"They won't see a thing. There are lead and copper plates around all the good stuff. Even the NSA couldn't see them. To any scan, we're just another boat with the standard gear. Oh, well the boat has a Loran unit, but that's nothing they'd be concerned with. No big deal. But maybe I will take a look and see what they have. Sara, could you take the wheel for a few minutes?"

Sara, happy to be involved, replied, "Sure thing, Bud."

She got up and moved toward the wheel.

"I just steer the boat, right?"

"Yup, that's it," Grant said as he went down the steps into the cabin.

"Want the binoculars?" offered Harper.

"No thanks. Got my own."

He opened the aft compartment and slid out a metal box. He unhitched the top, opened the lid, and took out a high-tech viewer. Then he closed the box and moved toward the steps.

Grant switched the viewer on and was soon targeting the boat following them. He whistled.

"Wow, that is one fine boat. It's a Benship, and they have all kinds of goodies onboard. I would *love* to see their gear."

"I wonder if there's drugs," mused Harper.

"I can't tell you that, but based on the antenna array, they have some super-sophisticated ComSat stuff, strictly military issue, and other stuff I've never even seen before. This is some kind of ship on our tail. "

"Interesting," observed Harper. "If they have that kind of gear, then we should watch our step."

"The *Salty Dog* is small potatoes," said Jill. "They're just the delivery boys. But I think Robert Guerra had a key role, since there were so many kilos at his house. The way I see it is . . . if they learned that he was with the FBI, that might be a reason to kill him. Or maybe they didn't know, and it was something else. Either way, the drugs got taken out of his house."

"Wonder where they are now," mused Grant.

"In a very safe place, I imagine," Harper said. "Jill, I need you to take another look at that boat behind us. You didn't go below, did you? You just stayed in the passenger area?"

"Right," said Jill. "Do you want me to go now?"

"Not yet," said Harper. "I want to take a look first. Maybe I can save you a trip."

"OK," said Jill. "While you're doing that, I need to call Cathy. She doesn't know I'm away, and I want to touch base."

"OK," said Harper, as Jill moved to the forward cabin and he moved to the galley.

Sitting at the galley table, Harper put on his headphones and started the MP3 player. A recording called "ThetaStream" began to send its powerful tones into Harper's brain. Before him was a piece of paper. He picked up a pencil and closed his eyes.

He sat in silent stillness for a full minute; then his pencil moved on the paper, making circles. Or was it the letter O? Harper's face suddenly registered alarm, and his mouth fell open in astonishment.

It can't be. Can it?

Stirring himself to normal consciousness, he rubbed his face, and then moved quickly to the helm doors.

"Bud, I need you to do something."

"Sure thing. Whaddya need?"

At that moment, Jill emerged, happy and buoyant.

"Hey, Cathy is going to be a field producer! It's just a tryout, but they like her at the TV station."

Harper turned and looked at her seriously.

"Jill, I need you to go out again. Right away."

Jill's smile vanished. They didn't want to hear about her daughter. Oh well.

"Sure. Why? What's going on?"

Harper looked at Jill, and then at Grant.

"I took a look at the boat. And . . . they are very aware of our presence, and we need to take action. Bud, can you disable their engines?"

"Probably," said Grant. "Unless they're using plasma or nuclear, which I doubt."

"OK, then. Please do that."

In the cabin, Grant opened the back hatch and pulled out a metal box. He raised its lid and took out a silver, circular device the size of a loaf of bread that had a small parabolic reflector on the top. It had dials, LEDs, and a couple of buttons. It also had a small port to plug in headphones.

"Let me borrow your headphones for a sec," Grant said over his shoulder.

"Right," Harper replied.

Harper moved to the table, unplugged the headphones from his player, and handed them to Grant.

Grant put on the headphones, plugged them in, and returned to the helm. He shouldered the gizmo so he could sight the boat, and then he used a dial to calculate its distance and speed. Listening carefully, Grant could determine the kinds of engines that were powering the large boat.

Harper watched with interest, then turned to Jill.

"Jill, I need you to do a complete sweep of that boat. But be *careful*. There is a possibility you could be detected."

"Are you serious?" asked Jill.

"Yes. The chances are slim, but you never know."

Jill, feeling a sudden return of anxiety, moved to the forward cabin. She lay on one of the berths, as before, and put the buds into her ears. She remembered what Mata and the man had said, that she was guided and she was loved; the feelings of anxiety slightly lessened. Then she put on the sleep mask and pressed the player's button.

It took her longer than normal to relax, but a few minutes later, Jill was out of body, circling behind the enormous boat. She floated in through the back and moved quickly through the engine room and several compartments: pantry, laundry, a large freezer, and other service areas. She could hear the quiet *chug-chug-chug* of the giant engines as she moved toward the forward compartments.

Wow, this is some boat.

There were no drugs to be found; at least, there were none on the lower levels. Next, Jill moved back to the middle of the boat and into a long corridor that had metal stairs going up. She floated upwards and came to another corridor. It had beige carpeting and recessed lighting and was far more luxurious. She began to float through the first of three bedrooms. They were being used, but the beds had been made. Men's clothes were draped on the back of a chair. The next bedroom was somewhat similar, as was the third, which had bunk beds but no sign of occupancy.

When she reached an aft compartment, a large room with an array of computers and technical gear, she saw three men. One looked like a distinguished professor; a second looked small and boyish; the third looked like a naval seaman, attired in khaki shirt, pants, and web belt. The small, boyish man suddenly looked in Jill's direction, as though he could see her. But then something caught his attention.

The *Sea Shadow* had suddenly become eerily quiet.

"What was that?" asked the distinguished-looking man.

"I'm not sure," the man in khaki replied. He paused for a few seconds before moving to a console. He pushed a button and spoke into a microphone.

"Bob, it sounds like the engines just shut down."

"I heard it, too. I'm going to the bridge," Webster said tersely.

"Can't believe it," exclaimed the man in khaki. "This ship was just checked out."

"Well, isn't this exciting!" drawled the small man. "Forty million bucks for a tub that conks out."

"*I did it!*" exclaimed Grant. "She's *dead!*"

"Yeah?" said Harper.

"Yup."

Harper peered at the big boat through the binoculars. It began to recede in the distance as the *Keuka Maiden* moved forward. Yes, Grant *had* done it.

"What did you do?" asked Harper.

"You *stopped* that big boat?" asked Sara incredulously.

"I believe *so*," said Grant. "Unless they cut their engines for the hell of it."

"What *was* that you used?" asked Harper.

"I call it my Gizmo," began Grant, "It's a high-voltage flux compression transformer coupled to an electromagnetic pulse generator."

Harper nodded. It was all Greek to him.

Sara nodded and said, "Sorta like a low-frequency sonic oscillator, with a piezoelectric transducer."

Grant replied, "Well, yes, but . . . *Hey!* You know about this stuff?"

"Yeah," smiled Sara. "Don't get to talk about it much, though. Mostly guys just look at my boobs."

There was grave concern on the *Sea Shadow*. For such a well-equipped vessel—with the most up-to-date technology in communications, satellite recon, and propulsion systems—it should *not* be dead in the water.

As engineers scurried below to get to the engines, Jill floated uneasily through the large, beautiful rooms; she remembered what Harper had said about possibly being detected.

If that happens, I'll just wake myself up and disappear.

She arrived at the bridge, where Webster and the young pilot were trying to figure out what had happened. The young man in khakis and a buzz cut looked at the dual computer screens—one on each side of the helm—and just shook his head.

"What caused this?" asked Webster as he peered at the readouts.

"Probably just a malfunction," the pilot said.

Webster pushed a button on the console and said, "Who's in the engine room?"

"Gilbert here, Sir. I'm here with Haidle. We just arrived and haven't had a chance to figure out what the problem is," came the reply.

"How soon can you fix it?" asked Webster, seething.

"As I said, Sir, we just got here. We'll know in a few minutes. I hope."

"Very well," said Webster. He punched another button on the console and barked, "Prepare a Hellfire for launch."

"Yes, sir. Right away," came the startled reply.

A Hellfire? Oh shit, what is that?

Webster picked up his binoculars and peered at the *Keuka Maiden*. It was now a speck in the river. Webster set down the binoculars, picked up the handset to the ComSat radio, and pushed a speed-dial button. Moments later, a ringtone chirped in a silver Acura.

When Jill emerged from the forward berth, Harper was seated at the galley table. He was clearly rattled.

"What's the matter?" asked Jill.

"Some old ghosts have come back to haunt me," he said grimly. "So. What did you find out?"

"Well, if there are drugs aboard, I didn't see them. It would probably take an hour to check out every nook and cranny."

"Yeah," nodded Harper. "I didn't see any drugs either. Doesn't mean they're not there, though. But I found out something important."

"What?"

"This operation is far, far more than simple drug smuggling. There are people from the government involved."

"Oh boy," said Jill. "Maybe we should just back off."

"Too late for that," said Harper. "They're aware of us. We can run, but we can't hide."

"But we have fast motors on this boat," pleaded Jill. "Why should we hang around and risk getting killed? And what's a Hellfire?"

Harper's expression became grave. "It's an antitank rocket. Very deadly. It would vaporize the boat and all of us. Is that what they have?"

"I think so. We better get out of here while there's still time!"

Harper held up a finger, indicating that Jill should be patient, and he moved quickly to the back deck to take a look. The *Sea Shadow* was a speck in the distance. He sighed with relief and returned to the cabin, where he saw Jill with an expression of anxiety on her face.

"We are way out of range, so don't worry . . . yet."

Jill took a deep breath, sat down at the table, and said, "OK. If you say so."

"So, what else did you see? Tell me about the people you saw."

Jill described Webster, the redhead, the skinny man with blond hair, and the various men in khaki. Then she described the professor and the small man with the high voice.

Harper nodded. He knew two of them all too well: *Miller and Petit.*

Meanwhile, Grant had resumed his duties as the *Keuka Maiden's* pilot, while Sara sat across from him, looking at him with barely concealed admiration.

"So how did you get interested in high-tech stuff?" Grant asked.

"My dad was an electrical engineer, and my high school science projects were always electrical stuff."

"Like what?" said Grant, pausing to look astern. There was no sign of the big boat. That was a relief.

Sara began, "Oh various things. I wired up our house to remote controls that would respond to vocal commands. So all you'd have to say is, "drapes closed," and the drapes would close. Or the lights would dim, or the radio would go on. Simple stuff, really."

"How old were you when you did this?" asked Grant.

"I don't know, maybe sixteen," smiled Sara, taking the binoculars and looking through the forward window.

"Very cool. I had no idea."

"Well," began Sara, "as I said, I don't talk about it much,

CHAPTER EIGHT

and I haven't done anything with electronics for a long time. Maybe ten years. Hey, I think I see the *Salty Dog*."

The *Salty Dog* was docked at a small marina about a quarter of a mile away. She stuck her head in the cabin and announced to Harper and Jill, "One *Salty Dog*, with mustard: dead ahead."

Harper moved up the steps and into the helm, taking the binoculars from Sara. He looked toward the *Salty Dog,* which was now docked. There was a man standing near it, but he was too far away for Harper to distinguish any features.

"Yeah, that's it," he said. "Looks pretty quiet. I think we should just pull in alongside and see what's going on."

"Think that's wise, Captain?" Grant asked.

"If the *Sea Shadow* were operational, I'd say no. But it's just us and them. Besides, we don't have to do anything. We can just buy some Cokes at the store."

"I'm about ready for lunch," Sara announced. "You wanna buy stuff? We brought all kinds of food along."

"Oh that doesn't matter," smiled Harper. "We'll just take a little look at the boat and act like we don't know anything."

"I bet you could get some bait there," Grant said.

"Yeah, that's the only thing we forgot," observed Sara.

A few minutes later, Sara was standing on the front deck of the *Keuka Maiden*, Grant on the back, each holding a line, ready to throw it to the young, pretty dock attendant. They had reached Sistersville, West Virginia, and Harper stood at the helm, cutting the power as the boat drifted in.

"Hope you guys don't need gas," the young woman called.

"That's OK, honey," yelled Sara. "We're just gonna get some bait. Ya got some?"

Sara flung the rope to the young woman, who drew in the bow and cinched it to an upright, four-by-four post.

"Well, yeah. We have regular lures and night crawlers," said the young woman. "I don't know if we have any minnows."

"That's fine, thanks," Sara replied.

The young woman moved down the dock toward the stern of the *Keuka Maiden* and caught the rope Grant flung to her. The *Salty Dog* was just across the dock, and nobody seemed to be around.

"How they bitin'?" asked the young woman.

"Well, bait helps enormously," said Grant.

"You'll find some inside," said the young woman as she moved down the dock toward a shabby, dark green house with white shutters.

The house was similar to the gray Nantucket-style shack they had seen near Grandview, but this one was much bigger. There was only one dock shaped like a sideways H. Its boards were gray and worn. The house was an old, rambling, two-story structure with an ice machine out front.

Jill emerged from the cabin and went up on deck. She waved to Sara.

"Going to the store?"

"Yep," Sara said as she edged her way down the side of the boat and jumped on the dock. She offered a hand to Jill, who climbed out.

"The girls are going to the store," Grant noticed.

"Should be OK," Harper said.

Grant looked at the *Salty Dog*, which lay on the far side of the dock.

"The *Dog* looks deserted. Wonder where the people are?"

"They can't be far."

Sara and Jill walked carefully down the dock.

"We'd better be real careful in here," Jill said quietly.

"Why? Are worms dangerous?" cracked Sara.

Jill stopped walking and put her hands on her hips. Sara turned to look at Jill, who looked tense.

"The people on that boat are *dangerous*. You know? They could be in here. We could be walking into a trap," Jill said.

"Oh shit, I'm sorry!" said Sara in a loud whisper. "Never even occurred to me."

"So we'll just stay close together, OK?"

Sara nodded.

"If there's any trouble, we make a dash back to the boat."

"*Absolutely*," said Sara, nervously.

Arriving at the house, Sara grabbed the screen door handle and held it open for Jill.

Inside, the little store was dark and cool. Florescent lights sputtered overhead; the place was dingy and old. It was empty except for an old man with a beard and a baseball cap.

"Can I help you girls?"

"Yeah," Sara said. "We need some bait. And . . . maybe a couple of Cokes."

"We got worms. In the back, near the sink," wheezed the old man.

"Do you have a ladies' room?" asked Jill.

"Yeah. Go to the back where the bait is; there's a hallway on your right."

Jill and Sara walked toward the back of the house.

Sara saw the bucket of worms. Over it was a sign that said, "Angle W Ranch—1 pint $3.50, 1 quart $5.00."

"Oh, they are really icky," Jill said, scrunching up her nose.

"I don't much like them, either, but if we're gonna catch . . ." Sara said as she extended her pale fingers into the slimy black loam.

"Be right back," said Jill as she headed down the dark hallway.

As she reached its end, a side door quietly opened, and something struck Jill hard on the head, knocking her unconscious. As she slumped, she was caught, lifted up, and silently carried up the stairs of the house. Sara, busy with the worms, heard nothing.

Aboard the *Keuka Maiden*, the radio crackled to life.

"This is the Sea Shadow *calling for Patrick Waterhouse . . . or James Lee Harper."*

Harper froze; Grant looked around.

"What?" Grant gasped. "How the hell did they find you?"

"*Shit*," Harper said, resigned.

"Fear not, my liege," Grant said as he leapt into the cabin, flung open the cabinet, and drew out his metal case. He picked up the Gizmo and leapt to the helm. Then he grabbed the microphone and held down the button on its side.

"I'm sorry, I didn't quite get your CQ. What was that again?"

"This is the Sea Shadow *calling for Patrick Waterhouse, or James Lee Harper. If he is there, put him on, please."*

Harper waited anxiously as Grant sighted the black boat. It was hard to see, more than a thousand yards out, and, because of the curvature of the river, there were trees in the way.

"Damn!" said Grant, "I can't get a clear line. Any idea who's trying to reach you?"

"Yes," said Harper. "My old friends from OSI. They found me."

"What would they be doing on that boat?" asked Grant.

"Remember, years ago, when we were 'skimming the pool?'"

Grant nodded, "Yeah."

"And I 'saw' some heroin shipments and knew that they were connected to the CIA? This was years ago; you probably don't remember."

"No, I remember," insisted Grant. "So your old associates were involved with that?

"Yeah. I see it now. They were providing covert intel. I stumbled onto it accidentally, and they must have recognized me. So when I had a sit-down with Miller, he was covering his butt. At the time, it never occurred to me that OSI was involved in drugs. And, of course, I stopped viewing that stuff afterward."

"I thought your, ah, death in Vegas would have thrown them off."

"It was a good effort, but they're pros. It probably only pulled them off course for a few days, if that."

"So now what?"

"We have to stop them."

"Right. How we gonna do that?"

"I don't know," Harper sighed.

He took the microphone from Grant and said, "This is Waterhouse."

A few seconds passed before the voice of Nathan Miller was heard.

"*Patrick!* We wondered what happened to you. Are you all right?"

"I'm fine, thanks," said Harper.

"Why don't you and your friends just come on back to the *Sea Shadow*, and we'll have cocktails?"

"Gee, that sounds swell," said Harper, "but we're kind of busy right now."

Sara suddenly bounced over the gunwale and landed on the back deck. Grant and Harper reacted in surprise.

"Hey! I got some worms!"

Grant waved to her that something serious was going on, and she quickly got the message.

"Well, what can I say?" came Miller's reply. "No matter. We'll meet . . . sooner or later."

"Maybe we will," said Harper. "If you can ever get your boat started."

"Repair crews are on it now. Thanks for asking about it, though," said Miller.

"Nice talking with you Nathan. Gotta go," said Harper. Then he replaced the mic on its hook.

"Well, at least we have a little time, with their boat out of commission."

"Yeah," Grant said, musing.

"Where's Jill?" Sara asked.

"I thought she was with you," Harper said.

"No, I thought she came back."

"You better get her," Grant urged. "We may have to leave soon."

"OK," Sara said as she climbed out of the boat and walked quickly down the dock toward the shabby green house. As she walked, she heard the overhead sound of a helicopter. She looked up. There it was: a tiny speck, high over the river. Then it disappeared from view.

On the bridge of the *Sea Shadow*, Webster was on a secure ComSat frequency, talking with an admiral at the Office of Naval Intelligence. The bridge windows were open, and a river breeze ruffled the lapels of Webster's shirt.

"Yes, Sir, this is a national security issue, and we need the launch code for one Hellfire missile. The boat represents a threat to the security of the United States."

"You are standing by," replied the voice.

"I am standing by, Sir," said Webster.

"You are authorized to destroy the target with a one-time use of a single Hellfire missile. You will have a window of one hour. After that, the launch code will be invalid."

"I understand," Webster said. He took out a pen and looked around for a notepad. There was none, but there were a few loose sheets of paper on the front of the console. He took the top one and wrote down the numbers the admiral had related: G57A02. Then he set it back where he could find it later.

"Got it. Thank you, Sir."

"Out," said the admiral.

The bridge radio crackled to life again.

"Mr. Webster, we found the problem with the engines, and we have to replace two rotors. We need the key to the supply closet."

"Be right down," said Webster, and he quickly left the bridge, heading down a flight of stairs.

Sara cautiously approached the dark green house and opened the front door. *Jill was right. Why hadn't I watched her more carefully? Will I be next?*

The old man with the baseball cap and beard sat behind the counter; now he was reading a magazine.

Sara nervously walked to the back of the store, looking around past the array of bait bins and down the hallway to the ladies' room. Pausing, she rapped lightly on the door.

"Jill?"

There was no reply.

Sara looked around anxiously and knocked again.

"*Jill!*"

Nothing.

Sara opened the door to the ladies' room.

It was empty.

Sara quickly returned to the store and looked briefly over the shelves, calling, "Jill?" Then she stepped over to the old man and asked, "Did you see where my friend went?"

"No."

Sara ran out the door and looked around the docks. Jill was gone; something *had* happened to her. Then Sara ran back down the gray wooden planks to the *Keuka Maiden* and yelled into the boat.

"Something's happened to Jill! She's gone!"

Harper looked at Grant and grimaced.

"Are you positive?"

"Absolutely," cried Sara. "She's not in the store, or the ladies' room. She wouldn't have just . . . gone off!"

"No, she wouldn't. Not her style," Harper said. "Somebody got her."

"Oh, this is not good," said Grant. "But they didn't get Sara."

"We still have some options," Harper said tensely.

He pulled out his cell phone and punched in a number.

"Who you calling?" asked Grant.

"The cavalry," said Harper. "Hope they're not fishing."

Below decks on the *Sea Shadow*, Webster was at the supply locker while two mechanics waited for him to open it.

"Glad you can fix the motors," Webster said.

"We're pretty sure we can do it, Sir. The rest of the engines looked fine. Just the rotors."

The door swung open, and one of the young men stepped quickly inside. There was only one box of the needed spare part. A young man took the box from the shelf and looked, without success, for another.

"Looks like we'll be on one engine, Sir," the young man said.

"Well, one engine is better than none," Webster said, closing the door as the young men moved aft toward the giant gray Ford diesels, carrying the replacement part.

Webster then moved down the hallway, passing a small elevator, to a forward compartment. He quickly arrived at the munitions locker, where a young man in a blue jumpsuit was waiting. He had a small dolly, ready to transport the three-foot-long Hellfire missile to a top deck, where a launcher assembly lay under a taut white tarp.

Webster unlocked the door and entered the munitions room. Around the edge of the room were metal cages housing various munitions and armaments. There were six Hellfire missiles on a tall rack in one of the cages.

Webster unlocked the cage, then unlocked one of the springs that held the missile fast to its berth. Webster and the man in the jumpsuit carefully lifted the missile and set it upright on the dolly. While the man in the jumpsuit strapped the missile to the dolly's top and moved out of the cage, Webster quickly closed the door. Then the men moved out of the munitions room, toward the waiting elevator.

"How long will it take you to prepare the missile for launch?"

"Ten minutes, Sir. I have to set up a back shield so the flame from the Hellfire doesn't scorch the ship and set her afire."

"Very well."

"We're kind of shorthanded now, Sir, so if you could help me, that would save us some time."

"OK," nodded Webster. "Let's go."

Jill awoke in darkness. Her eyes had been bandaged with something thick and tight, and a hard knot pressed into the back of her neck. Her hands were bound by a sturdy strap, and her ankles were also bound together. Her head throbbed with pain, and a rag had been shoved into her mouth. She had been knocked unconscious and then taken—where? She listened for any identifying sounds, but the house was dead quiet. Wherever she was, she had never been so terrified. A clammy, horrible fear prickled her; the sound of her heart pounded in her ears. It was *excruciating*. Nobody knew where she was, and these people— whoever they were—had killed before. Would they kill her?

Stay calm stay calm stay calm stay calm!

She immediately thought of Harper and Sara and Bud Grant. They were probably looking for her right now. They were highly perceptive; they'd figure it out . . . wouldn't they?

She had only one option, and she knew it: she had to— somehow—get *out*. Her past attempts had been fruitless. Calling Mata would be of no use.

She began to breathe deeply, trying to make herself relax. She imagined hearing the soothing voice of Robert Madison: *You are going on a voyage of discovery. All you need do . . . is to listen . . . and to pay attention. As you listen to the soothing sounds of the stream, make yourself as comfortable as possible—on your back, on your side—whatever is best for you . . .*

"Ever done this before?" asked Webster, as he watched the technician wheel the dolly toward the launcher. Another man removed the launcher's white tarp and stowed it.

The man in the jumpsuit replied, "Not from a ship, Sir. Only on land, from the back of a Hummer. It's pretty much the same."

"Good," said Webster, as the men gingerly took the Hellfire missile from the dolly and gently loaded it into the steel-framed launcher that would hold the projectile.

"You have the launch code?"

"Yes, it's on the bridge. We'll fire from there."

"Yes, Sir."

Jill was quickly descending into a relaxed, altered state, reminding herself that she was guided and loved. She imagined that she was hearing the tones as she had so many times before. She held the intention of lifting . . . *out.*

Nothing happened.

Harper and Grant stood before the old man in the shabby green house. Harper began to speak in an offhand manner.

"Excuse me," began Harper. "We're trying to find our friend. Pretty girl who used the restroom. Any idea where she might be?"

"Nope."

"What about the people on the other boat, the *Salty Dog?* Any idea where they are?"

"Nope. There's a parking lot out back. Mebbe they went there."

"Right," said Harper, as he and Grant went back out the door and around the corner of the building toward the parking lot. There were only a few cars and no sign of Jill.

They looked up at the house.

"Think we should go in?" Grant asked.

"Not yet. Maybe we can find some answers on the *Salty Dog.*"

"OK," Grant said as they quickly moved back toward the docks. When they had rounded the corner, Lawrence sat upright in his car and reached for his ComSat phone.

"Any sign of her?" asked Sara as Harper and Grant jumped aboard the *Keuka Maiden*.

"No," said Grant, as he nodded to the *Salty Dog* across the dock. "But I bet *they* know."

"Let me take care of this," said Sara, as she climbed out of the *Keuka Maiden* and crossed the dock.

"Sara!" yelled Grant, "I don't think that's a good idea!"

"I have to do *something*," Sara insisted as she waved and then stepped onto the back deck of the *Salty Dog*.

"You are going on a voyage of discovery . . . all you need do is to relax . . . let go . . ."

At these imagined words, Jill felt her body relax and sink into the cot below. She had achieved the preliminary state of relaxation. At home, it was easy, effortless. But now it required an astonishing effort of mind over matter. She maintained her relaxation, and the intention of relaxing further, to the point of letting go. She began to tone *Ahhh* quietly, which was nearly impossible with her mouth gagged. With each exhalation of *Ahhh*, she felt herself going deeper and deeper. Then, as before, the vibrations started . . .

Suddenly Jill was floating above her body—she had done it! *Thank God!*

She floated up, through the ceiling, through the roof, and into broad daylight. She had been taken to an upstairs room in the shabby green house. Now she had to find Harper and the others.

"I hope Sara knows what's she's doing," Grant said as he took his high-tech viewer and moved toward the back of the ship.

"This thing can scan for heat signatures, so if there are others aboard the *Dog*, we'll know."

Harper nodded. "Maybe you should scan the house. See if Jill's there."

"Yeah, yeah, in a second," Grant said as he aimed his viewer at the *Salty Dog*.

But before he could activate the viewer, something caught Grant's attention. The *Sea Shadow* had restarted and was sailing toward them. Grant turned the viewer to the large boat, which was now three hundred yards away and closing.

"Oh shit," said Grant. "That big boat is coming down fast."

"Can you knock it out again?" said Harper.

"Maybe," said Grant and he scrambled into the cabin to grab the Gizmo.

Suddenly, Jill floated in through the top of the *Keuka Maiden*.

"James! It's Jill! It's Jill!"

Harper cocked his head and looked up anxiously.

"Jill? Where are you?

"I'm right next to you!"

Grant looked up, his eyes wide.

"You OK? What happened to you?"

"They knocked me out. My body is upstairs in the house, but don't go there yet. I need to find out a few things!"

"Is Jill here?" asked Grant.

"Yeah!" yelled Harper.

"I think she better take a look at that ship!" cried Grant.

272

"We could be in harm's way very soon."

"Jill?" said Harper intensely, "Did you get that?"

"OK! Yes! Going!"

"She's going now," said Harper. Grant sighed.

Jill floated up and saw the large, ominous boat bearing down on the Sistersville marina. She quickly zoomed above the Ohio River and was soon directly above the *Sea Shadow*. She saw two men on the top of the boat, holding a small missile. The wind nearly blew the cap off the young man in a jumpsuit, but he caught it and pulled it down tight.

This is not good!

She floated near them as the rocket was secured into the track, its firing pin put into place and the wires to the computer secured to the control panel.

"Ready to fire, Sir."

"Very well. All I have to do is to punch in the numbers, and we'll blast the *Keuka Maiden* out of the water."

Not my boat!

Jill was suddenly overcome with rage: these two men, whoever they were, were lousy bastards. She began to scream and punch them with all of her might.

"You are not going to shoot my boat! You are not! I won't let you!"

Her punches and kicks had no effect, and the two men were oblivious to Jill's tirade.

"You lousy goddamn assholes! I will not let you shoot my boat! Do you hear! I will stop you! I will stop you! I will do everything in my power to stop you! Ahhhhh!!!"

"She's ready to launch," said Webster. "We'll go down to the bridge and fire it from there."

"Yes, Sir!"

"I won't let you! I won't let you! I will prevent this! You are not going to kill my boat and my friends!"

The two men quickly walked down the deck toward a hatch with a ladder leading down.

Enraged, Jill floated straight down to the lower deck and into the bridge. There were papers on the console. She didn't know what she was looking for, but she was in no mood to start reading! With massive energy, Jill began to wave her hands and arms around the bridge, causing a whirlwind of psychic energy. The few papers on the console—including the page with the launch code—went up into the air and swirled around her head.

"There! There! There! There!" screamed Jill.

She heard the footsteps of the approaching men in the corridor. As they opened the door, Jill kept waving her arms and yelling. Then, with the change in air pressure, Jill pushed the papers out the window with her hands. They floated out to the breeze and into the churning river below.

Fire this, Buddy!

"Oh shit!" yelled Webster as he tried to reach the paper.

It was too late.

"Damn!" exclaimed Webster.

"Was that the code, Sir?"

"Shut up."

Jill slapped the face of Webster repeatedly, screaming, *"I beat you! I beat you, goddamn it! I beat you!!"*

He felt nothing, but she didn't care: she had *triumphed*.

Still furious, Jill moved through the *Sea Shadow* to see what else might threaten her friends and her boat. In the aft room, where she had seen the professor and the small man, she found them seated at a table. The small man appeared to be remotely viewing something, but Jill could not tell what it was. The paper before him only had a few lines on it.

"Are you getting anything?" asked the professor.

"Two people aboard the *Keuka Maiden*."

"Well, she won't be there long. A rocket will be hitting her very soon."

"And . . . the girl is upstairs in the house. She's not going anywhere . . ."

"You're not going to do this! You can't do this! You're a jerk!"

The young man jolted back as though struck hard.

"What the *hell* is *that*?"

"What the hell is what?" asked the professor.

"I heard a woman yelling."

"What?"

"No! It stopped," said the young man, his face flushed. "That was weird. That was weird. I can do this."

He looked at the blank paper before him and began to clear his mind.

"You can't do this! You're a jerk! You're an asshole! I am not going to let you do this!"

Jill pushed the man's paper off the table. Both men sprang to their feet in alarm.

"Holy shit! What is this? What is this?"

"You're all through messing with me, you got that? You got that?"

Aboard the *Keuka Maiden*, Harper was at the cabin table, a piece of paper before him. He was sketching quickly: the house, the *Sea Shadow*, and the *Salty Dog*. There was only one person aboard the *Salty Dog*, but he could not determine who it was.

Hope it's Sara.

Targeting the house, Harper saw several people: one in the front, three in a back room. He could not tell who they were. On a side table were twelve white bricks, kilos of heroin.

The *Sea Shadow* was now within 100 yards of the Sistersville marina. Grant had his Gizmo ready and another high-tech device resting on the helm table.

Harper viewed the house again and noticed two motorcycles entering the parking lot behind it. There was another man in the parking lot. Friends or foes? He had better find out.

He leapt from the cabin seat, ran up to the helm, and out to the back deck; then he vaulted over the gunwale and began to run down the dock toward the shabby green house.

As Harper ran past Grant, Grant yelled.

"Hey!"

But Harper was halfway down the dock, headed for the house.

Grant, puzzling over Harper's sudden departure, waited for the enormous *Sea Shadow* to glide within range. He could see several men in khaki—standing on the front deck—holding automatic weapons. They had shouldered their weapons and were taking aim at the *Keuka Maiden.*

Grant shouldered the Gizmo, sighted it, and pressed a button. A loud wavering sound filled the deck of the *Sea Shadow.* The men in khaki began to wobble and keel over, their weapons clattering to the deck. Above them, on the bridge, the young man with the buzz cut also fell from sight.

Grant then picked up the other Gizmo, aimed it at the *Sea Shadow,* and held the button down for a long time. Aboard the large boat, the massive Ford diesel engine seized and ground to a stop.

"Now, they'll never work," thought Grant.

"Nice job, Bud!" yelled Jill. Then she lifted out of the boat and zoomed toward the parking lot and James Harper.

Rounding the corner toward the parking lot, Harper saw Lawrence get out of his car. Harper did not see the pistol Lawrence held behind the door. As Harper came into view, Lawrence swung up the pistol and took aim.

"James! Get down!"

Harper hit the ground hard as a shot rang out, the bullet missing Harper by several feet. Terry Buckman came up behind Lawrence, grabbed him by the collar and belt, and flung him backwards, high over the car. He splattered with a thud on the trunk. Then Preston Caldwell grabbed Lawrence, stood him up, and, with a large meaty fist, delivered a devastating jab to Lawrence's face, breaking his nose and knocking the man unconscious.

Terry picked up Lawrence's pistol as Harper cried, "Jill! Are you still here?"

"Yes, I'm right here."

"Are there people in the house?"

"*Yes, three. You go in the back door, it's the first room on the left. I am upstairs tied to a bed. You'll find me . . .*"

Harper turned toward Terry and Preston and motioned toward the back door of the house. They nodded and followed him.

At the door, Harper whispered, "I don't know if they're armed or not, but my friend Jill is upstairs, and she's tied down.

Harper, followed by Terry and Preston, entered the back of the house.

In a back room, the bald fat man said, "I think that's Dave now."

"Not quite," said Harper as he entered the room and held his weapon on them.

The bald fat man exclaimed, "Oh *shit*."

Harper handed the gun to Preston and said, "Keep these guys covered. I have to find Jill."

Emerging into the dark corridor, Harper looked for a staircase. It was at the end of the hall. He vaulted up the steps until he reached the top. Then he moved carefully down the hall. At last he came to a locked door. He stepped back, kicked it hard, and the door gave way.

Inside, Jill was bound to a cot. Harper quickly moved to her and took off the blindfold; then, using a pocket knife, he slit the bands that held her feet and wrists.

"Jill! Jill!" said Harper intensely. "Wake up!"

Groggily, Jill stirred to life.

"Are you OK?" asked Harper.

Jill took a breath, and started to cry.

"They were going to blast the boat! They had a missile! They were going to blow it up, and kill you and Bud, and . . . but I stopped 'em! I stopped 'em dead! They are such assholes!"

Harper helped her stand up, looking at her with deep admiration. Jill had saved them all.

"Give me a second," she said, rubbing her face and eyes.

"Take all the time you need," he replied. "We've got the others covered."

The both heard a noise outside.

"We'd better get out of here," said Jill.

"Yeah," agreed Harper.

Outside, two black sedans pulled into the parking lot, and four men in dark suits got out. Two moved toward the house; the other two, with pistols drawn, ran toward the docks.

As Jill and Harper walked down the stairs to the lower level, they heard voices.

"FBI. You're under arrest."

When Jill and Harper arrived at the back room, the federal agents had the bald fat man and two other men in handcuffs.

Harper said, "Those big guys are with me."

"Yeah, we know," said the agent. "We have photo IDs."

The other agent, a tall man with a chiseled face, turned to Jill and Harper.

"We knew about you, too. Agent Guerra told us you were investigating. Normally we do not like civilians interfering in Bureau affairs, but we couldn't reveal ourselves. Besides, it seems you handled the situation . . . adequately."

"Adequately," repeated Jill, looking toward Harper.

"There's something else," said the agent. "There's something big behind this drug-running operation; and we know that money is getting out of the country."

"Yeah? So?" asked Jill.

"So it's outside of our jurisdiction. That's all I'm saying. Here's my card if you should . . . hear anything."

Was that a hint?

"This bust will be reported to the media. We need to let people know that the Bureau is tough on drugs and that we're capable of stopping a major trafficking operation."

Harper shot a glance at Jill.

"So when the press talks to you, I wouldn't tell them very much about . . . well, you know. I'm sure you'll be fine. Anyhow, thanks for your help."

The agent shook hands with Jill and Harper and then nodded to the other agent, who led the suspects outside and into one of the cars.

Harper turned to Terry and gave him an affectionate slap on the shoulder.

"Good thing you showed up."

"A mere bag of shells," Terry said, smiling.

"Always good to have a little fun," nodded Preston.

"We're gonna get some barbecue. Wanna come?" asked Terry.

"We'll take a rain check," said Harper.

"Another time then," smiled Terry, his gold tooth glinting.

As Jill and Harper walked back toward the *Keuka Maiden*, Harper asked, "What happened on the boat? What did you do back there?"

Jill stopped walking, put her hands on her hips, and said, "Oh man, I was *pissed!* I don't know when I've been so angry. I'm still angry. I could *kill* those lousy bastards!"

"I'm glad you're on our side."

"I don't know if I want to talk to the press, either," Jill said hotly.

"Yeah, and they don't care. Whatever it is, it's just another story," observed Harper. "Too bad we don't know any reporters."

They walked silently for a few moments, and then Jill looked up.

"Hey, James, let me borrow your cell . . ."

When Harper and Jill reached the *Keuka Maiden*, there was an agent on the back deck talking with Grant.

"You *made* these devices?" he asked incredulously.

"*May-be*," smiled Grant. "I call 'em 'Gizmos.'"

The agent blinked. He was not pleased with Grant's casual demeanor.

"Do you have a permit to own and fire these weapons?"

"They're not weapons," Grant said hotly. "They're duck decoys."

Jill and Harper, stepping into the back deck, noticed that a U.S. Coast Guard vessel had arrived and had attached tow lines to the *Sea Shadow*. Coast Guard personnel were aboard the big boat and were rounding up those on board.

As Webster came into view, he was heard shouting indignantly, "I have top security clearance! I have Q-5 clearance!"

"Not for missiles, you don't," came the terse reply.

Jill, watching from the back deck, called to Webster. "*Hey, Bob!*"

He turned to see who it was.

Jill held up a finger.

In short order, the Coast Guard vessel had towed the *Sea Shadow* downstream and out of view. In a holding cell below were the twelve members of the *Sea Shadow* crew, including Webster, Petit, and Miller. Lawrence, the old man with the beard, the fat man, and the others were bundled into the back of the FBI vehicles and driven away.

Standing on the back deck of the *Keuka Maiden*, Grant said, "Well. I guess we had our fun for the day."

Harper nodded. "For the summer, I hope."

Jill said quietly, "I don't ever want to go through that again as long as I live."

"Yeah," replied Harper. "That was a little rough."

Grant spoke up, "On the bright side, the FBI might buy my Gizmos."

"Really? You're gonna sell 'em?"

"*May-be,*" said Grant. "But I'll want a lot of money for them."

"Oh God . . ." exclaimed Jill. "What happened to Sara?"

"Shit," moaned Grant. "She *was* on the *Salty Dog* at one point . . ."

Harper looked around.

"Oh damn," moaned Grant. "I should have kept a better eye on her. But in the excitement . . . What's the matter with me? If anything happened to her . . ."

"There she is," exclaimed Harper.

Grant wheeled around. There was Sara, chocolate smeared on her lips, holding several packages of cupcakes, walking down the dock toward the *Keuka Maiden*. Grant breathed a sigh of relief.

"Are you OK?"

"Oh yeah," smiled Sara. "I'm just fine. The FBI didn't lock the store."

Grant smiled and nodded; Harper and Jill looked at each other.

"Want a cupcake, Bud?"

CHAPTER NINE

The next afternoon, at the Newport Marina, Jill, Harper, Sara, and Grant reassembled on the back deck of the *Keuka Maiden*. Each had gotten spruced up for what would be a very special occasion. Standing on the dock was Jill's daughter Cathy, with an NBC video crew. Parked behind Lawrence's small office was a large van with a microwave dish on the top.

As the technicians were setting up, Grant whispered to Harper, "You know, this could be my big break. I may need an agent after this."

"Either that or a parole officer," quipped Harper.

"Shhh. *Guys*," Jill hissed.

"OK!" yelled Cathy. "That's good. We need a master shot of you all on the boat. Why don't you all stand in the back?"

Dutifully, Jill, Harper, Grant, and Sara moved back and stood in a row.

Jill was thrilled about Cathy; she was no longer a mousy college student, but an attractive, professional woman. She had her hair nicely cut and wore a smart navy suit with a crisp white blouse.

The NBC cameraman moved into position to get the best angle as the audio technician handed Cathy, still on the dock, a wireless stick mic.

"Okay," said Cathy, with a professional tone, "I am going to stand on the back deck with these people, and we'll do the interview from there. I'll do the voice-over narration from there, too."

Then Cathy took a pair of high-heeled shoes from a bag and flung them into the back of the boat. Then she climbed aboard, kicking off her sneakers and putting on the heels.

"Gotta look tall for this, Mom," Cathy said, smiling.

"You're six feet tall to me, Cath," replied Jill with a look of pride.

"Well, let's hope this goes well," Cathy said. Then she looked up to the stage manager and said, "OK. Let's do it, Mitch."

Mitch, standing on the dock and wearing a headset, began a countdown.

"Quiet please! Stand by people! All singing, all dancing, *in . . . three . . . two . . .*"

The stage manager pointed to Cathy and she began to speak, looking directly into the camera.

"Yesterday, a massive FBI operation halted the largest single heroin-smuggling operation in the United States. Nearly eight tons of drugs were seized by Federal agents in various locations in Ohio and West Virginia, and more are expected in the next few days."

"However, the FBI stated that they could not have accomplished their goal without the assistance and courage of four concerned Ohio residents . . ."

It was a little before 6:00 p.m. when Sara's red minivan pulled up in front of Jill's house.

"So, ya think we'll be on TV?" asked Sara.

"I don't know, Sara. This is her first big break, and it may not make the cut. At least that's what Cathy said. Maybe she was just being modest."

"When will you know? Will you call me?"

"Absolutely."

"Say, what'll we do with all the food we bought?"

"Oh, let's worry about that later," said Jill. "I'm going to take a shower, wash my hair, and just relax."

"Well, thanks for a real exciting couple of days," said Sara. "This was probably the most exciting thing that ever happened to me. Being taped for NBC news . . . and meeting Bud and James . . . well it's just *all* good. Maybe I'll make the guys a pecan pie."

"The way to a man's heart . . ."

"Yeah. Well, that's *one* way," laughed Sara, as Jill slowly walked up the steps to her house.

Jill entered her quiet house and walked straight back to the kitchen to get a glass of iced tea. She noticed a flashing light on her answering machine and pressed the button. Cathy's voice burst through the speaker.

"Mom, I don't know if you're back yet, but my story about you and the FBI is going to be the top story on *Nightly!* So if you're back in time and get this message, maybe you can see it? We're still on the road. We're staying at a hotel in Wheeling tonight, and then I'm going to NBC in New York on Monday. They loved the piece and want to talk to me about a full-time position! *Yay!* You have my cell number, right? Hope so! Love ya! Bye!"

Jill smoothed away a tear.

She glanced at the clock on the stove: 6:01. *NBC Nightly News* was broadcast at 6:30; she had time for a shower . . . but she wanted to tell the others first. Picking up the phone, she excitedly dialed Sara's number.

At 6:28, Jill was wrapped in her soft, pink, terry-cloth bathrobe, curled up on the sofa, a vodka tonic in her hand. She sipped it. It felt good. After what she'd been through, she wanted a drink.

Those bastards. I hope they hang.

She reached for the remote control and switched on the TV.

"Our top story tonight . . ." Brian Williams began, "is a massive drug bust, with far-reaching consequences, that has sent shock waves through the drug-smuggling community. This afternoon, on the Ohio River, Federal agents intercepted a yacht that was at the center of operations for a nationwide drug-trafficking operation. But the FBI didn't do it alone. Cathy Messenger, in Newport, Ohio, picks up the story of how four ordinary citizens helped bring the bad guys to justice."

There they were—Cathy, Sara, Harper, Grant, and Jill—looking quite serious, standing on the back of the *Keuka Maiden*. Cathy looked great: professional and in command.

Why didn't I brush my hair?

I should have put on makeup!

James looks so handsome.

Bud looks so serious.

Sara really needs a better bra.

When the program went to a commercial, Jill got up and went into the kitchen to call Cathy. She'd made the big time!

Jill took another sip of her drink; she didn't want it any more. She walked back to the kitchen and poured it down the drain. As she was rinsing out the glass, the phone rang.

"Hello?"

"Hey, Jill, James. Well, I guess we're TV stars now!" he laughed.

"Yeah," she smiled. "I think we had better start wearing sunglasses, or we'll be mobbed for autographs."

"Let's do dinner sometime soon," Harper said.

"Sure," replied Jill. "Tell you what. We have all this food we never ate. Why don't you and Bud come over here tomorrow night, and we'll do another cookout?"

There was a brief pause. "Well, sure. Would you mind if a couple of other guys came along? You saw them yesterday, the guys with the motorcycles."

"Oh those big guys. Are they safe?" asked Jill.

"Oh yeah," laughed Harper. "They're pussycats, despite appearances."

"Well, why not? Might as well celebrate. I'll give Cathy a call to see if she can join us, too. We have tons of food, so we might as well have a crowd. Oh, Cathy might have a job with NBC in New York!"

"You mean, because of the TV thing?"

"Yes—she has an interview with them next Monday."

"Fantastic!" said Harper. "You must be really proud."

"Words don't even begin."

Tired, but excited, Jill walked slowly upstairs. She had not been *out* since her harrowing experience, but she wanted to see Mata. She wanted something . . . she wasn't sure what. She needed a little closure on the events of recent days. Maybe reassurance was a better word—reassurance that there would be no more intrigue . . . for a while, anyway.

Soon, Jill was lying on her bed, the big earphones on her ears. She settled back and pressed the play button.

The familiar sounds of the babbling brook soothed her immediately. She closed her eyes, took a deep breath, and settled back on the pillow.

She barely heard the voice of Robert Madison before she was floating at the foot of her bed. She hovered momentarily and stretched out her arms and fingers.

She wanted to see Mata but not just yet. Maybe she would make the rounds of the places she had seen, the friends she had met, as a kind of final check-in. It would wrap up the events of recent days, like a final goodbye.

Jill floated leisurely through the outside bedroom wall, across Sixth Street, pausing to notice how lovely everything looked. It was still daylight, and she could hear kids playing down the street. Next, she floated over to Sara's house and found her on her sofa, chatting happily on the phone.

"Yes it was quite an adventure. I'm lucky to be alive. Oh. I met a man. A nice one, for a change. Sure, I can work the waffle booth. What time?"

Jill had no idea who Sara was talking to, but it didn't matter. She lifted herself up and floated high, circling over the Mound Cemetery, flying north, and then swooping down to Ridgewood Court, toward Harper's apartment.

Grant was on the couch, leaning forward, his hands clasped together. Harper was in a chair he had drawn in close. Bottles of beer rested on the coffee table.

The men appeared to be having an intense discussion. Grant was speaking.

"We could set up a little shop, that place behind your friend Terry's house, and I could make a few Gizmos."

"You sure you want to part with your inventions?"

"What the hell. If I don't make some money off it, the Israelis will do it. Besides, I could use the dough."

Jill smiled as she lifted up and out of Ridgewood Court.

She flew high above the buildings and soared southward. She turned at the Muskingum River and noted all the pleasure craft that were out on this summer evening. She banked north at the Ohio River and noticed that below her the river was full of sternwheelers for the festival. There were probably twenty or more crisp white boats with colorful paddle wheels dotting the banks of the Ohio, and she saw little Buckley Island in the middle. She looked back and saw that Front Street and Second Street were beginning to fill with booths for the festival.

Oh right . . . This is the weekend!

Jill continued to fly upstream, enjoying the experience of being free as a sparrow.

Maybe I should fly south for the winter?

Soon she was at the Newport marina. She saw the *Keuka Maiden* bobbing lightly under its tarp, and she hovered over it.

Oh baby, we nearly lost you. I am so glad to see you.

The boat rocked a sweet reply.

Maybe someday they'd go on a real fishing trip. She'd like that.

She lifted out and flew toward the little shed that was Lawrence's office. No one was around and the door was open. Apparently, the FBI liked to leave places open to the public. She moved inside and stuck her head through the cabinet behind the desk. The map with the colored pins was gone; the filing cabinets were empty and had been left partially open; the office had been stripped.

All that remained for Jill to check out was Robert Guerra's house. She flew high in the sky, heading slightly southwest, over the treetops and trailer parks.

Soon, the roof of the house appeared. It looked completely deserted; no cars were in the driveway, and no lights were on.

She floated in through the back door as before and began to move though the rooms. They had been stripped of all furniture, though the carpeting remained. She wondered about the basement, the locked room, and the closet with the porno and uniforms. She floated down through the floor and was in the large basement room.

Before her was the locked door. She moved through it into the secret room. As before, it was empty. She looked in the locked closet; it too had been cleared out—no more porn or uniforms on a rack. The house was clean, completely devoid of any trace of Robert. Except, she *thought* she smelled that nice cologne he always wore. That was a little odd.

She lifted herself up, floating directly into the living room. By now, the light was beginning to fade, causing deep shadows.

"This is a really nice house."

"Hello, Jill."

Startled, Jill looked around—*someone* saw *her?*

"Over here," said the voice.

Jill looked toward the back of the room.

It was Robert Guerra: a *younger* Robert Guerra, attired in casual clothes.

"Bob? I thought you were dead!"

"I guess I *am*," smiled Robert. "But when I saw you were here, I asked for permission to visit, to see you."

"Oh."

"I had so much more to tell you that night. Once you told me what you knew, I wanted to entrust the rest to you, so that it might help you. I had no idea you could go out of body."

"I had to be careful."

"Well, Jill, many people from the other side were watching you with great interest, following your progress. Dave, Jamie, your parents, your spirit guides . . . many others."

"They could see what I was doing?"

"When we chose to. You really *are* guided and loved, you know."

"Robert . . ." began Jill. "I knew about the drugs, but what was the porn?"

Robert laughed. It sounded like an echo.

"That was for Dave Lawrence. Guy's a perv. I didn't want to arouse suspicion, so when he asked if I could get some, I contacted HQ and they shipped some down. They coulda nailed him for all kinds of things, but he was—is—pretty clever."

"Is he going to jail with the others?"

"I don't know."

"What about watching that porno movie with the redhead?"

"She was an associate of Lawrence and Webster's. Her name is Angela Bennett. She asked me to get some dirty movies, so I did. I kind of enjoyed it, actually. Being an agent has its perks."

"So you really are a sleaze . . ." teased Jill.

"Well, once in a while, maybe," said Robert. "But if I have learned anything lately, though, it is that there is no judgment . . . by others, that is. No matter what one does, in the end, we are forgiven. If we make mistakes, we're not sent to hell. There's always another chance. By the way, your going out to see the trifecta results isn't exactly playing fair."

"Yeah," said Jill. "I know. I probably shouldn't have done it."

"On the contrary," laughed Robert. "The mob runs the track, and if you can, take them for every last cent."

Jill smiled.

"Come with me," said Robert, extending a hand.

"Where to?"

"There is someone who wants to see you."

Jill took Guerra's outstretched hand and, as before, they were in a dark tunnel, traveling at a high rate of speed.

"I *hate* this!" yelled Jill.

Then Jill and Robert were in the garden, the place where she had first seen Dave and Jamie. Robert turned and waved, and moved to join a group of people. And, for a moment, Jill was alone.

"You did well, Jill."

Jill turned around to see Mata, who was smiling slightly.

"Oh, Mata," began Jill. "I was wondering . . ."

"Yes, I know. Come with me."

The two women walked down a path that seemed to glow underfoot; then the pathway rose up, as though it was a magic carpet, and—on either side of the pathway—the vista began to race by, as though they were on a speeding train. It continued to accelerate to a dizzying speed; then it suddenly slowed down and they were, once again, in the Hall of Records.

"Do you recognize this place?" asked Mata.

"Yes. We were here before," replied Jill.

Mata led Jill toward a familiar lectern and paused briefly before speaking.

"You have accomplished an important mission. You and

your friends. Your powers are restored. And yet, greater challenges await you."

"Oh, *please*," Jill said wearily. "I am tired of adventures. I don't want to save the world. I just want to live a normal life."

"There is no mandate, of course. You are free to choose. But first, I want you to see something."

Mata opened the large book on the lectern and turned to a page near the end.

"Look."

What Jill saw made her gasp.

"Is that what's going to happen?" she asked.

"It *could*."

Jill was astonished. "Any idea of when these things are to occur?"

"I can't tell you exactly," said Mata. "But unless there is an intercession, then I would say . . . within two years."

"And I can prevent that?"

"You can *help* prevent that."

"Is there a connection between what I just saw and the men in Europe?"

"Most definitely."

Mata paused and looked at Jill. "We're proud of you, Jill. You have proven yourself. You summoned enormous energy to save your friends and your boat."

"Oh, I was angry. There's a part of me that's still angry, with those men, and what they tried to do."

"Anger is a form of energy; usually it's negative, but you used it constructively."

"I don't want to go through that again. It was terrible."

"You will have a long break. Rest. Have fun. Socialize with your friends. Go shopping."

"That is exactly what I intend to do," Jill said, "but I want to thank you for your help and guidance."

"It's not necessary, but I appreciate it," said Mata. "Can you hear the voices singing?"

"Yes, I hear something beautiful, lovely," said Jill. "What is that?"

"That's for you."

Jill's mouth dropped open and her eyes grew wide. She placed her hands over her heart and gasped.

They're singing for me?

The next morning, a welcoming cool breeze wafted through the streets of Marietta, Ohio, driving out the humidity and making the temperature ideal for the Sternwheel Festival.

Jill sat at her kitchen table, thumbing through her address book.

If I'm going to have a party, I might as well invite everybody.

She picked up the phone and began to make calls.

Two hours later, Jill, Harper, and Grant ambled down Front Street. It was late morning and the crowds had begun to gather. Young children scurried toward the amusement park rides that had been set up at the bottom of the street.

Harper noticed the P.R.I.D.E. Dojo and Training Center—

the martial arts establishment—and said to Jill and Grant, "I want to go in and take a look."

"Fine with me," Grant said.

When the three entered the Dojo, they saw racks of tie-dyed shirts, plastic milk crates that had been turned on their sides to serve as shelving, incense, Asian flags, and other interesting stuff.

Harper moved toward the back to see the large, empty room where the classes were held. There were three human-oid dummies. Even though they were plastic and rubber, they looked mean.

"They're for practice," said John, the owner, who had followed Harper into the back room.

"I assumed as much," said Harper.

"Say, aren't you the guy in the paper?"

"I was one of them."

"That was very cool. Listen, if you'd like to take classes, I can give you a special rate. All I want is to take a photo with you and the others. If I put it in the window, maybe it will help business."

"Well, I'll have to ask them. I'll let you know, OK?"

"Sure thing. Thanks for stopping by."

Up front, Jill was purchasing a tie-dyed shirt.

"I love the hippie stuff," she said to Grant.

"Me too," he replied, flashing the peace sign. "Peace, love, and black lights, man."

A little while later, they ambled down Front Street, where a number of small food kiosks had been set up. They noticed

Sara, her face moist with sweat, making Belgian waffles in a little booth.

"Hey, kids," she beamed. "Are we ever going on a real fishing trip?"

"Geez, I dunno," said Jill, looking at the others. "Ya wanna?"

"Not right now," grinned Harper.

"What time is the shindig tonight?"

"Any time after 7:00," Jill said.

"Should I bring the guitar?" Sara asked.

"If you don't, I'll spank you," smiled Grant.

"OK," replied Sara. "Can we do both?"

Grant laughed and pointed to Sara, waving a finger. Jill smiled and shook her head.

By 6:30, Jill's backyard and driveway had been set up with tables and chairs. Neighbors had brought food—large bowls of potato salad, macaroni salad, coleslaw, bags of potato chips, and several identical bottles of yellow mustard. The boys from Sig Ep had set up a PA system, and music was playing—too loudly at first, until Jill yelled at them.

Grant had unpacked his keyboard, taken out his guitar, and was waiting for Sara to arrive. In the kitchen, Harper was helping Jill make hamburger patties.

"I want to show you a trick," he said as he grabbed a ball of fresh hamburger. "Have any waxed paper?"

"Yeah, there's a roll in that drawer over there," Jill pointed.

"I need a pie plate, too," said Harper.

Jill opened a low cupboard, took out a pie plate, and handed it to Harper.

"Watch this," he said, ripping off some waxed paper.

He put the ball of hamburger on the piece of waxed paper. Then he put another piece of waxed paper on top, and then squished it flat with the pie plate.

"Presto!" he said, smiling.

"Well, now," said Jill, impressed. "That's a time saver."

"Plus, they cook faster when they're thin."

"Oh the things I'm learning. I want to learn to do the samba next. I'm feeling, like, in a samba mood."

"I was feeling samba once, but I cheered up," cracked Harper.

Jill groaned.

Soon Jill's backyard was filled with happy neighbors, fraternity boys, Terry Buckman, Preston Coleman and his wife Grace, Dr. Singh, Jack and Barb from across the street, some of Sara's friends from the library, even Willie Pindar and Flash. Everyone had a good time eating the burgers and hot dogs and drinking some fairly lethal punch Grant had made.

"It's *fantastic*," said Sara. "What's in it?"

"Well," began Grant. "It's orange juice, vodka, Cointreau, and orange sherbet. Got the recipe from a Tibetan monk. If you drink enough you become incandescent."

Later, Grant and Sara were playing their guitars and singing to the others seated in folding lawn chairs. The Sig Ep boys, bored with folk music, had retreated to their house, taking their PA system and the punch bowl, which was still half full.

Sara saw them sneak off and pointed to them, as she nudged Grant with her elbow.

Grant watched them leave and said to Sara, "I would expect no less of those fine young men."

But the older people stayed to listen; the evening, like the dying embers of the charcoal, had become warm and comfortable. Preston and Grace smiled and nodded.

"This is a fine evening," he said to Harper. "I'm glad to be here with you and the others."

"Me, too," said Terry. He turned to Jampa Singh, who was seated next to him, and asked, "So what is it you do?"

"Oh, I'm just a doctor," Dr. Singh said, smiling.

Dr. Singh was watching Jill, who was seated next to some of Sara's friends from the library. A brief expression of concern crossed his face, and he rose from his chair and moved quickly to Jill.

She looked up and smiled, expecting him to speak to her.

"Don't move!"

Dr. Singh, with an instant wave of his hand, batted a wasp to the driveway pavement and then stepped on it. Jill began to get up, but Dr. Singh put a hand on her shoulder and gently pushed her back in the chair.

"It was a wasp, but I took care of it." Then he gave her a brief smile. She paused for a moment, and then nodded back, her eyes sparkling knowingly.

By midnight, all that remained were Sara, Grant, Harper, and Jill.

"This was a perfect evening," Harper said. "I don't know when I've had a nicer time."

"That goes terabytes for me," said Grant, slightly drunk.

"'N' that goes . . . for me too," said Sara, also quite tipsy.

Jill stood up and said, "Well, I guess I'd better start taking things inside."

"I'll give you a hand," Harper volunteered.

As Jill carried a stack of kitchen items up the steps to the kitchen, Harper began to fold up the remaining chairs.

Sara turned to Grant and smiled.

"Hey, Buddy. Can you help me carry some of the stuff back to my place?"

"It would be my unbounded pleasure," replied Grant, as he rose unsteadily to his feet, a grin on his face.

Gripping his arm for support, and carrying an empty bowl with her other hand, Sara walked with Grant slowly down Jill's driveway, across Sixth Street, and up Sara's sidewalk to her front door.

"I had fun singing with you, Bud," she said, looking at Grant earnestly. "I hope we can do that again."

"Me too. You're a sweetie," smiled Grant.

"C'mere, you," said Sara, wound an arm around Grant's neck. She drew him to her and gave him a kiss he would long remember.

Jill was just coming out of the back door when Harper extended a thumb toward Sara's house.

302

"Looks like they're happy," smiled Harper.

Jill went up to Harper and wrapped her arms around him.

"You know, I'd like that too. But it's just . . . a little too soon for me. I hope you don't mind."

"No, I don't mind," said Harper. Then he kissed Jill on the mouth. It was not a passionate kiss, but a sweet, sincere one. She rested her face on his shoulder and drew him close. They stood in each other's arms.

"So what's next?" asked Harper quietly.

Jill looked up and blinked.

Then she said, "I think we should go to the racetrack and clean 'em out. I'll get the winning numbers beforehand, and we'll all go."

"Sounds like fun," smiled Harper. "Then what'll we do?"

Jill thought for a moment.

"Well, we could . . . go fishing. We could . . . work for the FBI. We could . . ."

"I guess," said Harper. "There's no end to what we can do."

"We could save the world."

Harper laughed and nodded.

Jill smiled.

And, somewhere in the Netherlands, a phone rang.

AFTERWORD

This book is not entirely fictional, though the story and the characters are made up.

Marietta, Ohio, is a real town located in Washington County in southeastern Ohio. All of the Marietta establishments and locations are real. If you go to Marietta, you can visit most of them. There is no marina in Newport, Ohio, however, nor in the West Virginia towns mentioned (though the towns are real). There is a marina next to the *Becky Thatcher*, as described.

The CDs that Jill uses are based on Hemi-Sync® CDs, which are made by Monroe Products (Lovingston, Virginia). Listening to any of the CDs with headphones will provide you with a unique experience—especially the MindFood series, which are guided meditations. The story's references to Robert Madison are actually to Robert A. Monroe, a pioneer in out-of-body travel, and the author of several books on the subject. Perhaps the best book is Monroe's *Journeys Out of the Body* (Doubleday, 1971). It is still in print and well worth reading.

The ability to go out of body is a real phenomenon, and, according to Robert Monroe, anyone can do it. It takes time, dedication, and practice. I can't do it. I have tried. Maybe someday I will, however. Additionally, Bob Monroe (and others) insists that each of us go "out" each night while we are asleep and dreaming. This is especially true if we dream of flight or even of being on an airplane.

Remote viewing is also a real phenomenon. It is a learned skill and Joseph McMoneagle ("Remote Viewer Number 1") says that anyone can do it. It is something that can be learned, but it takes practice to get a high percentage of correct "hits." Joseph is in the 80% range, and he has written several books on the subject. F. Holmes "Skip" Atwater, who is currently the president of The Monroe Institute, has also written a book about his remote viewing activities and how he became involved with Monroe.

The U.S. government established a program of psychic spies and called it Project Stargate. Both McMoneagle and Atwater were part of it, and it lasted eleven years, until it was disbanded. Other similar programs have since been created.

Last, Mata is based on a true *Avatar*, Mataji. She is the sister of Babaji. Both are highly evolved beings who appear on the earth from time to time to assist humanity. They do great work and keep low profiles.

ACKNOWLEDGMENTS

Thanks are due to the many people affiliated with The Monroe Institute (Faber, Virginia) and Monroe Products (Lovingston, Virginia), who provided encouragement and support: Laurie A. Monroe, Skip Atwater, Darlene Miller, Ph.D., Brian Dailey, M.D., Carol Moore, and Nancy McMoneagle.

Thanks to Jack and Barb Moberg of Marietta, Ohio, and its fine citizens, for making me feel welcome.

I would like to thank Annette Maxberry-Carrera, Publisher of Two Moons Press, for many years of extraordinary friendship and spiritual fireworks; Deanne Lachner, for her fastidious copy editing and lessons in grammar; Ted Ruybal, for his inspired cover and interior design; Richard Truitt and David Castor, for providing excellent feedback during the preparation of the manuscript; Maria Whitehead, for the beautiful cover art; and, though he passed away in 1995, Robert A. Monroe, a pioneer in higher consciousness. His influence endures.

ABOUT THE AUTHOR

Russ Mason was born and raised in upstate New York, not far from Lake Ontario. After attending college in Boston, he traveled to Dublin, Ireland, to write, compose, and direct its first rock musical, *Stephanie.* The run sold out, and Mason realized that he could write things that others might enjoy. He later moved to New York and tried his hand at stand-up comedy (*The New York Times* said he was "marvelous"); created shows for many New York City church groups, and worked at NBC on *Today* and *Dateline.* Tired of city life, he relocated to New Hampshire and became a commercial boat pilot. In 2004, after writing a magazine article about higher consciousness, Mason visited The Monroe Institute (Faber, Virginia), and it was there he learned about out-of-body experiences, remote viewing, and other psychic phenomena. It was also at the Institute that he first had the idea for a book about a housewife who learns to go out of body and who has many interesting adventures. He currently resides in the Commonwealth of the Northern Marianas, on an island in the Pacific Ocean.

The Monroe Institute has generously extended a $100 discount to readers of *Jill Messenger: Out of Body* who wish to take The Gateway Voyage®, a 6-day intensive, experiential learning adventure.

The Gateway Voyage provides tools that enable development and exploration of human consciousness, deeper levels of self-discovery, expansion of one's awareness, willful control of that awareness, and communication with and visits to other energy systems and realities.

You may find out more about The Monroe Institute, its programs, its various research initiatives, and its publications at the site below.

www.MonroeInstitute.com

If you are interested in taking The Gateway Voyage at a reduced rate, phone the Institute at one of the numbers below. Inform the Monroe representative of promotional code "Jill." Your name will be added to a special list. Then, when you send in the application—available for download at www.MonroeInstitute.com—attach a copy of either the sales receipt for the book, or a photocopy of the back of the book, with the bar code visible. The $100 will be deducted at the time of payment.

The Monroe Institute
365 Roberts Mountain Road
Faber, VA 22938

Local: 434-361-1252

Toll-Free: 866-881-3440

Fax: 434-361-1237

The Monroe Institute is a non-profit 501(c) (3) charitable organization furthering the evolution of human consciousness through its educational programs and associated research. The Institute is internationally known for its participatory educational programs that provide opportunities for the personal exploration of expanded states of consciousness.

Printed in the United States
130666LV00004B/21/P